D1106022

Love

Arty

Approaches to Teaching
Narrative of the Life
of Frederick Douglass

Approaches to Teaching
World Literature

Joseph Gibaldi, series editor

For a complete listing of titles,
see the last pages of this book.

Approaches to Teaching
Narrative of the Life
of Frederick Douglass

Edited by

James C. Hall

The Modern Language Association of America
New York   1999

©1999 by The Modern Language Association of America
All rights reserved
Printed in the United States of America

For information about obtaining permission to reprint material from
MLA book publications, send your request by mail (see address below),
e-mail (permissions@mla.org), or fax (212 477-9863).

Library of Congress Cataloging-in-Publication Data

Approaches to teaching Narrative of the life of Frederick Douglass /
edited by James C. Hall.
    p.   cm. — (Approaches to teaching world literature ; 63)
    Includes bibliographical references (p.   ) and index.
    ISBN 0-87352-749-6. — ISBN 0-87352-750-X (pbk.)
    1. Douglass, Frederick, 1817?–1895. Narrative of the life of
Frederick Douglass, an American slave. 2. Slaves' writings,
American—Study and teaching. 3. Afro-American abolitionists
Biography—History and criticism. 4. Slaves—United States
Biography—History and criticism. I. Hall, James C., 1960–
    II. Series.
            E449.D75A66   1999
    973.8'092—dc21   [B]   99-35483

ISSN 1059-1133

Cover illustration for the paperback edition: frontispiece engraving of
Frederick Douglass from *My Bondage and My Freedom* (New York: Miller, Orton,
and Mulligan, 1855). Source for this engraving and for others in the Folsom essay
is the Special Collections Department, The University of Iowa Libraries.

Set in Caledonia and Bodoni. Printed on recycled paper

Published by The Modern Language Association of America
10 Astor Place, New York, New York 10003-6981

CONTENTS

ACKNOWLEDGMENTS

Thanks to the Institute for the Humanities, University of Illinois, Chicago, for financial assistance in the preparation of this volume. Eva Bednarowicz provided invaluable editorial and research support. Thanks to William Andrews, James Olney, and Eric Sundquist for collegial encouragement. Finally, special thanks to Albert E. Stone for his contributions to the study of American autobiography and, more important, for his teaching and friendship.

PREFACE TO THE SERIES

In *The Art of Teaching* Gilbert Highet wrote, "Bad teaching wastes a great deal of effort, and spoils many lives which might have been full of energy and happiness." All too many teachers have failed in their work, Highet argued, simply "because they have not thought about it." We hope that the Approaches to Teaching World Literature series, sponsored by the Modern Language Association's Publications Committee, will not only improve the craft—as well as the art—of teaching but also encourage serious and continuing discussion of the aims and methods of teaching literature.

The principal objective of the series is to collect within each volume different points of view on teaching a specific literary work, a literary tradition, or a writer widely taught at the undergraduate level. The preparation of each volume begins with a wide-ranging survey of instructors, thus enabling us to include in the volume the philosophies and approaches, thoughts and methods of scores of experienced teachers. The result is a sourcebook of material, information, and ideas on teaching the subject of the volume to undergraduates.

The series is intended to serve nonspecialists as well as specialists, inexperienced as well as experienced teachers, graduate students who wish to learn effective ways of teaching as well as senior professors who wish to compare their own approaches with the approaches of colleagues in other schools. Of course, no volume in the series can ever substitute for erudition, intelligence, creativity, and sensitivity in teaching. We hope merely that each book will point readers in useful directions; at most each will offer only a first step in the long journey to successful teaching.

Joseph Gibaldi
Series Editor

PREFACE TO THE VOLUME

Our understanding of the nineteenth-century American literary canon has changed dramatically over the past thirty years. In particular, the diverse literature of slavery—abolitionist novels, poems, tracts, and speeches, narratives written by fugitive and freed slaves, postbellum memoirs of slavery, and so on—has come to play a much more central role in our syllabi and teaching. Of these varied texts and traditions, it has been that group of "authentic" first-person accounts of the conditions of slavery that has most vigorously asserted itself in the American literature classroom. Teachers and scholars have found that the desire of the nineteenth-century slave and ex-slave narrators to motivate audiences to examine the ethical grounding of American culture has great resonance in the last years of the twentieth century. All the narrators' successes (and occasional failures) in literary artfulness, in entertainment, and in converting sympathizers to the abolitionist cause, appropriately attract our attention as students of the American experience. The narratives are eminently teachable: students engage deeply with the psychological drama, suspenseful adventure, and moral rhetoric found in slave narratives. The survey of instructors undertaken for this volume revealed that these narratives are taught in a wonderful diversity of classroom settings: introductions to American and African American literature; graduate and undergraduate literature seminar and topics courses; American studies, American history, women's studies, and African American studies courses; and literature surveys of many configurations, including surveys of British literature. Most striking, these first-person accounts of slavery are often assigned in composition courses.

The desire to diversify syllabi with this literature is commendable. To make the most of this rereading of American culture, however, teachers must become aware of a complex history of reception and interpretation. From the very beginnings of this literature, questions of cultural authority and historical authenticity have made these accounts difficult interpretive terrain. The racial chasm across which the writers attempted to speak has narrowed slightly, although it is arguable whether the question of who gets to speak for whom has been settled. Even as literary critics began to celebrate the rhetorical and artistic accomplishment of "the slave's narrative," historians registered anxious cautions about the accuracy and reliability of the narratives as documents of the historical record. Although much groundbreaking work has been done in the study of this literature, it remains unclear whether this diverse group of narratives (diverse in the conditions of their writing, distribution, adoption of literary models, etc.) should be treated as a separate genre, with particular rules and conventions. Teachers willing to step out on this shaky ground will need to engage in a certain amount of retraining; these texts are easily misrepresented and misunderstood. It is the purpose of this volume to provide first-time and experienced teachers with access to the appropriate historical resources and informed discussion necessary to confidently present these important texts to students.

Narrative of the Life of Frederick Douglass makes sense as the focus for a teaching volume, as it is available in many affordable paperback editions and is regularly excerpted in introductory American literature and composition anthologies. Douglass's *Narrative* illustrates the most fundamental of literary and historical debates surrounding the status and literary character of the slave's narrative. The presence of the "authorizing" preface by William Lloyd Garrison raises issues of the slave narrative as a meeting place for the negotiation of cultural authority. The structural complexity of the *Narrative* makes it ideal for exploring the artistic accomplishment of the slave narrator. Differences in the factual accounts of the author's life in the *Narrative* and subsequent autobiographical texts by Douglass invite investigations of the imperfect and intricate literary act of memory, thus making the *Narrative* problematic as a source for historical record. Finally, *Narrative of the Life of Frederick Douglass* suggests a number of intertextual relations, both at the level of genre (sentimental fiction, captivity narratives, adventure stories, etc.) and at the level of direct connection to other American canonical and noncanonical texts (works by David Walker, Benjamin Franklin, Thoreau, Emerson, etc.).

There is, however, a danger in this focus. By no means should the constitution of this volume suggest that *Narrative of the Life of Frederick Douglass* is somehow the ur-text of a slave narrative tradition or that the question of the text's quality or authority vis-à-vis other similar narratives is somehow settled. Deborah McDowell, in particular, has criticized limited genealogical models of the slave's narrative (and African American literature, more generally) that unquestioningly put Douglass at the head of a line. The place of Douglass's *Narrative* (if not of Douglass himself) in the African American and American literary canon is hotly contested right now, and it is hoped this volume will give teachers some sense of the vitality of that healthy debate rather than assert its conclusion. The constitution of the volume is meant, then, to perform a difficult double task: to affirm, however self-consciously, the position of Douglass's *Narrative* as a classic text (i.e., taught often) while giving voice to contending forces, the contributions of other slave narrators (often women) and their pedagogical champions. I am trying to acknowledge one hundred years of American literary education and study without necessarily reinforcing its hegemony.

The volume is divided in two parts. The first part, "Materials," describes contextual studies in African American and American literary criticism, background works in cultural history and the historiography of slavery, pertinent information about contemporary editions of a variety of slave narratives, and audiovisual resources. This section of the book is possible because of the generous contributions of more than fifty instructors who responded to a survey sent to randomly selected members of the MLA's Black American Literature and Culture and Nineteenth-Century American Literature divisions. Survey participants are acknowledged at the end of the book. The second part of the book, "Approaches," consists of sixteen essays by a diverse group of scholars, representing African American and American studies, American literature, women's studies, and American history. These essays testify to the complexity of the slave's narrative and its possibilities in the classroom.

William L. Andrews has written:

> Given the uncertain status of Negroes, especially fugitive slaves, in the so-called free states of the ante-bellum United States, the definition of freedom for black people remained open. Autobiography became a very public way of declaring oneself free, of redefining freedom and then assigning it to oneself in defiance of one's bonds to the past or to the social, political, and sometimes even the moral exigencies of the present.
>
> (*To Tell* xi)

Needless to say, this account suggests a complex public literary act that imposes significant ethical responsibilities on teachers and students. Educating ourselves about the challenges presented by Douglass's *Narrative* (and the narratives of countless other men and women who documented and transcended slavery) and taking that knowledge to the classroom are two ways by which we, as teachers, give witness to the New World holocaust. This action does not complete our responsibility but it is a good place to start.

As this volume goes to press, a new edition of Douglass's *Narrative* (New Haven: Yale UP, 1999), edited by John W. Blassingame, John R. McKivigan, Peter P. Hinks, and the textual editor Gerald Fulkerson, has just been published as part of the scholarly edition The Frederick Douglass Papers.

Note   Unless stated otherwise, the edition of Douglass's *Narrative* to which all essays refer is that contained in Henry Louis Gates, Jr., editor, *The Classic Slave Narratives*. All quotations from students' writings are used with permission.

James C. Hall

Part One

MATERIALS

Editions

Not surprisingly, instructors report that they use many different editions of Douglass's *Narrative* and of other narratives as well. Two developments are, however, of particular import. First is the growing popularity of *The Classic Slave Narratives*, edited by Henry Louis Gates, Jr. In addition to the effectiveness of Gates's introduction, many instructors commented on the desirability of having the narratives of Douglass, Mary Prince, Olaudah Equiano, and Harriet Jacobs in a single affordable edition. This response suggests that teaching the slave narrative is becoming very much a comparative enterprise. The second development is the Schomburg-Oxford publication project Nineteenth-Century African-American Women's Writers, also edited by Gates. Many instructors mentioned that their teaching has been transformed by the availability in affordable editions of these seemingly forgotten texts. The following Schomburg-Oxford series volumes deserve to be highlighted: Harriet Jacobs, *Incidents in the Life of a Slave Girl* (ed. Valerie Smith); *Narrative of Sojourner Truth* (ed. Jeffrey C. Stewart); Elizabeth Keckley, *Behind the Scenes* (ed. James Olney); *Collected Black Women's Narratives* (ed. Anthony Barthelemy); C. W. Larison, *Silvia DuBois* (ed. Jared Lobdell); *Spiritual Narratives* (edited by Sue Houchins); and *Six Women's Slaves Narratives* (ed. William L. Andrews).

Instructors gave a variety of reasons, historical and literary, for assigning other slave narratives in addition to the works in *Classic Slave Narratives*. Of note are the narratives of Henry Bibb, William Wells Brown, Briton Hammon, Elizabeth Keckley, Josiah Henson, Estaban Montejo, Solomon Northup, James W. C. Pennington, Moses Roper, and James Williams. Multiple paperback editions exist of many of these narratives, and instructors should consult *Books in Print* for information about availability. (Two paperback editions that collect early African American autobiography are of special note: Adam Potkay and Sandra Burr, *Black Atlantic Writers of the Eighteenth Century*, which includes abridged narratives by James Ukawsaw Gronniosaw, John Marrant, Quobna Ottobah Cugoano, and Olaudah Equiano, and Andrews, *Sisters of the Spirit: Three Black Women's Autobiographies of the Nineteenth Century*, which includes narratives of Zilpha Elaw, Jarena Lee, and Julia Foote; see also Vincent Carretta's recent anthology of eighteenth-century African American and Anglo-African writing, *Unchained Voices*.)

When citing specific editions of *Narrative of the Life of Frederick Douglass*, many instructors commended two editions, one edited by Houston Baker, Jr., and the other by David Blight. The Baker edition was praised for its introduction, and the Blight for its introduction and supportive apparatus. Since the survey was conducted, the Library of America has issued a paperback edition of Douglass's *Autobiographies* (with notes and a chronology by Gates), making it possible for students, at reasonable cost, to compare the *Narrative* with *My*

Bondage and My Freedom and *Life and Times of Frederick Douglass.* (Andrews's excellent edition of *My Bondage and My Freedom* is also worth mentioning here.) The *Narrative* appears unabridged in Gates's *Norton Anthology of African American Literature.* Another collection published since the survey was completed, the Norton Critical Edition of *Narrative of the Life of Frederick Douglass* (ed. Andrews and William McFeely), has great potential for the classroom. It includes reviews of the *Narrative,* letters and orations by Douglass, and six seminal literary and historical essays interpreting and explaining the text's importance.

The edition of a slave narrative that drew the most attention (besides Gates's *Classic Slave Narratives*) was Jean Fagan Yellin's edition of Harriet Jacobs's *Incidents in the Life of a Slave Girl.* Yellin's definitive introduction and the wonderful maps and photographs make this edition the most important scholarly and pedagogical accomplishment in the reconstruction of the slave narrative tradition.

Related Readings

The significant presence of Douglass's *Narrative* in the American literature survey led many instructors to describe the intertextual and comparative means by which they taught the slave narrative. In connection with Douglass's participation in a discourse of "rights," they introduced the founding documents of the United States as either dialogue partners or, more bluntly, as targets for Douglass. The Declaration of Independence, the Constitution, and selections from Thomas Jefferson's *Notes on the State of Virginia* are often used to locate Douglass's learning and the sources of his tropes. Similarly, some instructors introduce the Dred Scott decision (*Scott v. Sanford*) or the Fugitive Slave Act to contextualize the trajectory of the rights tradition as it responded to slavery (see Gregg Crane's essay in this volume). Other instructors note that most slave narrators participate in an emergent (and intercultural) tradition of protest writing (see Anita Patterson's essay in this volume) and surround the slave narratives with a variety of works, both Euro- and African American in origins. For these instructors, the slave narrative is a particular expression of a national tension, a dramatization of the struggle between the forces of conformity and resistance. The conversations that emerge are striking: the slave narrator and Walt Whitman, the slave narrator and David Walker, the slave narrator and Ralph Waldo Emerson, and so on. Another group of instructors considers that the most specific discourse community within which Douglass and other slave narrators participate is that of American (and sometimes transatlantic) abolitionism. For this group, Lydia Maria Child's *An Appeal in Favor of That Class of Americans Called Africans,* selections from William Lloyd

Garrison's newspaper the *Liberator*, and Henry Highland Garnet's *Address to the Slaves of the United States* are crucial contextualizing voices. (Douglass's own reading can be found in William Petrie's *Bibliography of the Frederick Douglass Library at Cedar Hill*.)

Instructors mentioned the usefulness of introducing other Douglass texts when teaching the *Narrative*. In addition to *My Bondage and My Freedom*, excerpts from *Life and Times of Frederick Douglass* draw attention to the process of constructing or inventing a life story. Other instructors (most notably Keith Miller and Ruth Ellen Kocher in this volume) comment on the importance of introducing famous Douglass speeches or orations like "What to the Slave Is the Fourth of July?"(1852) or "Lecture on Haiti." William L. Andrews's *The Oxford Frederick Douglass Reader* includes "The Rights of Women" (1848), "Letter to His Old Master" (1855), "Fourth of July," "Men of Color, to Arms!" (1863), and "The Lessons of the Hour" (1894). Andrews and McFeely's Norton Critical Edition of the *Narrative* includes "I Am Here to Spread Light on American Slavery" (1845), "Preface to the Second Dublin Edition of the Narrative[. . .]" (1846), and "Fourth of July." David Blight's edition of the *Narrative* includes "My Slave Experience in Maryland" (1845), "Letter to Thomas Auld" (1848), and "Fourth of July."

Charles Davis and Gates's *The Slave's Narrative* and Andrews's *Critical Essays on Frederick Douglass* include reviews of slave narratives written by authors who were contemporaries of the narrators. Andrews's *Critical Essays* and Andrews and McFeely's edition of the *Narrative* include Margaret Fuller's review of the *Narrative*; Andrews and McFeely also include an anonymous review from the *Spectator* (1845), A. C. C. Thompson's article in the *Liberator* challenging the veracity of the *Narrative*, and Douglass's subsequent response.

Finally, while not suggested by any instructor as a potential related reading, it is worth recording that Frederick Douglass's novella *The Heroic Slave* is included in Andrews's *The Oxford Frederick Douglass Reader* and in his *Three Classic African-American Novels*.

Historical Background: African American Literary and Cultural History

General Background

As African American history rapidly matures as a discipline, it is becoming more difficult to identify a single volume that is satisfying as a general historical overview. While John Hope Franklin and Alfred A. Moss's *From Slavery to Freedom*, Lerone Bennett's *Before the Mayflower*, Mary Berry and John Blassingame's *Long Memory: The Black Experience in America*, Peter Kolchin's

American Slavery, 1619–1877, and Vincent Harding's *There Is a River* are reliable standbys and useful for the beginning teacher, they do not reflect the ways in which African American history has been transformed by contributions from anthropology, labor studies, women's studies, musicology, and race relations. Of the previous generation of seminal texts, Blassingame's *The Slave Community* continues to stand up well and remains a good starting place.

Teachers with a general sense of the contours of African American history might be better advised to consider the following seminal (and sweeping) contributions in African American cultural history: Eugene Genovese's *Roll Jordan Roll: The World the Slaves Made*, Lawrence Levine's *Black Culture and Black Consciousness*, Sidney W. Mintz and Richard Price's *The Birth of African-American Culture: An Anthropological Perspective*, and Sterling Stuckey's *Slave Culture: Nationalist Theory and the Fundamentals of Black America*. Each of these texts is noteworthy for its sensitivity to oral tradition and its recognition of the processes by which displaced Africans (to use a much too benign phrase) formed a culture in the New World. Albert Raboteau's *Slave Religion* fits in this tradition too and is especially useful in explaining the complex dialogue that many of the slave narrators, including Douglass, maintained with institutional Christianity. In addition, and for many different reasons, contributing instructors note the usefulness of the following: R. J. M. Blackett, *Beating against the Barriers*; Angela Davis, *Women, Race, and Class*; Martin Duberman, *The Antislavery Vanguard*; Clement Eaton, *The Growth of Southern Civilization*; Louis Filler, *The Crusade against Slavery, 1830–1860*; Howard Floan, *The South in Northern Eyes, 1831–1861*; Robert Fogel, *The Rise and Fall of American Slavery*; George Fredrickson, *The Black Image in the White Mind: The Debate on Afro-American Character and Destiny, 1817–1914*; Elizabeth Fox Genovese, *Within the Plantation Household*; Winthrop Jordan, *White over Black: American Attitudes toward the Negro, 1550–1812*; Leon Litwack and August Meier, *Black Leaders of the Nineteenth Century*; Carleton Mabee, *Black Freedom*; Wilson J. Moses, *The Golden Age of Black Nationalism*; James Oakes, *The Ruling Race: A History of American Slaveholders*; Dorothy Sterling, *We Are Your Sisters: Black Women in the Nineteenth Century*; Deborah Gray White, *Ar'n't I a Woman: Female Slaves in the Plantation South*; and Shirley Yee, *Black Women Abolitionists*. Of this long list, Fredrickson and Jordan are worth highlighting for their attention to the ideologies of race supremacy to which Douglass (and other slave narrators) responded. Again, because of the terrific growth and dynamism of African American history as a field, literary scholars would be well advised to consult with colleagues in history to ascertain which works would be most useful in meeting and supporting the instructor's pedagogical aims.

Teachers interested in utilizing primary documents (outside the scope of, say, those provided in the Norton Critical Edition, *The Slave's Narrative*, or *The Frederick Douglass Reader*) might look at Herbert Aptheker's *A Documentary History of the Negro People* or Willie Lee Rose's *A Documentary History of Slavery in North America*.

African American and American Literary History

Not surprisingly, the work of the critics Houston Baker, Jr., Hazel Carby, Frances Smith Foster, and Henry Louis Gates, Jr., was mentioned often by instructors in noting important contributions in African American literary criticism. In particular, Gates's *Figures in Black* (which includes the crucial essays "Binary Oppositions in Chapter One of the Narrative[. . .]" and "Frederick Douglass and the Language of the Self") was singled out for transforming instructors' understanding of Douglass's artistic accomplishment. Other instructors were similarly enthusiastic about Baker's *The Journey Back*, *Long Black Song*, and *Blues, Ideology, and Afro-American Literature*; Carby's *Reconstructing Womanhood: The Emergence of the Afro-American Woman Novelist*; Foster's *Witnessing Slavery: The Development of Ante-bellum Slave Narratives*; and Gates's *The Signifying Monkey: A Theory of Afro-American Literary Criticism*. A more recent volume, edited by Maryemma Graham et al., *Teaching African American Literature: Theory and Practice* (which includes an essay by William Andrews, "Narrating Slavery"), is likely to be of great use in the classroom.

Beginning instructors looking for general background in nineteenth-century African-American literature might consider volume 1 of Blyden Jackson's *A History of Afro-American Literature, The Long Beginning, 1746–1895*. *Afro-American Literature: The Reconstruction of Instruction*, edited by Robert Stepto and Dexter Fisher, is a good place to discover the roots of the post–Black Arts era's approach to African American literature. Farah Griffin's *Who Set You Flowin': The African-American Migration Narrative*, Stepto's *From behind the Veil: A Study of Afro-American Narrative*, and Valerie Smith's *Self-Discovery and Authority in Afro-American Narrative* all provide excellent introductions to the development of African American narrative art in the nineteenth century. Carla Peterson's *"Doers of the Word": African-American Women Speakers and Writers in the North (1830–1880)* is also noteworthy, particularly for the way it reminds readers and critics about the importance of oral art forms in the nineteenth century.

Outside the immediate realm of African American literary studies, a number of scholars are beginning to devote significant efforts to documenting what the writer and critic Albert Murray has called the mulatto character of American literature and culture. Eric Sundquist's *To Wake the Nations: Race in the Making of American Literature*, Karen Sanchez-Eppler's *Touching Liberty: Abolition, Feminism and the Politics of the Body* (on Emily Dickinson, Walt Whitman, and Harriet Jacobs), and Dana Nelson's *The Word in Black and White: Reading "Race" in American Literature, 1638–1867* are excellent examples of this work. See Shelley Fisher Fishkin's essay "Interrogating 'Whiteness,' Complicating 'Blackness': Remapping American Culture" for a good overview of this literature.

Other Pertinent Cultural History

Many instructors discussed the importance of Douglass's encounter and inter-pretation of African American music. Those interested in pursuing this topic should look at Dena Epstein's *Sinful Tunes and Spirituals: Black Folk Music to the Civil War*, Samuel Floyd's *The Power of Black Music: Interpreting Its History from Africa to the United States*, and Eileen Southern's *The Music of Black Americans: A History*. One instructor strongly recommended Joyce Jackson's "The Changing Nature of Gospel Music" as useful for understanding the impact of African American sacred music on Douglass. The previously mentioned *Black Culture and Black Consciousness*, by Lawrence Levine, is also superb on the topic.

The Slave Narrative

The testimony of slaves is included in more than the formal slave narratives. A variety of ethnographic and quasi-ethnographic projects have been pursued since emancipation for the purpose of getting the slave's story. The most famous of these projects were undertaken under the auspices of the Federal Writers Project of the Work Projects Administration in the 1930s. Instructors might do interesting comparative work by excerpting from *The American Slave: A Composite Autobiography*, edited by George Rawick; *Slave Testimony*, edited by John Blassingame; or *Lay My Burden Down: A Folk History of Slavery*, edited by B. A. Botkin. Each of these collections draws on these preservation projects. Davis and Gates's *The Slave's Narrative* contains a couple of fine essays that evaluate the legacy of this testimony, especially Paul Escott's "Art and Science of Reading WPA Slave Narratives" (40–47) and C. Vann Woodward's "History from Slave Sources" (48–58).

Studies of the Slave Narrative and African American Autobiography

The pioneering studies of the slave narrative and of African American autobi-ography were Marion Starling's *The Slave Narrative* and, to a lesser extent, Rebecca Chalmers Barton's *Witnesses for Freedom: Negro Americans in Autobiography*. Both remain useful monographs, although they have been supplanted by more recent criticism. Two collections of essays from the 1980s were especially important in moving the conversation forward: John Sekora and Darwin T. Turner's *The Art of the Slave Narrative* and the previously men-tioned Davis and Gates's *The Slave's Narrative*. While not focused exclusively on the slave narrative, Deborah McDowell and Arnold Rampersad's *Slavery and the Literary Imagination* raises important issues by building on the con-cerns of the Sekora and Turner volume and the Davis volume.

More recent collections or monographs have focused on the contributions of a particular slave narrator or on a subset of the slave narrative tradition: William L. Andrews's *Critical Essays on Frederick Douglass*, Angelo Costanzo's *Surprizing Narrative: Olaudah Equiano and the Beginnings of Black Autobiography*, Deborah Garfield and Rafia Zafar's *Harriet Jacobs and Incidents in the Life of A Slave Girl: New Critical Essays*, Eric Sundquist's *Frederick Douglass: New Literary and Historical Essays*, and Peter F. Walker's *Moral Choices: Memory, Desire, and Imagination in Nineteenth-Century American Abolition*. Ronald Judy's *Disforming the American Canon: Afro-Arabic Slave Narratives and the Vernacular*, a study of extant narratives of African Muslims in America in the nineteenth century, builds on the pioneering work of Allan Austin and dramatically revises our understanding of the limits of the slave narrative and, for that matter, American literary traditions as well. Jennifer Fleischner's *Mastering Slavery: Memory, Family, and Identity in Women's Slave Narratives* opens up the conversation about the slave narrative tradition with its introduction of psychoanalytic theory and its attention to the psychological dimension of the narratives. While not limited to the consideration of the slave narrative, John Ernest's *Resistance and Reformation in Nineteenth Century African American Literature* will engage instructors. Russ Castronovo's treatment of the slave narrative as a critical mode in *Fathering the Nation: American Genealogies of Slavery and Freedom* deserves much more attention than it has received so far. Special mention should also be made of *The Teachers and Writers Guide to Frederick Douglass*, edited by Wesley Brown. Although directed mainly to teachers of writing in the high schools, it includes many useful essays on presenting Frederick Douglass in the classroom.

For illuminating (and documenting) the slave narrative tradition, the text most cited by instructors was the seminal *To Tell a Free Story: The First Century of Afro-American Autobiography, 1760–1865*, by William L. Andrews. This is arguably the one indispensable text for any instructor interested in teaching Douglass's *Narrative* or the slave narrative tradition in general. Andrews's comprehensive historical detective work, his theorization of audience and response, and his compelling analysis of the ontological status of the narratives make *To Tell a Free Story* a must read.

A number of individual essays on the slave narrative tradition are also worth mentioning: Raymond Hedin, "The American Slave Narrative: The Justification of the Pícaro"; Joycelyn Moody, "Ripping Away the Veil of Slavery: Literacy, Communal Love, and Self-Esteem in Three Slave Women's Narratives"; John Sekora, "Black Message / White Envelope: Genre, Authenticity, and Authority in the Antebellum Slave Narrative"; John Sekora and Houston Baker, Jr., "Written Off: Narratives, Master Texts, and Afro-American Writing from 1760 to 1945"; and Maurice Wallace, "Constructing the Black Masculine: Frederick Douglass, Booker T. Washington, and the Sublimits of African American Autobiography." (Although Hedin, Moody, and Sekora have not produced monographs on the slave narrative tradition, each has been an extremely productive essayist. It would be worth consulting the database of the *MLA International Bibliography* to track down other excellent essays by these scholars.) Important general essays on the slave narrative tradition—especially on the question of its historicity—can be found in the Davis and Gates volume.

On Douglass in particular, instructors might seek out William L. Andrews, "Reunion in the Postbellum Slave Narrative: Frederick Douglass and Elizabeth Keckley"; Donald Gibson, "Reconciling Public and Private in Frederick Douglass's *Narrative*"; and Albert Stone, "Identity and Art in Frederick Douglass's *Narrative*." In the Norton Critical Edition of the *Narrative*, Andrews and McFeely include important essays by McFeely, Peter Ripley, Stepto, Andrews, Baker, and Deborah E. McDowell. McDowell's "In the First Place: Making Frederick Douglass and the Afro-American Narrative Tradition" (included in Andrews, *Critical Essays*) is required reading for all instructors, but, I would argue, especially for those who find themselves using the *Narrative* to diversify an otherwise all-white reading list. McDowell's essay is cited by at least half of the contributors to this volume. Again, Andrews's *Critical Essays* and Sundquist's *New Essays* are terrific starting points for new or experienced instructors.

Composition instructors may find a series of essays on Douglass and literacy to be of importance. In addition to Baker's work in *The Journey Back*, see John Burt, "Learning to Write: The Narrative of Frederick Douglass"; Leonard Cassuto, "Frederick Douglass and the Work of Freedom: Hegel's Master-Slave Dialectic in the Fugitive Slave Narrative"; Teresa Goddu and Craig V. Smith, "Scenes of Writing in Frederick Douglass's *Narrative*: Autobiography and the Creation of Self"; Lucinda MacKethan, "From Fugitive Slave to Man of Letters: The Conversion of Frederick Douglass"; and Eric Sundquist, "Frederick Douglass: Literacy and Paternalism."

Critical studies in African American autobiography were also important to the instructors surveyed. Joanne M. Braxton, *Black Women Writing Autobiography: A Tradition within a Tradition*; Stephen Butterfield, *Black Autobiography in America*; David Dudley, *My Father's Shadow: Intergenerational Conflict in African-American Men's Autobiography*; V. P. Franklin, *Living Our Stories, Telling Our Truths*; and Sidonie Smith, *Where I'm Bound: Patterns of Slavery and Freedom in Black American Autobiography*, all provide useful historical and literary context. For beginning instructors, the Andrews volume *African American Autobiography: A Collection of Critical Essays* is excellent. For a further sampling of essays, see the special issue of *Black American Literature Forum*, edited by Andrews and Nellie McKay.

Instructors might also find useful monographs or collections of essays that deal with autobiography (and American autobiography) in a more theoretical manner. James Olney, *Autobiography: Essays Theoretical and Critical*, and Albert Stone, *Autobiographical Occasions and Original Acts* and *American Autobiography*, are especially broad and erudite.

Bibliography

Instructors interested in lists of slave narratives should consult either Russell Brignano, *Black Americans in Autobiography* (rev. ed.), or the appendix to William L. Andrews's *To Tell a Free Story*. On Douglass in particular, see John Blassingame et al., *The Frederick Douglass Papers*, and Philip Foner, *Frederick Douglass: Selections from His Writings* and *The Life and Writings of Frederick Douglass*. Less comprehensive but obviously useful are Foner, *Frederick Douglass on Women's Rights*, and Barbara Ritchie, *Mind and Heart of Frederick Douglass*. It is also worth drawing the reader's attention to the volume edited by Jean Fagan Yellin and Cynthia Bond, *The Pen Is Ours: A Listing of Writings by and about African-American Women before 1910*.

Historical Background: Frederick Douglass and Other Slave Narrators

Biographies and Biographical Studies of Douglass

Among instructors who wrote that they made significant use of a Douglass biography either for classroom use or for personal knowledge, most chose William McFeely's *Frederick Douglass*. Other biographies did receive mention: Nathan Huggins's *Slave and Citizen: The Life of Frederick Douglass*, Philip Foner's *Frederick Douglass*, Dickson J. Preston's *Young Frederick Douglass*, Benjamin Quarles's, *Frederick Douglass*, and Booker T. Washington's *Frederick Douglass*, although these examples do not exhaust the accounts of this well-documented life. Waldo Martin's *The Mind of Frederick Douglass* was often singled out as especially useful in preparing to teach the *Narrative*. Gregory P. Lampe's *Frederick Douglass: Freedom's Voice, 1818–1845*, William Rogers's "*We Are All Together Now*": *Frederick Douglass, William Lloyd Garrison, and the Prophetic Tradition*, and David Blight's *Frederick Douglass's Civil War* explore more specific aspects of Douglass's life.

Not biographical in the usual sense but perhaps highly practical to the instructor would be *Frederick Douglass and the Fight for Freedom*, produced by Facts on File and edited by Douglass Miller. (Other chronologies of Douglass's life can be found in the editions of the *Narrative* edited by Blight and Andrews; in Gates's edition of Douglass's *Autobiographies*, Andrews, *Reader*; and Wesley Brown, *Teachers and Writers Guide*.)

Instructors might consider comparing Douglass's self-inscription with later attempts by others to represent Douglass in a literary fashion: Robert Hayden's poem "Frederick Douglass," William Branch's play *In Splendid Error*, and Edmund Fuller's novel *A Star Pointed North*. Historical representations might also be considered; see, for instance, John Thompson's *An Authentic History of the Douglass Monument*.

Biographical Studies of Other Slave Narrators

Jean Fagan Yellin is completing a biography of Harriet Jacobs. William Wells Brown is the subject of several biographies: L. H. Whelchel, *My Chains Fell Off*; J. Noel Heermance, *William Wells Brown and Clotelle*; and William Edward Farrison, *William Wells Brown: Author and Reformer*. See also Curtis Ellison and E. W. Metcalf, Jr., *William Wells Brown and Martin Delany: A Reference Guide*. Herman Thomas has written *James W. C. Pennington: African-American Churchman and Abolitionist*.

Audiovisual Materials

Frederick S. Voss's *Majestic in His Wrath: A Pictorial Life of Frederick Douglass* offers instructors the opportunity to explore with students the various ways in which Douglass has been portrayed visually. (See also Ed Folsom's essay in this volume.) Ellen Harkins Wheat has edited a volume that explores the African American artist Jacob Lawrence's Frederick Douglass and Harriet Tubman series of paintings.

A number of instructors noted the usefulness of Marlon Riggs's documentary *Ethnic Notions* for its exploration of nineteenth-century racial stereotypes. Many instructors also made use of the PBS-produced documentary on Douglass, *When the Lion Wrote History*. (Brown's *Teachers and Writers Guide* has a good list of other visual materials.) Many instructors noted the usefulness of episodes of the television film *Roots*, especially because so few students of the current generation saw the important adaptation of the Alex Haley novel. One instructor suggested Julie Dash's outstanding film about black life and the slave past, *Daughters of the Dust*.

While it is likely to be of limited pedagogical value—and will perhaps be difficult to find—instructors might make something of *The Autobiography of Frederick Douglass*, a mid-1960s Folkways recording of Ossie Davis reading selections from each of Douglass's autobiographies. The material on the recording and liner notes was edited by Philip Foner.

Part Two

APPROACHES

Introduction

When I teach Douglass's *Narrative*, I inevitably spend a great deal of time conversing about his dramatic apostrophe: "You have seen how a man was made a slave; you shall see how a slave was made a man" (294). It's an incredibly elegant rhetorical gesture, and undergraduate readers respond intensely and sincerely to its power. I am usually interested, however, in disrupting the very clarity that it invites or imposes. What is the relation between seeing and social status? How do we as twentieth-century readers understand the binary opposition of slave and man? Is gender incidental to our interpretations and understanding? What is the relation of the documentary function of the slave narrative to the advancement of a particular ideology? I am interested in getting students to experience the narrative as a language act grounded within a complex cultural history and subject to a particular set of material and interpersonal relations. In other words, I am interested in reminding students that Douglass—and other slave narrators—wrote from their experiences, according to and from their own literary educations, and that they wrote to sway, move, or challenge a readership with its own understanding and experience of race and slavery. Douglass's trope is the occasion, then, for both emotional engagement and sustained reflection.

The essays selected for this volume have been chosen in the spirit of this double experience. Indeed, much of the important scholarship of the 1970s and 1980s on the slave narrative challenged descriptions or evaluations of the tradition that assumed its meaning was readily transparent. Without disregarding or devaluing the specific role that the narratives had to play in the abolitionist struggle, critics asserted that the slave narratives, like all language acts, were complex and substantially open. Regardless of theoretical orientation, a consensus seemed to emerge that the evaluation (and, implicitly, the teaching) of the slave narrative could not be narrowly focused on authenticity. Responding to that critical challenge in a volume focused on pedagogy, I have tried to include essays that make clear that the slave narrative is a complex *literary* tradition; take seriously the slave narrative as a concrete artifact that expresses (by a variety of means) cultural value; take seriously the slave narrative as a discourse among discourses; recognize the ways in which the communication between narrator and audience is imperfect and often misread and the ways in which difference in the classroom makes such misreading both dangerous and of great pedagogical possibility; carefully document instability in our understanding of the tradition, that is, give some sense of a changing canon; and, finally, document the teaching of the slave narrative in a variety of contexts. As discussed in the preface, the volume focuses on Douglass's *Narrative* but also seeks to challenge that centering.

The first group of essays is brought together under the heading "Cultural Authority and the Teaching of the Slave Narrative." As a preface to more specific consideration of *Narrative of the Life of Frederick Douglass*, essays by

Joycelyn K. Moody, Lindon Barrett, and Russ Castronovo consider—from quite
different positions—the ways in which teachers need to be alert to the danger
of repeating within the classroom the very cultural dynamics that many of the
narratives sought to displace. Moody speaks passionately and reasonably about
the strange incongruity between the current vogue for "black texts" and the
continued invisibility of black (women) faculty members and students. She documents a complex social dynamic in the academy in which the relations among
students, teachers, the slave's narrative, and history are driven by the desire for
authority and by conflicting perceptions about where authority may lie. Barrett
discusses the situation of classrooms where students feel that the slave narrative
provides them direct access to authentic blackness. He describes reading and
interpretive strategies meant to highlight the ways in which each slave narrative
is unique and to encourage students to see "blackness (and whiteness) [. . .] as
strategies of cultural dominance or subversion." Castronovo assesses the somewhat ironic occurrence of the white instructor dutifully describing the "authorizing" function of texts like William Lloyd Garrison's preface to Douglass's
Narrative. Noting that a similar authorizing function is performed by the
instructor, Castronovo suggests that the slave narrative provides a unique
opportunity for students to explore the nature of pedagogical authority. These
essays are demanding but hold out great rewards for the instructor who takes
their challenges seriously and is willing to take on the intricate venture of teaching the slave narrative. By statement and implication, the essays offer compelling and ethically informed strategies to help the teacher encourage, rather
than discourage, intercultural, interracial, and intergender dialogue.

Essays in the second section of the book, "Douglass's *Narrative* in Historical
Context," introduce a variety of ways to provide students with relevant cultural
context. Context is interpreted broadly to include audience formation, discourse communities, the slave narrative as artifact, and "history." The section
opens with a contribution from the distinguished American historian of slavery
Arthur Zilversmit. He reflects on the use of the slave narrative in the American history classroom and, in particular, demonstrates for students of history
the nature of autobiography as a historical source and a literary form. Ed Folsom's essay deals with the slave narrative as artifact. For Folsom, the slave narrative as book often provides the aware teacher many opportunities to talk
about identity construction. His consideration of visual representations in editions of Douglass's book suggests a provocative (and practical) classroom practice. Jeffrey Steele explores a broad strand of nineteenth-century American
writing—the sentimental tradition—with which Douglass implicitly and explicitly enters into dialogue. Noting an affinity with Margaret Fuller, Steele points
out the importance for students of describing Douglass's efforts to politicize
this controversial and popular tradition. Gregg Crane describes the impact on
students when they get a chance to read, alongside the narratives of Douglass
and Jacobs, the various legal codes that enforced slavery. He argues that when
students read such legal materials as the Fugitive Slave Act and the Dred Scott

case, they acquire a sharper conception of Douglass's and Jacobs's polemic aims and figurative tools and an awareness that their own sense of what the Declaration of Independence and the Constitution mean depends in part on African American revisions of natural rights themes and tropes. Keith Miller and Ruth Ellen Kocher's essay builds on the desire of Zilversmit, Folsom, Steele, and Crane to radically contextualize the *Narrative* toward a consideration of the role of oratory in Douglass's *Narrative* and, by implication, in the slave narrative tradition as a whole. Miller and Kocher describe the pedagogical possibilities in explaining Douglass's reliance on a rich set of binary oppositions, a system they call interargumentation.

The essays grouped under the heading "Comparative and Intertextual Approaches to the *Narrative*" describe teaching strategies and situations shaped by the scholarly debates of the 1970s and 1980s and the exigencies of North American classrooms in the late twentieth century. Laura Hapke suggests using the framework, of labor studies to understand Douglass's accomplishment in the *Narrative* and raises questions similar to those of Barrett and Castronovo. Hapke is skeptical of studying race without studying class. Barbara McCaskill continues the resituating of Douglass begun by Hapke and considers the situation of women slave narrators addressing "mixed" audiences and the further difficulty of the black woman teacher presenting those narratives in mixed classrooms. Her discussion of the narrative of Ellen Craft suggests the ways in which the attitudes Douglass holds toward family, gender, and individualism can be revealed by placing his text side by side those of female narrators. Essays by Elizabeth Schultz and John Ernest revisit the tension involved in the current reconsideration of Douglass's place in the African American literary pantheon. Schultz describes the changes in her teaching of Douglass over twenty-five years, changes facilitated by her engagement with two important texts, Emerson's "Self-Reliance" and Harriet Jacobs's *Incidents in the Life of a Slave Girl*, and their evolving meaning in the culture at large. Schultz's essay suggests why the teaching of the slave narrative must become a dialogic venture. Ernest takes on the issue of students' valorizing Jacobs's important contribution without giving the text the close reading it demands and deserves. He insists that Jacobs prepares the reader to participate in a genuinely reciprocal relationship between text and reader, the mutual exchange necessary for genuine understanding. Most important, Ernest makes clear—as do Schultz and McCaskill—the obvious benefits of pairing a Douglass text with that of a female slave narrator. Concluding this section, Anita Patterson describes a pedagogy in which Douglass's *Narrative* is seen as exemplary of American protest writing. Like Emerson, Thoreau, and Jacobs, Douglass inserts himself into a discourse of "exhortations to reform or revolution." To appreciate fully the accomplishment of the *Narrative*, Patterson argues, students need to recognize the philosophic tradition descending from Locke and Paine with which it engaged. Her essay argues elegantly for a substantive canon revision project.

The final section of essays examines the teaching of the slave narrative in specific contexts. Martin Klammer considers the use of slave narratives, and Douglass's *Narrative* in particular, in an introductory humanities course in a midwestern liberal arts college. He writes of how he uses Douglass's *Narrative* to get students to think about the ideologies of individualism and pluralism and, more important, of how the *Narrative* provides a means for allowing students to ask hard questions of the nation's founding fathers. David Dudley views Douglass in the context of a world literature course at a southern state university. He describes using the *Narrative* to open up a course on the durability of the individual in modern culture. He also assesses the limitations of surveys like his but concludes that Douglass's *Narrative* has a valuable role to play in general education. The last word goes to Bruce Mills, who looks at the use of the *Narrative* in a survey of American literature. He advocates a pedagogy that does not allow students to perceive the slave narrative as a historical curiosity, or as an aesthetic accomplishment less worthy than the supposedly more sophisticated texts that often bracket these narratives in the necessarily broad American literature survey.

While each of these essays tries to elaborate on a particular pedagogical problem, most contributors make clear the great pleasure and satisfaction that teaching slave narratives can generate. As teachers we seem to learn much about the responsible use of cultural authority and the ethics of reading and interpretation. Most important, we are gratified to participate in a process by which we get to reintroduce these books that have been so central in shaping American culture.

Personal Places:
Slavery and Mission in Graduate Seminars
Joycelyn K. Moody

> It is a mistake, I think, to define this persistent debate
> over who can read black female texts as strictly or
> primarily racial or cultural or gendered [. . .]. The most
> important questions may not be about essentialism and
> territoriality, biology, sociology, or even ideology but,
> rather, about professionalism; about cultural literacy
> and intellectual competence; about taking ourselves
> seriously and insisting that we be taken seriously not
> simply as objects in someone else's histories—as native
> informants—but as artists, scholars and critics reading
> and writing our own literature and history.
> —Ann duCille, "The Occult of True Black Womanhood"

This was not supposed to happen to me. This essay was not supposed to eat into the precious time this fellowship year provides me to write my tenure book.[1] It was supposed to be easy to write: a break in my new routine, a straightforward account of how I use slave women's narratives in graduate seminars. Yet, after twelve years of teaching in five very different, predominantly white colleges and universities, I should have known better. I should have known that my presence transforms the Ivory Tower into a Tower of Babel, whether I am on fellowship or not.

The difficulty I'd face in writing this chapter became clear when I began outlining the types of literature professors I wanted to read it. As it happened, none of the three colleagues I envisioned was African American, and none a trained African Americanist. Instantly, it seemed imperative that I consider what it meant that the professors I imagined myself writing for were whites, not faculty members of color.[2] There seem some apparent answers to this question, including the obviously erroneous supposition that African Americans and African Americanists already know whatever strategies I have to offer. My chimerical readership would also suggest that I am more concerned with influencing the approaches to teaching nineteenth-century African American literature that white (and other nonblack) professors generally adopt than I am with how black instructors teach it. I confess it. Admittedly, though, this fact exposes my hasty assumption that African American professors' experiences with oppression render them, if not activist, then at least aware that black literature can be used as a means of challenging and even transforming (white) students' preconceptions of black citizens. I believe that what and how I teach can effect progressive change in my students' attitudes and ultimately in their voting practices, which could mean the difference between a racist society and a moral one. Conceptualizing teaching as missionary work is now passé; some professors now contest such a conceptualization of teaching. (I'm thinking here of such debates as the acrimonious one between Gates, Baker, and Joyce in *New Literary History*, Winter 1987.) This criticism notwithstanding, I feel fortified by Barbara Christian's stalwart declaration in "The Race for Theory," which yet resonates with me: "What I write and how I write [and what and how I teach] is done in order to save my own life. And I mean that literally. [. . .] My readings [and my teaching] do presuppose a need, a desire among folk who, like me, also want to save their own lives" (77–78).

My academic endeavors have a do-or-die impact on my personal well-being; the place of the personal functions profoundly in my scholarship. However, using this phrase, which was the subject of a series of guest columns in the October 1996 issue of *PMLA*, puts me at risk. The feminist contention that the personal is political is now decades old, but I still fear being discounted as personal and thus absorbed with the private and thus with the *un*academic. My fear of this charge derives primarily from what Johnnetta Cole has condemned as the academy's beguiling inveiglement: "Many African-Americans entering the academy today do so because they have been lured by the promise of alternative models of research and action-oriented scholarship [. . .]. [But] anything not fitting the traditional model is considered less than scholarly" (qtd. in Christian, "Diminishing Returns" 176). Nevertheless, praxis, however heterodox, *is* personal to me. I read no distinction between the personal and the academic. As Cathy Davidson observes in one column of the *PMLA* Forum, "The phrase 'the place of the personal in scholarship' [. . .] seems to conceal an imputation that it is the impersonal that really makes scholarship go round and that *personal* and *scholarship* are dichotomous terms. I don't buy that dichotomy" (1072).

Another guest contributor to the *PMLA* Forum, David Palumbo-Liu, speaks more directly to the difference that race makes when one considers "the place

of the personal in scholarship" (1072). Palumbo-Liu writes, "The institutional-
ization of racially identified disciplines has everything to do with how the
racialized personal is called on to authenticate the academic enterprise in particular historical frameworks" (1077). He illustrates this claim with an anecdote
about a colleague who caustically expressed frustration with "you people" when
Palumbo-Liu was forced by overcommitment to decline her request that he
guest-lecture in her multiethnic literature course. Palumbo-Liu notes, "'We
people' includes all those sympathetic to the goals of multiculturalizing the
curriculum, but the term achieves specific force when it focuses on those not
only authorized but also obligated by their phenotypic identities to perform
that revisionary act. Again, this is a double-edged phenomenon, the problem
of who teaches 'ethnic' material" (1078). Finally, in an ironic and implicit shifting of pronoun references to "we people," he wonders, "If we insist on multiculturalizing the curriculum and, for good reason, on having ethnic studies
taught by folks who are seriously engaged in those subjects (and if we claim
that phenotypic markings authenticate the authority to teach such subjects),
what do we do when called on (over and over again) to guest-teach *The Woman
Warrior*? or *The Color Purple* or *Ceremony* and so on?" (1078).

Palumbo-Liu's question is one that I have asked myself repeatedly in writing
this essay. Why didn't I withdraw from the project once I realized precisely
what energy and emotion writing this chapter would entail?

Certainly, I had not intended to write an article that analyzes the issues I
address here. However, once it became clear to me that the ostensibly simple
construction of a narrative of past teaching terms would prove so enervating, I
could not forgo this critical opportunity. For writing this essay allows me to
contribute to the current analysis of black women in the academy. In "Diminishing Returns: Can Black Feminism(s) Survive the Academy?," an incisive,
impassioned article defining the perimeters of this analysis, Christian discusses
her "sister/colleagues [who] refuse to be what they call 'academic mules'"
(175). Like them, I am all too aware that "it is usually [black women's] own
communities who lose if we do not attempt to fulfill the demands of our
respective communities" (175). So, for me this essay represents an urgent task
to which I am called by the community of black feminist scholars: it serves as
activism, the kind by which my whole career has been marked (the only kind
my overtaxed professional life affords me), the kind that persistently impedes
my more traditional (read less-suspect) scholarship and that threatens to keep
me from finishing my book and from filling my tenure file with juried journal
articles. Given my limited personal power to vanquish the academy's unpro-
fessional practices of permitting those who are untrained to teach African
American literature, I must use what authority I do have to instruct those professors who seek assistance here. As Ann duCille sagely asserts, "Much of the
newfound interest in [it] that seems to honor the field of black feminist studies demeans it by treating it not like a discipline with a history and a body of
rigorous scholarship underpinning it, but like an anybody can play pickup game

played on an open field" (94–95). Consequently, although "icons are not granted tenure automatically" (duCille 97), I cannot *not* write this essay.

Indisputably, the most momentous implication of my having identified three white colleagues as the target audience for this essay has to do with numbers— both statistics and economics. It is no wonder that thinking about my graduate seminars and the methods I apply in teaching them led me immediately to faces of white associates, for white faces overwhelmingly make up the student population at the large research university where I teach. Moreover, there were white faces before me in 1991, when I first led workshops on teaching slave women's narratives for high school instructors in a small midwestern college town, as there are before me at the MLA convention and the other conferences where I present professional papers. In "Diminishing Returns," Christian offers some disquieting statistics from the *Journal of Blacks in Higher Education*— numbers that prove Hazel Carby's avowal elsewhere that "there are close and disturbing links between multiculturalism [and] affirmative action" ("Multicultural Wars" 190). Christian reports, for example, the *Journal's* assessment that "in 1987, African-American women received 54 per cent of the doctoral degrees awarded blacks, that is, two per cent of the doctorates awarded that year." Four years later, in 1991, "only 2.3 per cent of the Ph.D.'s in all academic disciplines awarded in this country went to blacks," prompting Christian to wonder, "Why are African-Americans, and especially women, not going into academic areas at a time when issues of race and gender have become increasingly acknowledged as central to intellectual inquiry?" ("Diminishing Returns" 173). In "A Troubled Peace," Nellie Y. McKay poses a more pointed question:

> Why this absence of black graduate students from English departments when there is such a demanding market for them? Is there a connection between the desperate competition of discipline departments in white universities and colleges for the few available black faculty and the absence of candidates to fill these positions? (21)

Whatever the answers, we cannot impugn Carby's conjecture that "if the black student population continues to decline at the undergraduate and graduate levels, the current black intellectual presence in academia, small as it is, will not be reproduced" ("Multicultural Wars" 189). Necessarily, then, the fate of black feminist studies rests largely with my white students and coconferees, that is, with my present implied readership. African American women currently account for only 2.1% of all full-time faculty members, both tenured and nontenured, in United States colleges and universities (Benjamin 5), and not all these women are feminists. Therefore, if black feminist studies is to have any proponents, any whose jobs—whose *missions*—it becomes to profess its tenets, few will be black women.

Thus I worry—not only about the longevity of the critical attention paid the nineteenth-century African American women, free-born and enslaved, whose narratives I teach[3] but also about the welfare of contemporary African American women, myself included. For, like Palumbo-Liu, in the often hostile climate of my home institution, I sense

> a larger context that includes the anti-affirmative action backlash, the critique of progressive multiculturalism as merely identity politics [. . .] and so on—all of which are predicated on an insistent ignorance of the abiding legacies of the United States' white supremacist ideology and an ignorance, in general, of the very idea of history.   (1078)

Writing now, I have to remind myself that I really do believe, however old-fashioned and ill advised it feels, that I, too, stand to gain from sharing my knowledge of African American literature. My professional survival is bound up with the empowerment of white academics, who dramatically outnumber me and my kind throughout higher education. Some of these academics' participation in or tolerance of antiaffirmative actions effectively delimits the presence of black students and professors across the academy. Their "interest" in teaching such slave testimonies as Douglass's, William Wells Brown's, and James Pennington's too often lies chiefly in fetishized notions of an essential Strong Black Presence. With Carby, I worry even more that

> in spite of the fact that the writing of black women is extraordinarily diverse, complex, and multifaceted, feminist theory has frequently used and abused this material to produce an essential black female subject for its own *consumption*, a black female subject that represents a single dimension—either the long-suffering or the triumphantly noble aspect of a black community throughout history.
>
>   ("Multicultural Wars" 192; my emphasis)[4]

I have tried to insinuate the importance of history throughout this essay thus far. To be sure, in my graduate seminars in nineteenth-century African American life writing, "history," and its present configuration as "theory," becomes one of the most crucial, most vexing factors we must confront. In a variation of the controversy about the dichotomous relationship of the personal to the scholarly, my (white) students and I never quite agree whether the assigned twelve or more black autobiographies, many of them by or about former slaves, constitute history. Needless to say, our debates about what theory is similarly disintegrate, falter precisely on the definition of theory as, in Christian's words, speculation "about the nature of life through pithy language that unmask[s] the power relations of the world [, . . .] [speculation] in the form of the hieroglyph, a written figure that is both sensual and abstract, both beautiful and communicative" ("Race" 68).

Let me specify the texts I have used in three graduate seminars in nineteenth-century African American literature. For the seminar Early African American

Spiritual Literature, I assign the narratives in Adam Potkay and Sandra Burr's *Black Atlantic Writers of the Eighteenth Century*, Thomas Gray's *"The Confessions of Nat Turner" and Related Documents*, the oral histories of former slaves in Clifton H. Johnson's *God Struck Me Dead*, the four autobiographies (by Maria Stewart, Jarena Lee, Julia Foote, and Virginia Broughton) in Sue Houchins's *Spiritual Narratives*, and along with the full life stories of Douglass (*Narrative*), James W. C. Pennington, and the evangelist Elizabeth (Andrews, *Six* 1–19), we read excerpts from the writings of Nancy Prince (Barthelmy 1–89) and Rebecca Jackson (Humez 1–194). Furthermore, I assign Janet Cornelius's *When I Can Read My Title Clear*, the critical essays in Paul E. Johnson's *African American Christianity*, and selected chapters from William Andrews's *To Tell a Free Story* and Frances Smith Foster's *Written by Herself*. We also study an audio text of slave spirituals and field "hollers," several recorded by former slaves in the early twentieth century. Upon my arrival at the University of Washington, librarians in the ethnomusicology department prepared this tape for me. The audio companion to the *Norton Anthology of African American Literature* provides recordings of early musical texts.

For the seminar called The Slave Narrative, I assign pertinent chapters from Dorothy Sterling's *We Are Your Sisters* and three complete self-written autobiographies from the antebellum period: Douglass's *Narrative*, William Wells Brown's *Narrative*, and Harriet Jacobs's *Incidents in the Life of a Slave Girl*. Working from William Andrews's proposition that postbellum slave narrators significantly transformed the image of slavery (from hell to haven) to meet a set of social, political, and rhetorical needs dramatically different from those faced by their antebellum counterparts (see "The Representation of Slavery" in *Slavery and the Literary Imagination*), we move from Jacobs to a variety of twentieth-century novels about slavery. These are Arna Bontemps's *Black Thunder*, Ishmael Reed's *Flight to Canada*, Octavia Butler's *Kindred*, Gayl Jones's *Corregidora*, Toni Morrison's *Beloved*, and Caryl Phillips's *Crossing the River*. The assigned critical readings consist primarily of Andrews's *To Tell a Free Story* and Foster's *Witnessing Slavery* (exp. ed.) and essays from Charles Davis and Henry Louis Gates's *The Slave's Narrative* and from Deborah McDowell and Arnold Rampersad's *Slavery and the Literary Imagination*. At the end of the course, we contrast our readings with the white filmmaker John Sayles's *Brother from Another Planet* (1984).

For the seminar called Spirit, Spunk, and Sentimentality, on nineteenth-century black holy women's autobiographies, I assign *Spiritual Narratives*, edited by Houchins; *Gifts of Power: The Writings of Rebecca Cox Jackson*, edited by Jean Humez; the three autobiographies in *Sisters of the Spirit*, edited by Andrews; the Schomburg series *Narrative of Sojourner Truth*; selected slave women's narratives in *God Struck Me Dead* (C. H. Johnson); *The Memphis Diary of Ida B. Wells*, edited by Miriam DeCosta-Willis; and two dictated life stories (those of Elizabeth and Mattie J. Jackson) in *Six Women's Slave Narratives*, also edited by Andrews. Furthermore, I assign the essays in Johnson's

African American Christianity as well as selected chapters in Foster's *Written by Herself*, in Carla Peterson's *"Doers of the Word"*, and in Nell I. Painter's *Sojourner Truth: A Life, a Symbol*. Finally, we view Julie Dash's film *Daughters of the Dust* (1995) and read Jacqueline Bobo's chapters on the film in *Black Women as Cultural Readers*. For each of my courses, I arrange a library reserve shelf where students can peruse additional critical texts, including Gates's pivotal essay "James Gronniosaw and the Trope of the Talking Book" (*Signifying* 127–69) and such influential feminist scholarship as Joanne Braxton's *Black Women Writing Autobiography*, Hazel Carby's *Reconstructing Womanhood*, Mae G. Henderson's "Speaking in Tongues," Valerie Smith's "Loopholes of Retreat," and Harryette Mullen's "Runaway Tongue."

My students' concern that the course texts (and my instruction) provide them inadequate "history," "theory," and "sociohistorical context" fascinates me. In their course evaluations they indicate sincere appreciation for being exposed to the autobiographies I assign and for the criticism they must read. However, they also indicate pressing "need" for "a basic history text like Benjamin Quarles's *Black Abolitionists* [that] would orient everyone to historical issues" or for more "autobiographical theory/criticism, perhaps even in place of some of the primary texts," or they otherwise advise me that "it might be useful to include specific theoretical essays along with the primary texts." On the one hand, their ardor impresses me: any student requesting more reading is rare enough. I'm aware, too, that their counsel stems from more than genuine diligence. As the student authors of an essay in the *Journal of American History* assert, "Larger historiographical surveys [. . .]—courses that graduate students want (to gain some sense of a synthetic whole) and need (to prepare for qualifying examinations that suppose knowledge of a synthetic whole)—are unpopular among faculty and therefore rarely offered" (Berry 1141).

On the other hand, however, my students' call for "more context—historical, musical, theoretical" (in courses requiring them to read a dozen or more nineteenth-century texts, to listen to original recordings of nineteenth-century songs and arrangements, to study contemporary film interpretations of historical situations, and so on) reveals that their conceptualizations of both history and theory differ significantly from my own.[5] Clearly, the texts they are willing to endorse as valid and authentic, the sources from which they can confidently postulate about the past, are texts other than those I assign. My students and I often seem willing to accede powers of inference and interpretation to very different others.

And for divergent purposes. While historians have published consistently on slavery since its inception in the Americas, little scholarship in any field exists on the slave women whose narratives I teach. (Fortunately, this becomes less true all the time.) While I often experience tremendous joy in my seminars, specifically because of the fervor of my (white) feminist students, I have also found that many of them exalt theory (by which they mean contemporary black feminist criticism) precisely because they perceive this scholarship to champion (the stereotype of) the Strong Black Woman. Some have taken more than one of my seminars, appraising as "exotic" the texts I teach, which in turn render *me* exotic, they seem to reason; quite naturally, then, their study of these texts effects their own exoticism. Repelled as much by passive racists as by white supremacists, these students appear arrested in what the sociopsychologist Beverly Daniel Tatum describes as the pseudo-independent stage of (positive) white identity development, in which "some white students may want to distance themselves psychologically from their own racial group by seeking out relationships with people of color" (468). Moreover, they parallel the white abolitionists whom Nell Painter unmasks when she writes:

> Well-intentioned reformers went to hear Sojourner Truth present herself as a slave mother and bought copies of her little book to express solidarity, to contribute to her well-being, and to indicate their own relative position and status in society. As Truth sold her being as a slave woman, her customers bought the proof of their social difference from her.
>
> ("Representing" 474)

Painter plays, of course, in her final prepositional phrase: the whites literally bought Truth's *Narrative* "from her," that is, Truth sold her book herself, and whites figuratively bought the *Narrative* as evidence that their social status was distinct "from hers." My inability to comprehend fully these student feminists' notion of theory—and my concern for the fate of black feminist studies—increases when I read some students' fetishizing dispositions in Painter's astute observation:

> The conjunction between money and morals worked to the advantage of Sojourner Truth, who embodied the linked causes of feminism and antislavery and had something to sell. The *Narrative of Sojourner Truth* promised its reader a story of one woman who had been a slave; it immediately assured its purchaser that information about her own virtue had been conveyed.   (474)

For some feminist students, the study of African American women writers seems to provide absolution and protection from recreant racism at the same time that it affords them superior job marketability. Ironically, their commodification of African American literature and theory effects these feminist students' own greater value as commodities within the academy.

Other nonfeminist (white) students who want more history or theory from my courses call for increased inclusion of recent advances in revisionary history and postcolonial and poststructural studies. I regard much of this new scholarship as exciting and revolutionary; however, some of it is simply, in Christian's words, "as hegemonic as the world it attacks" ("Race" 71). However, because of the current preeminence of this kind of work and because of the failure of prominent and esteemed scholars to recognize and to challenge its frequent misapplication to African American texts, students learn to venerate "theorists" but not to discern the critical methodologies most compatible with explorations into African American literary tradition(s). Indeed, regressive interpretations of the matter of history curtail analyses of African American literature by repudiating the validity and continuity of its traditions.

Confronted with their anxieties about coverage, I assure my graduate students that they do not necessarily need to read more theory or history but they do need to immerse themselves in the assigned autobiographies and to trust themselves, as I do, to discern and infer the historical contexts that emerge from persistent and perspicacious reading in the tradition. This is not to say that students do not need historical contextualization; they do. My pedagogical concern and responsibility are that they have access to it. The problem is that this knowledge is manifest in my courses in a medium that so many white students are inclined—indeed, have been trained—to suspect, to reject: the words of blacks themselves. Braxton asserts in *Black Women Writing Autobiography*, "For the [African American woman's] text is accessible to whoever would first establish its proper cultural context, thus gaining access to a sphere of privileged (and valuable) knowledge" (5–6). In other words, the difficulty of accessibility to African American texts diminishes with familiarity with African American cultural contexts. Appreciation of a culture requires a fundamental respect for that culture and its constituents.

While I have been very honored to teach gifted graduate students who esteem my professional skills, I must further acknowledge that, just as I involuntarily embody for some students the Strong Black Woman stereotype they desire, I represent perforce for some others the substandard product of a society that has excluded black women from higher education. Consequently, I read in some students' hesitation to recognize slave (women's) narratives as authentic history and theory a devaluation of my own legitimacy and expertise. These students do not regard our study of African American literature as serious enough, not erudite or historical or theoretical enough. Ironically, under my tutelage, some students seem to intuit the verity of Mae Henderson's claim that

> Black women enter into dialogue with other black women in a discourse that [one could] characterize as primarily testimonial, resulting from a similar discursive and social positionality. It is this commonality of history, culture, and language which, finally, constitutes the basis of a tradition of black women's expressive culture.   ("Speaking" 217n15)

That is, these students do sense the peculiarity and nonconformity of the complex alternative discursive community formed by the early African Americans they study and the professor leading them in that study. Regrettably, they often do not also comprehend the fulfillment and ascendancy of that community.

Though I have had very few African American graduate students, I have found that the few I have had enter my seminars are already fully aware of the centrality of tradition(s) to African American literature. They also bring profound, experiential comprehension of the racialized personal in the academy. Mary, a brilliant MIT fellow auditing my Harvard Divinity School seminar on nineteenth-century slave and spiritual literature, vividly clarified for me the gravity but also the sagacity of the racialized personal in the academy. Our casual, occasional e-mail exchange took a significant turn when I noted to her that she often appeared to be exhausted during class meetings. Her reply astonished me. "Concerning my seeming exhaustion in class," she wrote

> I think it has a lot to do with the subject matter [rather] than my physical strength. I actually take a pleasant stroll and get to class an hour ahead of time and sit and refresh myself of the readings for the day. That may be the mistake. The narratives are powerful and evoke a lot of feelings in me. I think I am in another place as the discussion goes to the [rhetorical] style and so on and sometimes I am left with all of these feelings.

Happily perceiving this as a teachable moment in which I was both pupil and instructor, I used my e-mail response to discuss with Mary the false binary of the emotional versus the academic, especially as exhibited in our class dynamics. Neither she nor I wanted our discussions of slave autobiographies circumscribed by traditional scholarly methodology: we were both, in Mary's words, "too close to the narratives perhaps because [the two of us] grew up in the South hearing about slavery in the flesh and realizing that that was not long ago and that things can revolve." However, later in class, when I invited the other students to analyze how and why we had restricted our studies to a hypercritical realm devoid of emotion, they resisted this analysis—and any expression, and thus any collective examination, of those emotions the course texts elicited in them. This valuable experience illustrated for me that the needs of my black students and my pedagogical responsibilities to them often differ substantially from the needs of and to my white students in the same courses; it also elucidated how much work remains if I am to fulfill either set of needs respectably. Meanwhile, Mary follows the example of her slave foreparents and achieves her own survival, for her e-mail went on to describe the reading community she has formed for herself by providing copies of our course texts to a group of friends and colleagues also interested in studying African American history. Instructively, she wrote:

> I sense that [the other seminar participants] are comfortable where the discussion goes. I think they take it to a place where they can discuss [the texts] intellectually rather than emotionally because that's the place where they can handle it. I'm okay understanding that. I just know I have to have an outlet in which I can talk about the narratives from a place of

emotions and the feelings [that the narratives] evoke in me. That doesn't have to happen in class. I am finding these places.

Mary's decision marks my failure with this particular class: she ought not to have had to go outside our seminar room to find the intellectual community she desired, one voluntarily engaging early African American Christian narratives in a complex discussion at once intellectual and emotional. Nothing absolved me from the responsibility of providing her and her compeers with a learning environment in which race is addressed not as an abstraction but as a fact of tremendous influence on all American lives; nothing ever does. Every astute and responsible professor must urge—and lead—all students of multi-ethnic American literature into the realm of feeling. Indeed, this is essential for a thorough comprehension of texts, including slave narratives, that have as their very aim the arousal of deep feeling and an appeal to a shared morality.

By calling attention to Mary's ironic desire that my class at the Harvard Divinity School attend as much to spiritual matters as to scholastic ones, I risk reinforcing a myth pervasive throughout the nineteenth century and extant yet: that whites seek out rational, theoretical matters while blacks, ever primitive and imbecilic, study only (through) emotion and sensation. Certainly, I do not mean to imply that Mary, or any student of color, is either ill equipped for theoretical discussions (as if those are always already devoid of passion) or uninterested in them (as if hers were a baser, more irrational nature than white students'). Rather, I believe that Mary's African American heritage, the legacy of racism, and her personal commitment to understanding the full complexity of her rich ancestry compel her to insist on a multifarious study of early African American literature. Such insistence in no way demonstrates that she cares less than her (white) colleagues about developing an exhaustive working knowledge of high literary theory or about becoming as proficient as possible for the literary studies job market and, after, the American literature classroom.

What exactly does *proficiency* for the African American literature classroom entail? Not "blackness," not an African phenotype. But also not simply a background in generic American literature, if such an entity exists. The instructor who would pick up, say, *The Norton Anthology of African American Literature* and presume to select a few items for inclusion in a syllabus, on the basis that they are, after all, literature, insults both the traditions from which the selections emerge and colleagues long trained in a holistic historical and theoretical contextualization of those traditions. More emphatically, this instructor disserves students. Let me draw a final parallel. I daresay most English teachers are familiar with students, as obstinate and erroneous as they are naive, who argue that interpretations of literature are boundless, who insist on an infinite number of "right" readings of any given text. The instructor who drops Sojourner Truth's *Narrative* or Harriet Jacobs's *Incidents* into a syllabus without qualification(s) is like those errant students. Perhaps especially in the literature classroom, where students are likely to insist on their own opinions (however uninformed) as precise explications and where the proclivity to challenge scholarly instruction seems so much more rampant than in other academic disciplines, educators must be thoroughly knowledgeable about the origins and distinctions of multiethnic traditions. Our work must be fastidiously, as duCille posits, "about professionalism[,] about cultural literacy and intellectual competence" (94). It must be about respect.

NOTES

This essay was written under the auspices of the Harvard University School of Divinity Women Studies in Religion Program, 1996–97.

[1] I am surely one of those Indira Karamcheti has called the "walking exemplars of ethnicity and race" (qtd. in duCille 97). Ann duCille has sardonically noted that this designation "is particularly true for black women scholars on white college campuses where they experience both hypervisibility and superisolation. Unfortunately, icons are not granted tenure automatically; when their canonical year rolls around, these same black female faculty members who have been drawn on as exemplars and used up as role models will find themselves chewed up and spit out because they didn't publish or conform to the rules in some way"(97).

[2] I use *faculty members of color* for expediency, though, like Hazel Carby, I am concerned that "we are all supposed to be familiar with who is being invoked by this term, but do we honestly think that some people lack color? [. . .] Are those without color not implicated in a society structured in dominance by race?" ("Multicultural Wars" 184).

[3] "For the literature of people who are not in power has always been in danger of extinction or of co-optation. [. . .] I know, from literary history, that writing disappears unless there is a response to it" (Christian, "Race" 78).

[4] On the "consumption" of African American women, see also bell hooks's "Eating the Other" and "Selling Hot Pussy," in *Black Looks* 21–39 and 61–77.

[5] I do not mean to imply that nineteenth-century literary texts constitute history by virtue of their date of publication. And certainly I acknowledge that literature differs from history in its imaginative, constructed, and creative properties. However, despite a scarcity of artifacts and documents that chronicle the (f)actual experiences of nineteenth-century African Americans and that are unassailable among scholars, blacks' self-representations and their own reports of their life experiences provide historical and sociological information.

The Experiences of Slave Narratives:
Reading against Authenticity

Lindon Barrett

Often students facing the task of having to read and consider African American slave narratives make a notable misstep. They look at slave narratives so intently as experiential records that they virtually neglect them as discursive artifacts. They expect to engage through their experiences of reading the narratives singularly representative or authentic experiences of "blackness" and "enslavement," and these expectations are problematic because they diminish intriguing textual negotiations undertaken by the narrators as well as the powerful sociopolitical imperatives overdetermining racial categorization. Expecting to hit experiential bedrock, students overlook the acts of textual representation with which they are confronted. If the cultural regime underwriting United States slavery is one that "cast[s] social practices as biological essences" (Saks 40), then its analog in these instances is the casting of social practices as experiential essences. The result is that the textual artifacts before the students are dismissed as transparencies, and the notion of race underpinning enduring United States cultural formations is hypostasized. Racialization is reconfirmed and reiterated as obdurate and monolithic. It is imagined as the untroubled and authentic bedrock of social and historical experience, even as the narratives both produce and question the effect of race in their efforts to document and alter a social and cultural landscape. The narratives, that is, propose race foremost as the vexed product of social interactions and delineate and query these interactions. These delineations and queries—not any authentic experience monopolizing blackness or slavery—are the most recuperable performances of the narratives. Because race is by no means a self-evident principle, the reader of the narratives must consider race on some level as a discursively mediated phenomenon and apparatus. Students must be led to understand that a central lesson to be gleaned from the exercise before them is the way in which race "organizes a range of discursive practices" (Chay 639), practices eminently more recuperable than the "authentic."

Arguably the most influential line of thought in contemporary criticism of slave narratives, the now widely articulated African American feminist critique offers a productive basis for classroom instruction. Raising questions of representativeness and authenticity along lines of gender, the critique of what formerly stood as the archetypal figure and archetypal heroism of slave narratives highlights the idea that "slave experience" and "blackness" are not recoverable as parcels of experience transparently preceding and redacted in the narratives. Dispelling the aim of reading to find a unitary condition of blackness or slavery underwriting the narratives, the critique foregrounds ways in which constructions of blackness (and whiteness) in the texts emerge principally as strategies of cultural dominance or subversion scripting what may come to be understood as totalized "experience." Slave narratives are artifacts in which political, discursive, and textual crises make up the most substantive signifiers of racial blackness (as well as whiteness) and slavery. In reading to recognize these crises, students learn to forgo simple expectations of authenticity and its apparent stability of categories and conditions. They must question self-evident matters like *race* and the ease with which its self-evidence is usually received.

Much of the self-evidence of race as well as the experience of enslavement represented in the narratives is, from the vantage of the African American feminist critique, insistently masculinist, since most slave narratives, in the words of Deborah McDowell, focus "studiously on making the slave a man, according to cultural norms of masculinity" (40). Readers are schooled to be suspicious of what most often passes as authentic slave experience. What passes as the whole story is, in fact, only part of it. In place of a singular, authentic slave or black experience, one discovers attempts to parallel dominant constructions of masculinity. In addition to attempts to authenticate brutal experiences of racial blackness and enslavement, postures central to the narratives complicate or overwhelm gestures at unproblematic authenticity, as demonstrated by the narratives of Douglass, James W. C. Pennington, and Elizabeth Keckley, for example. These contradictory gestures form points of textual crisis that trouble the specious self-evidence of race and the highly charged and enduring investment of United States culture in both the certainty of race and the notion of the limiting nature of blackness.

This is not to say that race should be imagined as a meaningless or insignificant concept. But it must not be conceived as an ontological condition either. Students must be reminded that, even in the circumstances of United States slavery, race is not a given but a deployed concept and that the peculiar dynamics of its deployment are especially well illustrated by textual moments that refuse the transparency of authenticity. One well-known example comes early in *Narrative of the Life of Frederick Douglass*. When Douglass recalls that slave songs provide one of the most powerful impressions of the anguish of enslavement, he characterizes them as an authentic measure of African American experience. He also claims that only his subsequent remove from the songs triggered in him recognition of them as such: "I did not, when a slave, understand the deep meaning of those rude and apparently incoherent songs. I was myself within the circle; so that I neither saw nor heard as those without might see and hear" (263). Douglass the ex-slave proclaims a proximity to his white readership that, in effect, alienates him from the condition of racial blackness he is purporting to document. Douglass stakes his authenticity as a cultural informant by marking a gulf between himself and the cultural phenomenon he aims to explicate from the inside. How is it possible, many critics have asked, that attaining the position of "those without" ultimately validates Douglass's ability to represent the experiences and meanings of those "within the circle"? Whatever the answer, the odd address to his readers compromises any apparent immediacy to racial blackness and to the condition of enslavement Douglass advertises. The advertised immediacy to blackness and to the condition of slavery remains finally a strategic appeal, a manner of speaking deployed as a peculiar textual event, a dramatic, emphatic flourish.

There emerge from these statements no self-evidence, no unassailable or strict measure of authentication. If in the context of the narrative and much nineteenth-century thought, racial blackness is powerfully related to the terms of enslavement and if Douglass clearly lines himself up with those distanced from enslavement, then his disclosures trouble or unsettle pervasive codifications of race. Where one is led to expect pure racial blackness, one finds appeals to whiteness, so that the stark racial distinction paramount to the narrative and to the cultural and political intrigue the narrative reports emerges, in these textual moments, as troublingly imprecise and unreliable. If Douglass's address to his readers abandons to some degree "those inarticulate norms and values that determine what can legitimately be said—or perceived—in any social structure" (Finke 164), then routine notions of race are in this instance abandoned.

The enduring United States investment in both the certainty of race and the certainty of the *limiting nature* of blackness is placed in crisis. This notion of the limiting nature of blackness has to do with the supposition that those designated *black* remain circumscribed within a very particular set of experiences of, attitudes toward, and perspectives on the world strikingly differentiating them from a broader population that bear a much more open-ended positioning to the world. In the context of slave narratives, this notion has to do with imagining the brutal physicality and anguish of enslavement as the only problem or revelation yielded by the texts; it has to do with belief in a singular, authentic experience monopolizing both the writing and reception of the narratives. The point here is not to minimize or discount the brutal physicality and anguish of either enslavement or racial blackness in United States history. Nor is it to espouse a kind of belated liberal humanism: all people ultimately are the same and the human condition transcends incidental social divisions. Certainly not. While the position forwarded here fully acknowledges that the anguish and brutality of United States racial regimes provide powerful materials for extended consideration in the classroom as they do in the slave narratives themselves, it also cautions that to conceive the horrors and angst of brutalized lives as the only materials offered for consideration by slave narratives amounts to reiterating notions of the limited nature of blackness contested by the narratives themselves but pervasive in both past and present United States culture.

One might ask what it means for students of any racial or ethnic makeup to imagine they might be capable of or charged with recovering the immediacy of the physical or other conditions of enslavement. This type of approach ultimately disengages the narratives from the historical, political, economic, and judicial circumstances that determine the problematic of race and are unaccountable in the terms of oversimple black/white bifurcations. This type of

orientation to the academic endeavor may too easily reinforce conceptualizations of racial blackness and African Americans that are comfortable and overly
familiar in the cultural imagination of the United States. How might this misstep fail to make students see that race—and here is the unacknowledged crux
of the matter—always has been and continues to be foremost an intellectual
matter, either within or without the classroom but most plainly so in the classroom? The conditions and anguish of enslavement, as the passage from Douglass implies, are never merely reducible to stark, simple bifurcations nor are
they fully recoverable or unmediated. The crux of reading these narratives,
then, must also reside elsewhere. In the essay "Stranger in the Village," James
Baldwin writes:

> The ideas on which American beliefs are based are not, though Ameri-
> cans often seem to think so, ideas which originated in America. They
> came out of Europe. And the establishment of democracy on the Amer-
> ican continent was scarcely a radical break with the past as was the neces-
> sity, which Americans faced, of broadening this concept to include black
> [people].   (171)

However ambiguous United States responses have been to this challenge to
expand the concept of democracy, slave narratives stand as ready documents of
one episode in this ongoing drama. An understanding of slave narratives that
esteems them for more than their supposed fidelity to an unrecoverable past
allows them to complicate what people in the United States believe and what
they think their beliefs are based on.

Two moments from innumerable possible examples, one from J. W. C. Pennington's *The Fugitive Blacksmith* and one from Elizabeth Keckley's *Behind
the Scenes*, underscore this circumstance. These moments offer students textual crises in which race proves highly equivocal. The crises or postures they
reveal are not necessarily indicative of any authentic or lived experience but
are discursive performances that frustrate readers searching for what might
easily pass as the authentic. As readers had in the moment of Douglass's curi-
ous consideration of slave songs, they discover not only markers of blackness
and slave experience but patent markers of whiteness as well. Pennington and
Keckley take up stances that confound uncomplicated expectations placed on
race. Pennington's reflections on a decisive moment in his personal quest for
freedom and Keckley's reflections on the mind-sets of newly emancipated
African Americans reverse routinely assumed premises of racialization.

In the example from Pennington, the peculiar moment of address is precipitated by his witnessing, as a young man, the beating of his father: "Being a
tradesman, and just at that time getting my breakfast, I was near enough to
hear the insolent words that were spoken to my father, and to hear, see, and
even count the savage stripes inflicted upon him" (211 [Beacon]). Witnessing
this event causes Pennington to repudiate his condition as a slave and to

resolve to escape. "Although it was some time after this event before I took the decisive step, yet in my mind and spirit, I never was a *Slave* after it" (211). At this heightened moment of his narrative, Pennington makes an unexpected and unusual racial appeal. The incident is recorded in a way that calls attention to more than the pronounced physical violence Pennington witnesses and its disturbing emotional effect on him and the rest of his family. Pennington justifies his determination to no longer be a slave with a rhetorical question: "Let me ask anyone of Anglo-Saxon blood and spirit, how you would expect a *son* to feel at such a sight?" (211).

Pennington's appeal is not to the feelings, judgments, or experiences of African Americans, as one might anticipate, but to the sensibilities and self-assurance of those most emphatically understood as white in the United States imagination. Rather than ask his readers to comprehend experiences and matters entirely foreign to them, Pennington asks that they consider what is most familiar in their own attitudes and self-understanding. He asks that, in order to understand his experiences, they draw on their own. He offers them no alien authenticity but a proclamation of shared sensibilities, a shared sense of an appropriate response to witnessing the injury and humiliation of a would-be patriarch. Moreover, Pennington not only poses the question but also implies he knows the answer. Without pausing to offer an explanation, he implies that he understands "Anglo-Saxon blood and spirit" and that he does so with no taxing or unusual effort. Even more, he insinuates that his rejection of slavery and his eventual escape from the United States slave regime is a justified, if not obvious, response to his trauma. He presents his readers with a critical reading of his situation forestalling the imagination of stark, impenetrable divisions between racial blackness and racial whiteness and the experiences of both.

Rather than polarized racial positions, masculinist, familial, and sociolegal imperatives that refer to a shared world and discourse are brought to bear on the episode. Much is common across the gulf of race, Pennington assumes, and the apparent effortlessness of the assumption must complicate readers' notions of the experiences documented in slave narratives as well as the experience of reading the texts themselves. A large portion of what Pennington shares with his readers are comprehensions of what they already possess. In documenting United States slavery, he offers a vision of an exorbitant "chattel principle" (198) exceeding individual suffering or terror and disturbing widely esteemed institutions such as the family and the sentiments the family fosters. Pennington assumes that, despite barriers of race, he and his readers revile such disturbances.

It is also worthwhile to recognize that Pennington's conception of shared cultural sensibilities underscores the apprehensions and insights of the feminist critique so influential in reforming the reception and teaching of slave narratives. Key to Pennington's trauma is the diminished entitlements of a "son" realized through demonstrations of the belittled circumstances of a "father." Pennington's recollection centers the drama of enslavement, repudiation, and escape in the postures assumed by men and the cultural commerce among men. However, for those not invested in such prerogatives promoted across racial lines such as African American women, this rendition of the travails and triumphs of enslavement is glaringly inadequate. The central figure of the slave presented by Pennington conforms, in this way, to Frances Foster's estimations of the typical figure to appear in slave narratives:

> The Heroic Slave narrates a success story. He has endured the most inhumane environment imaginable and, without stooping to revenge, has escaped with his life and his integrity. He is Everyslave, innocent, ignorant, and abused but a human being who needs only free soil in which to blossom into an industrious, literate, and totally moral citizen. [. . .] His is decidedly a temporal and essentially parochial theme—liberation in this life of those physically enslaved in the southern United States.
>
> The Heroic Slave struggles not only against physical brutality and oppression but also against the subjugation of his human spirit. [. . .] He knows only that he lives within an institution that denies his humanity and threatens his very survival and that he is willing to risk his life to save himself. ("Adding Color" 32)

These conventional portrayals, as Foster points out, marginalize the matters openly pursued by feminist considerations of the genre, the experiences and circumstances of enslaved African American women. Given what is excluded from the purview of this typical figure, one begins to understand the misdirection of reading the narratives to recover, as a matter of course, some unitary condition of blackness or enslavement. Slave narratives become—in intellectually rewarding ways—highly questionable.

Elizabeth Keckley's *Behind the Scenes* similarly illustrates the questionable nature of representative performances undertaken by the narratives. Written several years after the defeat of the South in the Civil War, *Behind the Scenes* recounts Keckley's life as both enslaved and free, including her occupation as a well-respected seamstress, an occupation that allowed her to purchase her freedom before the war. However, the episode of interest here concerns Keckley's commentary on the "extravagant hopes" (139) of African Americans emancipated during the massive military campaign of the midcentury. The initiative and responsibility implicit in her own process of manumission do not obtain. She writes, "Some of the freedmen and freedwomen had exaggerated ideas of liberty [. . . and] it was but natural that many of them should bitterly feel their disappointment" (139). Having visited many of these disappointed ex-slaves arriving in Washington, Keckley discovers that some of them claim to prefer slavery to their newfound freedom. This is so, she speculates, "because dependence had become a part of their second nature, and independence had brought with it the cares and vexations of poverty" (140). She illustrates the point with her recollection of an old black woman complaining that since she had arrived in Washington, Mrs. Lincoln had not handed down to her any old undergarments in the manner of southern plantation mistresses. Keckley explains to "Northern readers [who] may not fully understand the pith of the joke" (142) that the old woman does not recognize that this custom is no longer appropriate to her new circumstances.

Keckley, at this moment of her narrative, like Pennington in his, positions herself to underscore her proximity to her readers—their experiences, conditions, and understanding. She advertises that she holds a routine comprehension of United States citizenship with its assumptions of economic ingenuity and self-reliance. She shares with her readers the amusement of scoring "the pith of the joke," how alien the old woman's perceptions are. The woeful misunderstandings of the old woman are as unacceptable to Keckley as they are to her readers. The consequence of the remarks lies, then, in Keckley's negotiation of spaces for African Americans both within and without the circle of experience attributed to the dominant United States population. If there are a large number of African Americans as misinformed as the old woman Keckley does not so much privilege or unfold those experiences and sensibilities as repudiate them. Recapitulating postures her readers already hold, her anecdote does not so much pursue what is unknown to her readers in experience or conception, as provide them with familiar matters and the assurance that some African Americans can and do share those familiar matters:

> While some of the emancipated blacks pined for the old associations of slavery, and refused to help themselves, others went to work with commendable energy, and planned with remarkable forethought. They built themselves cabins, and each family cultivated for itself a patch of ground.
> (142)

The image drawn of an African American community is a divided one. Some African Americans fully recognize what their new circumstances entail, and some do not, and this twofold vision of Keckley's remarks makes any act of claiming the authentic much more complex than it might first appear. Which of the two positions is more "black"? How is the question resolved? By a mere accounting or tallying? Is Keckley even concerned with this issue? Certainties may be more elusive than available, especially in a text premised on such peculiar dynamics of address as *Behind the Scenes*. It is a text in which an ex-slave glosses in three chapters some thirty years of her life as a slave in order to provide extended and close consideration of four subsequent years spent in service to public figures. It is a text in which an ex-slave is able to provide her white readership with intimate details of the lives of captivating public figures and to take her readers repeatedly and at length into the White House, giving them a kind of access to the national monument and the Lincolns, an access they would never be able to obtain otherwise. In effect, Keckley bears greater proximity to central figures and institutions of the United States than does an audience that intently understands itself as holding much more direct claims and a much more direct relation to these figures and institutions. The address of this text dramatically reverses deeply assumed premises of racialization. The certainties of authentic racial location and experience are powerfully ruptured. Keckley possesses the freedom, knowledge, and access that place her in a position that by the logic of racialization is as troubling as it is intricate.

These dynamics of address, if the text is attended to appropriately, cannot fail to emerge in the classroom. They cannot fail to arise if one is attentive to the ways racial blackness is produced, or effected, in the very act of its textual representation. The discursive and the experiential are, of course, closely related but are, just as assuredly, not the same. Often the two are mutually constitutive, but students must be reminded that, although the purpose of discourse is frequently to convey or consolidate experience, that goal is never an uncomplicated or wholly attainable one. Considerable humanist thought following Saussure dedicates itself to demonstrating this discrepancy in detail. Taking an act of representation for the represented itself, no matter how seemingly commonsensical or compelling, constitutes a misjudgment albeit a widespread one. One must also point out to students, however, that the issue is not simply one of misperception but ineluctably one of power. There are significant consequences to tally when one considers the relation between discourse and its referents. Who has the means or occasion to govern the relation? to foster and benefit from equating the discursive and the authentic? At what moments and in what circumstances? In other words, the misstep of neglecting the dynamics and subtleties of discursive practices amounts to submitting to those practices too naïvely, and the literary classroom, one must insist, should never be a site for such submission.

Celebrating and questioning the pioneering work of the critic-activist Barbara Smith, Deborah Chay, in her discussion of the development and fortunes of black feminist criticism, considers how "accounting for differences by reference to experience [. . .] cannot then account for the ideological construction of experience itself" (639). When one considers social difference solely in terms of experience, the purview of what can be explained is limited. What is omitted, Chay argues, are "the conditions which *continue* to make an appeal to experience as a logical, appealing, and *invisible* foundation" so enticing (649). Insofar as experience seems the unimpeachable ground that situates one in the world, one is never prompted to consider how what stands as experience, in fact, comes to stand as experience, how it may be overdetermined by more than authentic lived *reality*. In accepting experience as the only or fundamental ground of difference, one is not prompted to consider how one comes to "know" an elephant, an African American, a slave, a woman, a gay man, a lesbian, or the destitute before one ever encounters them. One is not prompted to consider how the perceptions detailing experience may be groomed for and channeled to the experience before its occurrence or appearance. Experience, this is to say, may result as much from overdetermining representations as from any singular, undeniable, discrete moment or encounter. Ideological constructions of experience, Chay reminds her readers, define one's situation in the world as much as experiences themselves do, and Chay is concerned ultimately with the irony that "efforts to identify varieties of black feminist critical practice [. . .] obscure one of black feminism's most persistent commonalities and one which wants theorizing—the use of experience to ground claims about difference and to establish cultural legitimacy" (648).

While the goal here is not simply to reproduce some of the preeminent concerns of African American feminist criticism, the instructiveness of these concerns, as already suggested, cannot be ignored. It is equally important to make clear that the practice Chay identifies is by no means unique to African American feminist criticism but, rather, a pervasive symptom of the conception of social difference in the United States. The near monopoly granted experience in the consideration of social difference more often than not leaves unpursued crucial opportunities for "exploring how difference is established, how it operates, how and in what ways it constitutes subjects who see and act in the world" (Scott 399–400). It leaves unexamined crucial opportunities to uncover very subtle channels of social power. It should be made clear to students that the dangers of conflating the experiential and the discursive are the dangers of diminishing the issue of power. When these dangers remain unacknowledged, authenticity seems to emerge through the variables of space and time independent of all matters of social power and cultural regimes. Categories of meaning appear given rather than produced.

Thus, to gauge race and United States slavery primarily in terms of experience would be to see them as given terms of United States social reality, rather than as phenomena actively produced and maintained. The exercise or experience of reading slave narratives would seemingly highlight the disparity attributable to difference—rather than to the politics (organized and otherwise) swirling around difference. By transforming their expectations into more useful impulses, students might be prompted to ask what is to be gained by imagining racial blackness and slavery purely in terms of experience and authentication. And by whom?

What is the boon to the students themselves? The comfort of eluding confrontations with "inarticulate norms and values that determine what can legitimately be said—or perceived—in [their own] social structure" (Finke 164)? Is there a boon for them in neglecting the question of how difference manages to underwrite political, economic, moral, psychic, and even libidinal formations they take for granted? Which is to ask, Is there a boon in neglect of the crucial question of what is difference itself? There is an intellectual solace in this position that forecloses genuine critical engagement with the narratives and, accordingly, genuine critical inquiry into imperative social constructs like race, gender, sexuality, and class. Kim Hall recognizes as much, and in the appendix to her study *Things of Darkness* urges scholar-teachers to create in their classrooms an atmosphere in which students cannot easily assume comfortable

cultural positions that elsewhere are offered to them routinely. Hall proposes
a set of alternatives:

> We can create a cultural narrative for the white student based on a fam-
> ily tale of glorious origins and lost (but soon to be regained) power and
> make the student of color a Caliban, fit only to serve the psychic and
> social needs of those in power. Or, we can acknowledge the ongoing
> legacy of "this thing of darkness" [racialization in the New World] and
> use that knowledge to create new ways of thinking about difference that
> let students approach the texts of Western culture as equals. If we are
> successful, we can give students the critical tools for a more meaningful
> and complex dialogue on race, one that comprehends the intersections of
> categories without disregarding our differences and that moves beyond
> racial guilt—but not beyond justice.   (268)

   If students expected only to engage experience, they would fail to account for
the circumstances, addresses, and perceptions of the very narrators to whom they
surrender themselves in opening the text, as illustrated by the reflections of Pennington and Keckley. They would gloss rather than meaningfully attend to Pennington's peculiar appeal to fundamentals of racial whiteness and would never be
intrigued by Keckley's divided characterization of emancipated African Americans. Such misreadings are to be avoided because they more insistently foreclose
intellectual curiosity than foster it. They abrogate the textual authority of Pennington and Keckley in deference to more widespread expectations of what the
narrators' experiences must have been—experiences singularly of *difference*.
They replicate widespread gestures of "a cultural system in which authority—
self-authority or any other—has been traditionally denied" African Americans
especially in acts of self-declaration (Barrett 219). Pennington and Keckley would
be refused the authority to characterize their experiences as they chose.
   In teaching slave narratives, then, one does not want to make the mistake
made by the culture at large, the mistake of reifying United States racialization
and slavery as historical givens recalcitrant to serious questioning. One wants
to excavate the powers of representation that ex-slave narrators struggle to
assume not only in the nineteenth-century but also in the circumstances of
their current reception as writers in a cultural archive. Against common perception, the narrators struggle to represent through records of their experiences the certainty that race only "embodies a pragmatic recognition of how
someone's ancestors were socially defined" (Saks 45). Race does not so much
redact any necessary experience or aggregate of necessary experiences as it
does a powerful apparatus of social classification. A paramount vector for social
power routinely represented otherwise, race is determined by both experience
and the cultivation of experience, not necessarily in equal measure. The influence of each, not to mention the causal relation between them, is not to be
taken for granted, ex-slave narrators remind us.

If students can be made to imagine that Pennington and Keckley have the power to accomplish this feat, how much closer are they to imagining the power of others more consistently and unquestionably invested with the power to represent the meaning of race and other signal experiences? An imperative task for teachers of slave narratives is to help students recognize how unlikely it is that those bearing highly uncommon experiences of race would offer the connection between experience and race as the commonplace it is assumed to be in the United States. It is highly unlikely that these narrators would represent race as an experiential given defined solely by the parameters of their particular experiences or, for that matter, any set of experiences. Authentic experience consorts with authentic power. The burden lies in engaging and highlighting these unlikely performances and disclosures on the part of exslave narrators. It lies, as do much of the import and interest of the narratives, in crises of representation that include race itself.

Framing the Slave Narrative / Framing Discussion
Russ Castronovo

How teachers and students frame a discussion of the slave narrative can lead to a pedagogical minefield. A teacher's first response might gesture toward historical contexts where words like *literacy, race, authenticity,* and *rationality* play important roles. Clearly, this necessary contextualization involves research and background reading, but it overlooks the initial and deeply problematic desire to frame the slave narrative in the first place. When we teach early African American autobiography, uncomfortable convergences emerge as the literary history of the antebellum era repeats itself in uncanny ways in our contemporary settings of higher education: just as the instructor in the classroom outlines a discussion of the slave narrative in historical, thematic, or ideological terms, so too 150 years earlier white editors prepared northern audiences for the fugitive's story by providing prefaces, letters, and other supporting documents to frame black discourse. In all cases, cultural authorities stand outside the slave narrative, their positions of exteriority confirming the power to influence, if not direct, how texts enter a field of consumption and interpretation.

Of course, tremendous differences exist between white antislavery activists whose philanthropic endeavors did not rule out racist beliefs, and college teachers with commitments to diversity and multiculturalism. Frederick Douglass's uneasy recollections of the abolitionist introduction to his story, however, can caution us about the paternalism latent in any display of cooperation. "I was generally introduced as a *'chattel'*—a *'thing'*—a piece of southern *'property'*—the chairman assuring the audience that *it* could speak," remembered Douglass of his early days as a lecturer for the Massachusetts Anti-slavery Society (*My Bondage* [Dover] 360). His words suggest that authority and power always undergird the framing of African American expression, whether it is the abolitionist prefacing a slave narrative or a college teacher presenting the same text to contemporary students. This is the minefield: teaching the slave narrative confronts instructors with the occasion and image of their own power. An articulation so deeply concerned with freedom enters the classroom terrain under a series of cultural constraints coincident with the teacher's necessarily privileged position within the the classroom. It is ironic, then, that the slave narrator's struggle for authority and voice are always secondary, ready for presentation only once the authority of instructor or editor has been enacted.

Instructors can respond, on the one hand, by deftly sidestepping any interrogation of the authority they (increasingly) exercise over the slave's text as African American literature is institutionalized within the academy. After all, teaching is a matter not only of education but also of authority, and many accomplished professors have found it best carefully to preserve their authority. Or, on the other hand, teachers can tread through this dangerous terrain, picking their way among the various degrees of privilege that they and their students enjoy and that allow them to comment on African American literature. Such a strategy attempts to practice the radical pedagogy described by Chandra Talpade Mohanty, who sees the classroom as a zone of "accommodations and contestations over knowledge by differently empowered social constituencies" (147).

The remainder of this essay considers this second alternative, first by briefly examining white editorial control over two very different slave narratives, Hiram Mattison's *Louisa Picquet, the Octoroon* (1861) and *Narrative of the Life of Frederick Douglass* (1845), and then by thinking about some pragmatic paths to negotiating a discussion about the instructor's unquestioned entitlement not only to situate, categorize, and interpret the slave narrative but also to manage and regulate the student voices participating in that interpretation. Despite appearances, the minefield may offer fertile ground. Thinking about the too often undisclosed and unexamined posture of the accomplished instructor can reveal how the framing of our reading is inevitably invested with possibilities of domination as well as understanding.

Slave narratives are complex pedagogical acts. They seek to educate a largely white audience about the horrors of slavery by revealing what the fugitive has learned during his or her "career" as a slave. As Douglass writes, white speakers who preceded him on the abolitionist lectern introduced him as a "graduate from the peculiar institution [. . .] *with my diploma written on my back!*" (*My Bondage* [Dover] 359). At the same time, slave narratives educate Northerners about their own virtue by publishing what the fugitive has learned during his or her new life in the free states. In addition to this often clear didacticism, slave narratives also convey other, more subtle, messages about what the texts' editorial authorities have failed to learn about their own authority.

Such unlearned messages constitute much of the Reverend H. Mattison's *Louisa Picquet*. Not so much a slave autobiography as a strained exchange between an octoroon slave and a white male interlocutor, *Louisa Picquet* illustrates the blindness of privilege (in this case, the privilege conferred by Mattison's race, gender, and education to question a black woman) to its own power. At first glance, Mattison accords Picquet the rare opportunity of telling her story to white evangelical America. His text consists primarily of a series of conversations he had with Picquet. He asks questions and she responds; he regulates the drift of the discussion, determining which topics need further elaboration and which aspects of the slave's life need only passing mention. His desire to hear the personal, private details of a woman of "illustrious birth" (5)—his attempts to spark a discussion between him and his "pupil"—makes relentless use of the Socratic method. He does not see how his commentary and questions about Picquet's experience on the auction block—"It seems like a dream, don't it?"—tell more about his own distance from and romanticization of the harsh realities of bondage than they do about the woman he is interviewing (18). Picquet's answer, that being sold and separated from her mother does not seem like a dream, reveals a woman who refuses to accede to another's authority to represent her life.

On closer investigation of the narrative's frame, *Louisa Picquet* appears to be less about the magnanimous cooperation between white humanitarian and former slave than about the lurid interest that constrains the visibly white but legally black woman who is the focus of the text. Mattison begins Picquet's story in this way: "Louisa Picquet, the subject of the following narrative [. . . ,] is a little above the medium height, easy and graceful in her manners, of fair complexion and rosy cheeks, with dark eyes, a flowing head of hair with no perceptible inclination to curl" (5). She is "subject" to him; she is his text, her history of miscegenation providing titillation and romantic intrigue. Her life as a "concubine" offers him the occasion both to display his moral satisfaction and to indulge a fascination about a "white" woman sold for sexual purposes. Picquet fends off his curiosity about "fornication and adultery" (51) by responding with short, clipped phrases and by redirecting the original thrust of his questions. Her reticence not only indicates her abiding concern with self-respect and privacy but also serves as a marker of Mattison's unexamined privilege to intrude on her life. By the end of the narrative, however, the frame reappears and envelops her, and Mattison concludes by absorbing Picquet's life as an exemplar of a general moral lesson. The persistent tension between female slave and white male interlocutor underscores how framing a conversation is a matter not simply of extending authority to a speaker but also of exercising authority over that speaker.

A similar conflict between white editor and black author pervades Douglass's *Narrative*. Although William Lloyd Garrison's prefatory interventions are much less obtrusive than Mattison's constant questioning and moralizing, his preface situates Douglass within a larger cultural narrative not of Douglass's own choosing. Remembering the first time he heard Douglass speak, the editor of the *Liberator* writes, "As soon as he [Douglass] had taken his seat, filled with hope and admiration, I rose, and declared that PATRICK HENRY, of revolutionary fame, never made a speech more eloquent in the cause of liberty, than the one we had just listened to from the lips of that hunted fugitive" (246). Garrison's syntax reveals the power of framing: Garrison occupies an active, ascendant position while the fugitive slave is cordoned off in a dependent clause. Douglass contends against this professorial preface that evaluates and confirms the slave's story as worthy material. Douglass appears to accept Garrison's invocation of Patrick Henry, and yet his language both rejects and exceeds the terms with which his white patron oversees the *Narrative*: "In coming to a fixed determination to run away, we did *more* than Patrick Henry, when he resolved upon liberty or death" (306; my emphasis). The frame of traditional American heroism does not suit Douglass. Viewing his own prospects for freedom as much less certain than those of the Virginia slaveholder, Douglass deems that a traditional frame of reference offers the ex-slave only inadequate terms of comparison. This revision of Garrison's allusion implies that whiteness often fails to recognize its own privilege. Neither Henry nor Garrison is forced to hedge his confidence about liberty when white men seek to attain it; Douglass, in contrast, is ever mindful that "[w]ith us it was a doubtful liberty at most" (306). Such textual discord between editor and author points to a sharp disjunction between the person who authorizes a historical allusion and the person who is subject to that allusion, between the person who structures a discourse and the person structured by it.

A brief exercise that asks students to inscribe their own life within the mediated *form* of the slave narrative demonstrates the perils of editorial intervention. Students should be discouraged from attempting to make their lives adhere to the *content* of the slave narrative; indeed, their legally recognized existences should bear a plenitude of information unavailable to persons who "know as little of their ages as horses know of theirs" (*Narrative* 255). This exercise focuses on the structural relations of power that encircle the slave narrative. Working in pairs, students can represent a life by using the model of interaction provided by Mattison and Picquet. Even as the transcript they produce records cooperation, it also registers unequal speech positions of questioners and respondents, especially when compared with the students' autonomous narrations of their lives. The exercise need not be long; ten minutes should be ample time for students to reproduce the basic information that the opening "I was born" paragraph of many slave narratives contains. Meanwhile, other pairs of students can pattern a discourse after Douglass's text and Garrison's preface. Students' autobiographical statements that they were born, not in "Talbot county, Maryland" as Douglass tells us, but in Fresno County, California, or Dade County, Florida, are supplemented by another student's preface (*Narrative* 255). What happens to the student's autobiographical act when it is linked to another articulation in which the student appears in the third person? Is this link one of convenience or dependence? Has the authority to tell freely one's story been eroded?

Uneasy and conflicted, the asymmetrical relationships between editors-interlocutors and autobiographical subjects reveal the workings of narrative power if only because they are situations in which the distribution of power is so severely skewed. The framers set up the frame and stand back, seeking to exempt themselves from the analytic attention brought to the text or conversation they have initiated. Authority remains most secure when it avoids notice. For both Mattison and Garrison the slave narrative is an occasion to present and examine others in a public setting, but never once an opportunity to reflect on the opacity of their own social power that makes such a display possible. Still, the slaves in these narratives do not accede to such unquestioned authority; after all, they are loath to reinscribe themselves in a textual situation that structurally echoes the conditions of Southern paternalism. Picquet's and Douglass's silences, revisionary impulses, and corrections speak volumes, informing us about the rarely acknowledged desire to readjust, if only temporarily, the positions within any exchange. It is their desire to question their questioners, to include within the analytic ken of the slave's text the editors and activists who had the privilege to call for and introduce the slave's enterprise in the first place. What happens when teachers follow the lead of Picquet and Douglass and include the institutionally granted privilege to hover over, shape, and guide class discussion as a subject of interpretative analysis?

Discussion of editorial authority in the college classroom can excite no particular interest unless the pedagogical tension within the slave narrative is linked to the pedagogical tension between teacher and student. Vested with the authority of higher education, instructors often frame discussion, drawing on knowledge, experience—and at least one diploma—to prepare a topic, direct the ensuing conversation, and gather conclusions. As with the slave narrative the lines of authority are clear: the interpretative project usually begins with an introduction that shapes the classroom dialogue whether it is the overt injunction to break up into small groups and trace the use of biblical allusions in chapter 10 of *Narrative* or the more tentative suggestion that during the next few meetings the class may want to give some attention to gender relations in both Picquet and Douglass. The remarks made at the beginning of the classroom hour—like the words that preface the slave's narrative—in part engender the text or conversation that follows. No matter how encouraging, the teachers' spurs and prompts—like the questions put to the slave—display authority even as they keep discussion fluid and vibrant. In short, our teaching practices and strategies can replicate the editorial authority that borders many slave narratives. Structurally speaking, how different is Mattison's interrogation of Louisa Picquet from a teacher's management of a discussion about *Louisa Picquet*? How different is Garrison's preface from an instructor's prefatory remarks to a class session about Douglass's 1845 autobiography? A contest of authority always pervades the slave narrative and its transmission, whether that transmission occurs in nineteenth-century Boston or in a twenty-first-century classroom.

By considering not only the intermittent opposition between white sponsor and slave narrator but also the necessary structural ambivalence between teacher and student, a class can begin to investigate the often elided links between pedagogical authority and textual mastery. The racial difference between Picquet and Mattison is only one of several differences that allow for Mattison's enactment of authority. Differences in education, age, and gender between Northern minister and Southern slave woman make Mattison's "reading" of her story into an act that serves his sensational yet moralizing interests. Instructors can highlight some analogous differences in subject position between teacher and student in an effort to encourage students to see how statements accrue validity, not because of their content, but because of the location from which they are spoken. Other rifts can appear as students perceive how authority marks their own subject positions as well. Do women and men—even if they say the same thing—speak with equal amounts of authority? Socially privileged subject positions, which historically have been answerable to no one but themselves, come under the analytic gaze of a class examining its own conduits of information and patterns of discourse. The results of self-reflection may, for some students, paralyze speech; however, such difficulty appears absolutely vital when we consider the alternative of discussing African American literature in an academic setting satisfied with the politics of its position. Silences in a classroom are temporarily strategic, providing a commentary on power relations much as the moments of reticence and evasion do in the autobiographies of Picquet and Douglass.

In my own case, I emphasize the structural ambivalence that arises when a white instructor prefaces and frames African American literature in a classroom in which African American students often constitute a majority. Unspoken tension becomes spoken as critical and intelligent discomfort. Do I inevitably occupy the place of a latter-day Mattison or Garrison? By questioning socially privileged subject positions, the class studying the slave narrative can reproduce the pedagogical tension of the text within the classroom. Picquet and Douglass push against the editorial apparatus; students probe the professorial management of their education. The connection between these two operations may be considered tenuous, but it is tempting to ask if nonresponsiveness to a teacher's attempts to spark discussion bears any similarity to Picquet's defiance of Mattison's indelicate inquiries. Notwithstanding the parameters of institutional higher education, such self-reflective thinking by students about the day-to-day operations of education can enhance the democratic impulses that are at the heart of the slave narrative. The slave narrative refutes the dominant cultural authority that insisted slaves could not write about, rationally view, or rightfully criticize United States domestic institutions. The ex-slave, in short, argues for the validity and integrity of his or her own interpretation of the world. When students critically survey the norms and regularities that govern classroom speech, they, too, can understand interpretation as a question of their participation.

Surrendering classroom authority to student scrutiny, however, does not necessarily imply a democratic pedagogy. This exposure of authority may only be a celebratory parade of an authority confident enough to withstand investigation. Michael Awkward's acute reading of white critics' work on African American literature stresses the dangers of a "self-referentiality" that disguises "desires to dominate regions and discourses of blackness, to censor what they [white critics] view as insufficiently and seriously flawed black critical and cultural practices, and to direct black natives to more enlightened modes and forms of 'real life' and scholarly behavior" (600). Such comments shed light on the "unmasking" of my whiteness to a class as perhaps little more than a playful abdication of authority that has the purpose of justifying and normalizing my socially privileged reading and teaching practices. Even though students debate the workings of classroom authority, their debate is still largely framed by the classroom authority—the teacher. To pretend that the instructor's authority has been dissipated is an exercise in bad faith.

One way to guard against a suspect philanthropy of the self-reflective instructor and the self-reflective classroom is to ask what is gained by critically questioning pedagogical-editorial authority. Is the goal of examining classroom dynamics within a discussion of the slave narrative to achieve a more harmonious educational setting? Is it to dissipate the tension created by the structural ambivalence between professor and student? Possibly—but then again, one might inquire if Picquet told her story to Mattison so that she might settle down alongside the man who condescended to interview her. The slave narrator's thinly veiled distrust of the white editor suggests that prospects for interracial harmony were replaced by a much more immediate desire to confront the cultural authority and social privilege so intimately bound up with questions of voice and autonomy. As Mohanty writes, the point of talking about race in the classroom is not one of "merely *acknowledging* difference" but rather one of understanding how such differences are located within a history marked by power, conflict, and struggle (146). Subjecting the frame of the slave narrative, both in its nineteenth-century editorial guise and in its twenty-first-century incarnation, to critical analysis is not to dispel the existence of constraint and regulation. Instead, this project works to recognize that respect is found in discussions risking hard questions and lacking easy answers.

Douglass's "Perplexing Difficulty"

Arthur Zilversmit

Frederick Douglass's *Narrative* presents an effective way of showing students that slavery was more than a system of extorting labor—that it was a way of life. Slavery was an evil, but coherent, social system. A significant question we can raise with students, therefore, is how did this social system function and, most important, how was it established and maintained? Although slave owners could and did use harsh punishments to force their reluctant workers to produce the great cash crops of the plantation South, extensive whippings were debilitating and ultimately self-defeating. To raise crops, slave owners needed to secure at least a modest degree of cooperation from their workers. Slavery as a labor system could work only if its African American victims at least to some degree actually became slaves in their own minds. How were African Americans socialized into the roles that this system demanded? How did slave owners make men, women, and children into slaves?

These questions were not even asked by southern historians of the early twentieth century. Writing from the perspective of the slave owners, the pioneer historian of slavery, Ulrich B. Phillips, simply assumed that African Americans were inherently a primitive, childlike people who readily accepted the guidance of their masters: "the slaves were [. . .] for the most part [. . .] by racial quality submissive rather than defiant, lighthearted instead of gloomy, amiable and ingratiating instead of sullen, and [. . . their] very defects invited paternalism rather than repression" (341–42). Explaining slavery by assuming the racial inferiority of African Americans has a long history in America. Thomas Jefferson had described Negroes as inherently inferior, and as late as the 1940s American history textbooks described slavery in terms of happy, childlike Negroes and long-suffering paternal slave owners.[1]

After we reject the racist interpretations of slavery, however, I ask students to consider how slave owners could run large productive enterprises with the labor of large numbers of workers who had no economic incentives to work and might be expected to have many reasons to resist. Historians now recognize the role of socialization in maintaining the slave system, although they differ sharply on the impact of the socialization process. Some of them, following the lead of Stanley Elkins, argue that the harsh slave system actually reduced its victims to a slave-like personality—the stereotypical "Sambo" (128–31). Others, however, see "Sambo" as merely a role, adopted by slaves in the presence of whites and readily discarded in the slave quarters. They argue that even those African Americans whose docile, childlike behavior gave the appearance of having internalized their masters' image of the good slave could, when the occasion presented itself, remove the mask and become rebels (Stampp; Litwack, *Been in the Storm*).

Reading slave narratives permits students to confront directly the question of the psychological impact of slavery. *Narrative of the Life of Frederick Douglass* is especially valuable in this regard for it reveals how masters socialized young black children to become slaves, to become part of a complex social system. Students come to understand slavery as a process of socialization when they examine its impact on one of its most sensitive and articulate victims, Frederick Douglass.

Douglass was, of course, unusual. Although he was born *into* the slave system, he was not quite *of* it. As a young boy, he had been fortunate to have experiences that served to undermine the process of socialization and to give him a unique insight into the process he would later escape.

When he was seven or eight years old, Douglass left the plantation where he was born and went to live in Baltimore. In that bustling commercial city the hold of slavery was much more tenuous than on the plantation. In addition, Douglass had the good fortune to have a mistress from the North who had not yet learned that she should not teach young Frederick to read and write. When his master found out that his wife had begun to teach him, he angrily admonished her: "A nigger should know nothing but to obey his master—to do as he is told to do. Learning would *spoil* the best nigger in the world" (274). Douglass recalls that these words provided "a new and special revelation, explaining dark and mysterious things. [. . .] I now understood what had been to me a most perplexing difficulty—to wit, the white man's power to enslave the black man" (275).

In teaching Douglass's *Narrative*, I emphasize the light this book sheds on the process of socialization—the methods that slave owners used to teach their African Americans to become slaves and to turn them into efficient workers.[2] At the same time, I point out that Douglass also shows how the institution socialized white boys and girls to become mistresses and masters.[3]

From the opening of his *Narrative* Douglass begins to explain how small black children learned their position in plantation society: "I have no accurate knowledge of my age. [. . .] By far the larger part of the slaves know as little of their age as horses know of theirs, and it is the wish of most masters [. . .] to keep their slaves thus ignorant"(255).[4] Like the other slave children, young Frederick did not know when his birthday was—he had no special day to celebrate his individuality. He did not even know who his father was, although he suspected that it was his master. He was separated from his mother when he was still an infant; this was done purposefully, he says, "to hinder the development of the child's affection toward its mother" (256). He never saw his mother again by the light of day, and he reacted to the news of her death as if she were a stranger.

From their earliest years African American children were made to feel different from the white children on the plantation. Slave children, Douglass tells us, were given no shoes, jackets, or trousers until they were old enough to work in the fields. They were given only two shirts, and if these wore out they went naked. They had no beds. When they ate, they were fed from a trough "like so many pigs"(271). Another slave from Maryland, James W. C. Pennington, recalls comparable experiences. He "often suffered much from *hunger* and other similar causes." Unlike white children, however, he could not turn to his family for solace: "To estimate the sad state of a slave child you must look at it as a helpless human being thrown upon the world [. . .] without a social circle to flee to for hope, shelter, comfort, or instruction" (Pennington, *Fugitive Blacksmith*, ed. Katz, 2).

For Douglass, the links between slaves and farm animals were repeatedly reinforced. After his master's death the estate was evaluated: "Men and women, [. . .] pigs and children, all holding the same rank in the scale of being, [. . .] were all subjected to the same narrow examination. Silvery-headed age and sprightly youth, maids and matrons, had to undergo the same indelicate inspection" (282).

Slaves, Douglass tells us, did not easily bond with their fellow victims. In his account of his early childhood we get no sense of a slave community. He left for Baltimore with no regrets: "The ties that ordinarily bind children to their homes were all suspended in my case" (271). Although he lived with a brother and two sisters "the early separation of us from our mother had well nigh blotted the fact of our relationship from our memories" (272).

The techniques masters devised for hampering the development of a sense of identity and self-worth in the individual slave child could lead slaves to identify with the master. Douglass recalls that the slaves from his plantation welcomed the privilege of being selected to do errands at the Great Farm; such selection was seen as a sign of respect from the overseer. Moreover, slaves frequently quarreled about who had the better master: "They seemed to think that the greatness of their masters was transferable to themselves. It was considered as being bad enough to be a slave; but to be a poor man's slave was deemed a disgrace indeed!" (267).

Behind these instruments of socialization were, of course, the threat and reality of physical punishment. One of the most traumatic events of Douglass's early childhood was seeing an overseer's brutal whipping of his Aunt Hester: "It struck me with an awful force." For Douglass, this was "the blood-stained gate, the entrance to the hell of slavery" (258). Significantly, he adds, "I expected it to be my turn next" (259). Jacob Stroyer, another ex-slave who wrote an autobiography, recalls that when his mother tried to protect him from a whipping she herself was flogged: "Then the idea first came to me that I, with my dear mother and father and the rest of my fellow negroes, was doomed to cruel treatment through life, and was defenceless" (18). Stroyer's sense of vulnerability was compounded by the recognition that a slave child's family could not save him.

Any attempt at self-assertion was cause for punishment. Douglass's master "could not brook any contradiction from a slave. When he spoke, a slave must stand, listen, and tremble" (265). One overseer (appropriately named Mr. Gore) saw impudence in any gesture, allowed no answering back, and would not allow slaves to defend themselves even from false accusation: "It is better that a dozen slaves suffer under the lash, than that the overseer should be convicted, in the presence of the slaves, of having been at fault" (267). The ultimate challenge to Gore's authority was posed by Demby, a slave who ran away from a whipping and took refuge in a nearby creek. Gore gave him a count of three to come back and accept the rest of his lashes. When he did not, Gore coolly shot Demby dead. "A thrill of horror flashed through every soul upon the plantation, excepting Mr. Gore," who carefully explained to the slave owner the necessity for this deed. The defiant slave "was setting a dangerous example to the other slaves. [. . .] [I]f one slave refused to be corrected, and escaped with his life, the other slaves would soon copy the example" (268–69).[5]

The sheer terror of whipping was compounded by its capriciousness. Slaves "were frequently whipped when least deserving, and escaped whipping when most deserving" (264–65). No one was exempt from punishment. "Old Barney," a slave well over fifty years old, was forced to "uncover his bald head, kneel down upon the cold, damp ground, and receive upon his naked toil-worn shoulders more than thirty lashes at the time" (265).

In this world, slaves came to know that to survive they needed to learn the arts of deception. One slave was sold to a Georgia trader for the mistake of having given an honest answer to his master. In this way, Douglass tells us, a slave learns that "a still tongue makes a wise head" (266).

All the master's sons and sons-in-law had the right to beat any slave at any time. White children soon learned their lessons: "It was a common saying, even among little white boys, that it was worth a half-cent to kill a 'nigger,' and a half-cent to bury one" (270). Douglass shows most vividly the ways in which slavery socialized whites in his picture of the transformation of Mrs. Auld, the woman who had begun to teach him to read and write. "Slavery proved as injurious to her as it did to me. When I went there she was a pious, warm, and tender-hearted woman. [. . .] Slavery soon proved its ability to divest her of these heavenly attributes. Under its influence, the tender heart became stone, and the lamblike disposition gave away to one of tiger-like fierceness" (277). She became even more opposed to Douglass's efforts at self-education than her husband.

Learning to read and write and the liberating experience of living in Baltimore gave young Douglass a new perspective. By the time he left Baltimore he was determined to become free. Now, however, he became, for the first time, a field hand. He was turned over to Mr. Covey, a well-known "nigger-breaker" (289) who proceeded to resocialize him as a slave.

Covey worked his slaves in all kinds of weather from early morning to late at night up to the point of their endurance. A few months of this regimen and even Douglass lost his desire for freedom. The relentless toil and frequent punishment took their toll: "I was broken in body, soul, and spirit. [. . .The] dark night of slavery closed in upon me; and behold a man transformed into a brute!" (293).

Finally, however, Douglass found the courage to resist Covey. In recounting this central point of his story, Douglass tells his readers, "You have seen how a man was made a slave; you shall see how a slave was made a man!"(294). When he could stand it no longer, he "resolved to fight" (298).[6] It was this act of violence that reversed the process Covey had so successfully begun. Covey, whose reputation as a disciplinarian of slaves was the source of his livelihood, could not admit to others that Douglass had beaten him. Nonetheless, Covey never tried to whip him again, and Douglass thereafter was only nominally a slave.

As a field hand Douglass was able, for the first time, to form deep friendships with other slaves. Because the other slaves refused to come to Covey's aid, Douglass was able to attain his crucial victory. After leaving Covey, Douglass went to work for a more reasonable slave owner, Mr. Freeland. Here, once more, he formed close ties with the other slaves and began a Sabbath school to teach them how to read; after a while he was teaching more than forty slaves at the house of a freeman. "The work of instructing my dear fellow-slaves was the sweetest engagement with which I was ever blessed. We loved each other" (304). The slave community thus provided a refuge and a powerful antidote to the other forms of socialization. Yet friendship could cut both ways. Douglass believed that "thousands would escape from slavery, who now remain, but for the strong cords of affection that bind them to their friends" (319).

Douglass's final days in slavery were spent back in Baltimore. Eventually he was able to hire himself out as a skilled craftsman. Although he now had control of his own time, he had to hand over his earnings to his master. (From this, students can readily see how slavery expropriated the labor of its African American victims.) Ironically, while Covey's cruelty had resulted in temporarily breaking Douglass's spirit, the relatively good treatment he received from subsequent masters heightened his desire for freedom. "[W]henever my condition was improved, instead of its increasing my contentment, it only increased my desire to be free [. . .]. I have found that to make a contented slave, it is necessary to make a thoughtless one. [. . .] [H]e must be made to feel that slavery is right; and he can be brought to that only when he ceases to be a man" (314–15).

Even after he had escaped to the North, however, Douglass confesses, "I felt myself a slave" (326). It was the act of testifying against slavery and writing his autobiography that finally completed the process begun when he went to Baltimore and that liberated him from the role that had been imposed on him.

After we finish our discussion of *Narrative*, students can recognize that writing his story was in itself a revolutionary act for Douglass. Like the other refugees from slavery who wrote their stories, Douglass asserted the humanity of slaves in a society that had tried to deny it in every way possible. In a nation that denied that slaves were equal to whites, an African American who wrote candidly about his life as a slave issued a revolutionary declaration of personhood. When he had done that, Douglass was no longer a slave in any sense.[7]

NOTES

[1]Jefferson writes, "I advance it, therefore, as a suspicion only, that the blacks, whether originally a distinct race, or made distinct by time and circumstances, are inferior to whites in the endowments of body and mind" (*Notes* 143). John D. Hicks argues, "The lot of the slave on a southern planation was ordinarily quite tolerable. [. . .] Indeed the slaves got much positive enjoyment out of life. Extremely gregarious, they delighted in the community life of the plantation, and on special occasions were permitted to indulge in picnics, barbecues, and various other types of celebration" (495). And Samuel Eliot Morison and Henry Steele Commager note, "As for Sambo, those wrongs that moved the abolitionists to wrath and tears, there is some reason to believe that he suffered less than any other class in the South from its peculiar institution" (433).

[2]Stampp outlines the four steps that slave owners were advised to take to socialize their slaves: first, "establish and maintain strict discipline"; second, "implant in the bondsmen themselves a consciousness of personal inferiority"; third, "awe them with a sense of their master's enormous power"; and, finally, "impress Negroes with their helplessness" (144, 145, 146, 147).

[3]It might be argued that slavery in Maryland, a border state, was not typical of the institution in the deep South. The best account of slavery in Maryland, by Barbara Jeanne Fields, *Slavery and Freedom on the Middle Ground*, disputes this view, arguing that Maryland slaves were exposed to the full range of slave experiences.

[4]In direct contrast to Douglass, Lunsford Lane, who also wrote about his years in slavery, did know his date of birth, and it was not until he was ten or eleven that he "discovered the difference between myself and my master's white children" (7).

[5]For a similar incident, see William Wells Brown, *Narrative* 181–82.

[6]Solomon Northup was another slave who attacked his master and survived the experience; see his memoir *Twelve Years a Slave* 294–302. The psychiatrist Frantz Fanon pointed out in his *Wretched of the Earth* the importance of violence in the liberation of an oppressed people: "At the level of individuals, violence is a cleansing force. It frees the native from his inferiority complex and from his despair and inaction; it makes him fearless and restores his self-respect" (94).

[7]Douglass recognized the importance of writing his autobiography. He confided to his editor, "I see, too, that there are special reasons why I should write my own biography, in preference to employing another to do it. Not only is slavery on trial, but unfortunately, the enslaved people are also on trial. It is alleged, that they are, naturally, inferior; that they are *so low* in the scale of humanity, and so utterly stupid, that they are unconscious of their wrongs, and do not apprehend their rights" (*My Bondage* [Arno] vii). Sidonie Smith points out, "The act of writing an autobiography was yet another act of rebellion against the slave system, for the choice of autobiography presupposes a belief in the primacy of the self. In writing his autobiography, the ex-slave affirmed his belief in his self-worth and forced a society that denied him full humanity to recognize him" (10).

Portrait of the Artist as a Young Slave: Douglass's Frontispiece Engravings

Ed Folsom

I most often teach *Narrative of the Life of Frederick Douglass, an American Slave, Written by Himself* in an advanced undergraduate course on the literature and culture of nineteenth-century America. After students have completed their reading of the *Narrative* and we have spent at least one class period talking about the historical and political issues surrounding Douglass's text, I begin the next class by projecting a slide of the 1845 frontispiece portrait (fig. 1). I tell the students I'd like them to *read* this portrait, to view it not only as a key physical element of the *book* that appeared in 1845 but also as an important component of the *text*, an image that has meaning in relation to the patterns of verbal imagery in Douglass's narrative. How, I ask my students, does this visual representation of Douglass correspond to his verbal self-representation in the narrative proper? How, in fact, does it function as part of the narrative? The portrait, I remind them, would have been very much a part of the original readers' experience of the text—the first representation of Douglass that they would have encountered and one that they no doubt returned to as they read and thought about the book. I quote Douglass's own statements about the importance of visual art: "Man is the only picture making and picture appreciating animal in the world," he wrote, going on to observe that visual art spans our individual lifetimes ("for childhood delights in pictures") and our history (art rises "with the first dawnings of [. . .] civilization, lifting the thoughts and sentiments of men higher by every one of its triumphs") and thus must be "diligently cultivated" (qtd. in Wheat [iii]). Douglass, then, would have been keenly aware of the impact the frontispiece picture of himself would have on readers.

I show my class a few slides of other examples of contemporary authors' portraits—Lowell and Whittier and Emerson and Longfellow (I save Whitman for later)—all of them framing the head and shoulders only, all of them presenting the author in formal dress, as the exemplar of decorum. These are portraits of the artist as a privileged man. Then I show the class some of the painful J. T. Zealy daguerreotypes of slaves taken in 1850—naked or half-naked, stripped of their right to dignity even as their eyes register defiance, the very emblems of violated civilized decorum. I explain to my students that few contemporary visual representations exist of individual slaves and that these Zealy portraits were taken to serve as specimens to support the scientist Louis Agassiz's racist polygenesis theories.[1]

Coming back to Douglass's portrait, I ask my students what they see now and how what they see relates to what they've read, and then I stand back and let the responses come. Someone always mentions the clothes, how the dress and fashion seem too formal for a former slave and affiliate him too closely with the

Figure 1. Frontispiece engraving of Frederick Douglass for *Narrative of the Life of Frederick Douglass, an American Slave, Written by Himself*. Boston: Anti-slavery Office, 1845.

privileged white authors. If I'm lucky, someone else will respond that that's just what some white people in the mid–nineteenth century said about Douglass's manner of speaking and manner of writing—that it was too "white," too "learned" and refined to sound authentic. One abolitionist friend told Douglass he needed "a little of the plantation speech" in his writing to give it a realistic edge: "it is not best that you seem too learned" (qtd. in Foner, *Frederick Douglass* 59). And it was not only whites who felt this way: Douglass recalled that Sojourner Truth always considered it "her duty [. . .] to ridicule my efforts to speak and act like a person of cultivation" (qtd. in McFeely 97).

Questions follow: Could part of the impact of Douglass's portrait, then, be a shock of recognition for white readers, a sudden and surprising realization that an African American could assume the status and dress (and voice) of the privileged white author? Is the portrait a conservative gesture that tries to reassure a white readership by portraying Douglass as safe and familiar (a black man certifying white dominance by playing at being white), or is it a radically disorienting gesture that makes Douglass seem dangerously insurgent (a black man essentially altering the power hierarchy by claiming an identity previously reserved for whites)? Has the institution of white authorship usurped Douglass and co-opted his identity, or has Douglass, the black slave, invaded and undermined the all-white establishment of privileged authorship? Could the portrait have functioned for antebellum readers as a kind of optical illusion, at one moment comforting them with an image of assimilation, at the next challenging them with an image of inversion and invasion?

I try to raise questions that broaden the discussion into issues of cultural identity: What range of possibilities for identity formation do the visual representations we've looked at suggest for people living in mid-nineteenth-century America? Do the Zealy portraits of South Carolina slaves and the various portraits of America's successful white male authors in some way set the poles of social identity in America—from the powerless to the powerful, from those denied any education to those who enjoy the privileges of a Harvard education, from those whose portraits were made for "scientific" categorizing and who thus remain nameless or recalled only with a first name to those whose portraits were signs of their fame, familiar faces that accompanied their famous names? If these are the poles of identity in antebellum America, how far could a black man travel from the Zealy slave portraits toward the Boston Brahmin portraits? Does Douglass make the complete journey?

Some students will note that while at first glance Douglass's portrait looks more like those of the successful authors than like those of the slaves, his portrait actually unsettles the bipolar sense of separate and even opposite identities that one assumes when looking at the two sets of images. Douglass's portrait seems to enact an impossible melding of the slave portrait with the successful author portrait. His face and hair join him to the slave portraits, but his clothing and his manner and his firm and elegant signature—the sign of his self-authoring—tie him to the author portraits. It's as if Douglass was demonstrating the fluidity of self-fashioning, literally posing the possibility that one's race could no longer prevent an ascent to cultural power and influence.

I ask students to consider, too, the way this portrait fits into the developing notions of cultural celebrity. The 1840s were the period of America's first celebrity authors, the decade that marked the appearance of what Michael Newbury has called "the mixed feelings about celebrity and exposure in the cultural sphere that simultaneously gave prominent figures power over while leaving them vulnerable to" their new fans (182). Newbury discusses the ways that "celebrity-as-slave figurations" (162) appear at this time, as celebrities become not those who produce commodities but instead commodities themselves. Douglass's striking portrait makes him the first "slave-as-celebrity," and his fame made him identifiable on the street, an obviously dangerous result for an escaped slave. In the warped mirror world of slavery, even celebrity was distorted: America's first celebrity stalkers may have been slave catchers. Douglass's growing celebrity, in fact, led him to flee the country for England, where he purchased his freedom. But by becoming a freedman he entered a new kind of enslavement, an enslavement to a fetishized image of himself that the portrait helped create. That problematic developing dynamic of former-slave/current-celebrity suggests some promising approaches to reading Douglass's 1892 *Life and Times of Frederick Douglass*, where we see the author struggling with what fame has brought and made him.

At this point I invite my class to examine the portrait even more closely. I tell them the 1845 engraving was based on an oil portrait of Douglass completed in the early 1840s by an unidentified artist (Voss 22). The anonymous engraver managed to stiffen and strengthen the gentler face that appears in the painting, but the major change the engraver made was to empty out or half-erase the bottom half of the portrait. Instead of making an engraving that pretended to be a copy of the oil portrait, the engraver emphasized (rather than disguised) the artificial and constructed nature of his steelcut image. While the engraving renders Douglass's face in photographic detail, its intensity of realistic detail quickly fades as our eyes descend; verisimilitude evaporates and we're left with a rough sketch. The total effect of the portrait emerges, then, from an intriguing tension between a half-sketched quality that emphasizes the artificial, constructed nature of the image and a finished, highly detailed quality that approaches photographic realism. I ask students to think about the implications of this oddly bifurcated image.

I explain that the emphasis on process, on the artifice of constructing detailed identity out of initial bare sketches, is part of the tradition of portrait engraving. Most portrait engravings in the nineteenth century emphasize to some extent the artifice of the engraving by leaving some part of the image unfinished or barely sketched in. The Douglass engraving, however, exaggerates this convention of having a detailed portrait arise out of a rough sketch; from the shoulders down Douglass is represented only by a bare, primitive line drawing, while from the shoulders up he emerges suddenly into a fully realized presence. Peter Dorsey describes the engraving as representing "a disappear-ing body" (445), but the dynamics of this portrait (mirroring the narrative) actually make it a self in the process of *appearing*. Like all visual art for Doug-lass, this portrait is about "lifting the thoughts and sentiments of men higher" by "rising" from the primitive to the "cultivated" (qtd. in Wheat [iii]).

At this point, students can begin to draw the connections between visual text and written text and to see how such a portrait enhances the pattern of Doug-lass's narrative, where Douglass the successful author and orator emerges from a slave who is prevented from having any access to his own personal history, whose ability to learn and form an identity is stunted by slavery's restrictions on movement and education. Douglass's book traces his rise from a generic "American slave" with an empty identity to "Frederick Douglass," a newly named and fully realized individual who has taken control of his life and is now the agent of his narrative instead of a faceless product of the slavery system, a servant in someone else's master narrative. His ability to gain access to writing and reading, to learn to "write by himself," brings his past under his own guid-ance and control, and his signature under his half-sketched, half-realized por-trait is ink affirming a literacy that creates and verifies identity; for a significant part of Douglass's life, that signature was impossible, because the name and the ability to sign it were absent. His page was blank; his narrative is the story of learning to sign his name, at first literally and later figuratively, and to fill the blank pages with his identity. His book is his signature, and it ends with the act of signing his name, a full circle back to the frontispiece page. The visual emblem of himself imitates his emergence from blank, absent, or sketchy beginnings into a distinctive and distinguished selfhood.

If we look at the title page that appears opposite the portrait in the 1845 *Narrative*, we can see that the placement of the words underscores the signif-icance of the portrait: the words "Frederick Douglass" appear in large type across from the singular, fully delineated face, while, in smaller type, "Ameri-can Slave" appears opposite the part of the portrait that is not fleshed out. The words "Written by Himself" appear opposite Douglass's verifying signature. The pattern of words on the title page mirrors the portrait. Douglass's barely visible hands resting on the single line of his leg form the fade-out lower bor-der of the portrait, but those hands are affirmed as active by the signature, which appears clearly just below and which is, along with the entire narrative, the visible work of those hands. A student once suggested that in reading "up" the portrait, we move from a nondescript outline of a body through more fully realized imitative clothing—the white man's uniform of success—and on up to the most detailed and individualized part of the portrait—the face and hair that distinguish this from all previous portraits of authors. The imitativeness (of dress, style, manner, voice) ultimately yields distinction, and the portrait emphasizes the irony of cultural identity that one must embrace imitation to emerge as an individual. As Dorsey notes in his fine study of Douglass's "self-fashioning process," any attempt at "acquiring mastery—whether of human, material, or textual resources—presupposes mimesis." Thus, Dorsey says, "Douglass emphasizes that resistance to oppression requires a degree of imitation; to change their position, the oppressed must at some level copy the metaphors, the behaviors, and even the thought processes of the oppressor"—only through such imitation can the oppressed gain "access to political exchanges that can alter social structures" (436–37).

Engraved portraits, then, served as particularly appropriate openings to slave narratives, a genre centered on confirmations of identity and celebrations of free individuals emerging from an institution that strove to keep such individuality invisible, blank, and unformed. Engravings—with their emphasis on the process of creating verisimilitude, their habit of incorporating in the same image various stages of composition (from rough sketch to finished portrait)—were thus more effective vehicles than photographs or paintings would have been in representing identity as an act of labor and artistry.

After the class finishes discussing the 1845 image, I show students another slide, this one of Walt Whitman, the writer we will study after Douglass. All the effects we've talked about in portrait engravings are famously captured in Samuel Hollyer's 1855 frontispiece engraving of Whitman for the first edition of *Leaves of Grass* (fig. 2). (I discuss this portrait in more detail and compare it with Douglass's 1845 portrait in Folsom 135–45. I offer a summary of that discussion here.)

All through his poetic career, Whitman carefully coordinated illustrations of himself with the song of himself: every portrait, he once noted, "has some relation to the text" (Traubel 2: 536); "the portrait," Whitman said, "in fact is involved as part of the poem" (Kennedy 248). For Whitman the inclusion of his portrait was not a decoration or badge but, rather, a challenge to the reader to work, to struggle for meaning, to respond. As with Douglass's portrait, it was as essential a part of the book as the written text was and demanded the same kind of involvement from the reader, who was required to actively interpret not only the words but the visual images as well.

This 1855 frontispiece portrait has become the most familiar of all the images of Whitman—hat on, shirt open, head cocked, arm akimbo. Early reviewers often commented on Whitman's oddly *un*cultivated self-presentation: "the damaged hat, the rough beard, the naked throat, the shirt exposed to the waist, are each and all presented to show that the man to whom these articles belong scorns the delicate art of civilization" (Leaves of Grass *Imprints* 42). The 1855 portrait makes its point in a number of ways: it is in sharp contrast to the expected iconography of authors' portraits, portraits that conventionally emphasized formality and the face instead of this rough informality where arms, legs, and body diminish the centrality of the head. Authors' portraits in the nineteenth century indicated that writing was a function of the intellect, a formal business conducted in book-lined rooms where ideas fed the head through words. Whitman, of course, was out to undermine this conception, to move poetry to the streets, to deformalize it, to yank it away from the authority of

Figure 2. Frontispiece engraving of Walt Whitman for *Leaves of Grass*. Brooklyn, 1855.

tradition, and to insist that poetry emerges from the heart, lungs, genitals, and hands, as much as from the head. He wanted the representative democratic poet to speak in his poems, and the absence of his own name from the title page allowed the representative portrait to speak to authorship. These were poems written by a representative democratic person living life in the world and experiencing life through the five senses—a self that found authority in experience, that doffed its hat to no one, that refused to follow the decorum of removing one's hat indoors or even in books. Just as the appearance of Douglass's name in large type and his signature in a firm hand was crucial for the identity formation

Douglass needed to represent, so is the absence of these nominal signs crucial for Whitman's quite different needs. As a white man speaking for the culture as a whole, Whitman could luxuriate in the absorption of his individual self into the communal identity of "America."

The engraved portrait, in one sense, works very much like Douglass's 1845 portrait. While Hollyer's engraving renders Whitman's face and upper torso in photographic detail, the intensity of its realistic detail fades toward the bottom of the image; Whitman's legs are rendered with less and less detail until they diminish to simple sketch lines, then fade into the blankness of the paper itself. The image advertises its constructedness. As with Douglass's portrait, Whitman's emerges from an intriguing tension between a rough, half-sketched quality that emphasizes the artificiality of the image and a finished, highly detailed quality that imitates the verisimilitude of the original daguerreotype on which it is based. It is as if Hollyer (and Whitman) want to underscore the process, the labor involved in making ink turn into identity, in making lines turn into humanity, in making a book turn into a man.

Whitman was familiar with Douglass's work, and the poems of the 1855 *Leaves* were in some ways based on what Whitman learned from slave narratives like Douglass's. Whitman's 1855 poems in fact incorporate a slave narrative, from the "runaway slave [who] came to my house and stopped outside" and "staid with me a week, before he was recuperated and passed north, / I had him sit next me at the table" (36) to the moments when Whitman speaks as the slave: "I am the hounded slave . . . . I wince at the bite of the dogs" (65) and "I hate him that oppresses me, / [. . .] How he informs against my brother and sister and takes pay for their blood, / How he laughs when I look down the bend after the steamboat that carries away my woman" (*Complete Poetry* 113). Whitman appropriated aspects of slave narratives to make concrete the expression of desire for freedom and equality in his poetry. Like a slave narrative, *Leaves* was the record of a human being seeking a new name, an unfettered identity, an open road that would lead away from all forms of enslavement— whether social conventions, literary traditions, or actual institutions of slavery.

Fittingly, Whitman's frontispiece portrait echoes certain aspects of Douglass's even as it differs from Douglass's in other ways: for Douglass, the escape was from work clothes to formal clothing, a change that signaled success and the acquisition of education and manners; for Whitman, the escape was in the opposite direction. Whitman, the white man, seeking democratic expression, could profitably fashion himself *down*, could take on the garb of the worker and seek to imaginatively identify with the slave's experience; Douglass, the black man, seeking cultural authority, had to fashion himself *up*, discovering identity in an escape from slavery. The same social conventions that marked an achievement of identity for Douglass threatened identity for Whitman. An African American posing as a distinguished writer was every bit as singular in the culture of mid-nineteenth-century America as a white poet posing as a day laborer. Just as Douglass's portrait undermined the generally expected image of a slave, Whitman's portrait undermined the expectations that his readers would have brought to an engraving of an author.

The same year that Whitman's *Leaves of Grass* appeared, Douglass published *My Bondage and My Freedom* and included a new frontispiece portrait, by J. C. Battre (fig. 3). At the end of our class discussion about *Narrative*, I show my students a slide of this engraving. Like Whitman's portrait, Douglass's 1855 engraving was based on a daguerreotype, and an intense photographic realism is apparent in this image. True to the engraving tradition, however, the lower part of the portrait fades into simple lines, though the rough-to-finished effect is much more subtle than in the 1845 frontispiece. Here Douglass's clothes— more elegant and formal than those in the earlier engraving—are emphasized even more and given a finish that the clothing in the 1845 image lacked. Also emphasized is Douglass's rigid bearing: it is not a formal rigidity so much as stiff discomfort, as if the clothes are forcing a manner on a body that resists it. As in the 1845 image, Douglass's hands are muted, faded, but unlike the earlier portrait, here they are fisted and tensed. Douglass's narration of his life moves from his use of his fists to enforce his freedom and "rekindle in [his] breast the smouldering embers of liberty" (246) to his discovery of how to use words as his weapons of freedom. In *My Bondage and My Freedom*, Douglass apologizes for the roughness of his physical fight with Covey and the roughness of his writing about the fight—"undignified as it was, and as I fear my narration of it is" (246)—but at the same time he expands his description of the encounter. He is both beyond that roughness and essentially formed by it, and his portrait captures this quality precisely. The faded but fisted hands are subdued but still visible and are vital parts of Douglass's newer, more refined identity: the fully realized face, intelligent and serious and black, unites the clothes and the fists and gives coherence to the author and the slave. Peter Dorsey observes:

> The title of *My Bondage and My Freedom* [. . .] contains the poles of a metaphorical equation: a self inevitably bound by the figures he and others used but simultaneously liberated from those chains, not just by the realization that he was (and is) always more than the metaphors attached to him but by his own mastery of the possibilities of self-figuration.
>
> (447)

So, too, Douglass's title serves as a fitting caption for his frontispiece image. His pose and his costume represent both his bondage and his freedom, the brute physicality of his slave past and the straitened refinement of his celebrity present. In his bondage Douglass found freedom, and in his freedom he finds other kinds of bondage. His frontispiece portraits, read as textual images, represent these tensions and ambiguities and serve as visual analogues of Douglass's narratives. By 1855, Douglass had become, as William L. Andrews says, "an accomplished man of letters, a sophisticated journalist as well as orator" (*To Tell* 218), but this accomplishment and erudition rose from and remained

Figure 3. Frontispiece engraving of Frederick Douglass for *My Bondage and My Freedom*. New York: Miller, Orton, and Mulligan, 1855.

attached to a life that began in denial of accomplishment and learning. Doug-lass's portraits manifest these tensions of origin and result, of what Dorsey calls "becoming the other" (435). When a reporter for the *Herald of Freedom* in 1844 tried to describe Douglass's "impressive speech," his analysis breaks at the seams of these very tensions:

> It was not what you could describe as oratory or eloquence. It was sterner, darker, deeper than these. It was a storm of insurrection. [. . .] He stalked to and fro on the platform, roused up like the Numidian lion. [. . .] There was great oratory in his speech. [. . .] He was not up as a speaker, performing. He was an insurgent slave, taking hold on the right of speech, and charging on his tyrants the bondage of his race. [. . .] He is a surprising lecturer. I would not praise him, or describe him; but he is a colored man, a slave, of the race who can't take care of themselves— our inferiors, and therefore to be kept in slavery. [. . .] He is one of the most impressive and majestic speakers I have ever heard. [. . .] I have never seen a man leave the platform, or close a speech, with more real dignity, and eloquent majesty.   (qtd. in Foner, *Frederick Douglass* 58)

Here once again is Douglass as a maddening, shifting optical illusion—not an orator, a great orator; not eloquent, majestically eloquent; a wild animal, a dig-nified man; an ignorant slave, an accomplished speaker. Douglass's emergence into eminence and accomplishment and fame always carried with it the ragged and rugged delineations of his past. His portraits are always about the rela-tionship of the author to (and as) the young slave.

NOTE

[1]Instructors can make slides of the Douglass portraits from public-domain copies of the 1845 *Narrative* and the 1855 *My Bondage and My Freedom*, available in the special collections departments of many public and university libraries. (The illustrations for this essay are from the University of Iowa Special Collections.) The portraits are repro-duced in several modern editions of Douglass's work and are also available in Dorsey and in Voss. The Zealy daguerreotypes are in the Peabody Museum at Harvard Uni-versity, and several are reproduced and discussed by Trachtenberg (52–60), in Reichlin, and in Wallis.

Douglass and Sentimental Rhetoric
Jeffrey Steele

At the center of Frederick Douglass's *Narrative* lies a powerful appeal to the reader's "heart." Presenting himself as a man of deep feeling, Douglass constructs a persona whose self-dramatization taps familiar veins of sentiment. William Lloyd Garrison, in his preface, draws special attention to this quality, commenting on "the multitudes [. . .] who have been melted to tears by his pathos" (245). "He who can peruse it without a tearful eye, a heaving breast, an afflicted spirit," Garrison adds several pages later, "[. . .] must have a flinty heart, and be qualified to act the part of a trafficker 'in slaves and the souls of men'" (248–49). Using sentimental terminology, Garrison identifies sympathetic emotional responsiveness as the core of morality. To fight against the evil of slavery, he suggests, one must be able to feel the pain it inflicts. The great excellence of Douglass's style, he observes, lies in the "union of head and heart, which is indispensable to an enlightenment of the heads and a winning of the hearts of others" (247).

Garrison's commendation of Douglass's expressive style reflected the literary and cultural standards of 1840s America. A decade before the emotional exorbitance of the 1850s, reformers began to use the emerging rhetoric of sentimentality as a powerful tool that had the potential to bridge class and racial barriers. A staple of sentimental literature was the scene of pathos (from the Greek word for suffering) in which readers mourned the plight of orphans, the grieving, or the poor. In *Godey's Lady's Book* and other periodicals, numerous poems and stories mobilized readers' sympathy for an expanding range of suffering victims. Reformers quickly learned the advantage of using available sentimental modes "to help the public perceive situations [. . .] in a new, emotionally charged way" (Walters 100). Taking advantage of structures of sentiment that luxuriated in the outpouring of mournful sympathy, reformers were able to shift attention from individual victims to groups of sufferers.

By the 1840s, reform leaders were adapting expressions of sentiment to new political ends. In 1843, two years before the publication of Douglass's *Narrative*, Dorothea Dix proclaimed in her report to the Massachusetts legislature, "I come to present the strong claims of suffering humanity"—"the condition of the miserable, the desolate, the outcast" (69). Recounting the sufferings of American women in the 1845 treatise *Woman in the Nineteenth Century*, Margaret Fuller, despite her avowed resistance to sentimentality, dramatized herself as being overcome by feeling: "I said, we will not speak of this now, yet I have spoken, for the subject makes me feel too much" (258). Even the reserved Ralph Waldo Emerson declared in his 1841 Boston lecture "Man the Reformer," "Let our affection flow out to our fellows, it would operate in a day the greatest of all revolutions" (*Nature* 158). When Douglass joined the Garrisonian circle of abolitionists, he entered a group of reformers whose commitment to the expression of "fervent sentiments" was derived partly from evangelical Christian sources (Yacovone 86). Such Christian fervor and sympathy influenced the antislavery fiction of the day—tales in which the "tears of the reader" were "pledged [. . .] as a means of rescuing the bodies of slaves" (Sánchez-Eppler, "Bodily Bonds" 99).

Analysis of the sentimental side of Douglass's rhetoric complicates the familiar critical argument that his "manly narrative text" enacts the triumph of a masculine power achieved at the expense of female values (Gates, "From Wheatley" 63). David Leverenz, for example, argues that "Douglass's preoccupation with manhood and power all but erases any self-representation linking him to women, family, and intimacy" (109). Along the same lines, Jenny Franchot comments on "the repression of the feminine required by the middle-class virility that Douglass emulated" (149). Such critical observations reinforce the image of Douglass as an independent figure invested in a stereotyped model of nineteenth-century American manhood—a "self-made man" who downplayed his emotional ties with others (Zafar 108). But we are now discovering that "antebellum Americans accepted no single definition of manhood" and "displayed a variety of [. . .] styles of masculinity" (Yacovone 86). As a result, the line between "masculine" and "feminine" discourse has become increasingly difficult to draw. Although sentimentalized literary forms that stressed relational ties have been associated with women's writing by twentieth-century critics, such forms were consumed and utilized by both men and women.

The image of Douglass's triumphant "manhood" picks out only one thread of the complex intertextual weave of his *Narrative*, while such a critical focus erases the narrative complexity of a book in which Franklinesque echoes blend with a variety of other discourses. On one level, Douglass does present a seemingly objective account of his life, thus satisfying the criterion (as expressed by Garrison) that the slave narrator present "his case" as a "specimen of the treatment of slaves" (249). But, as already mentioned, Garrison approved of Douglass's pathos—an emotional expressiveness exceeding mere documentation. In addition, Douglass complicates the straightforward account of his life by blending together a variety of discourses, including numerous biblical allusions, a parody of the language of jurisprudence ("seat of government" and "high misdemeanor" [260]), an echo of an African folktale ("touching tar" [264]), the language of domesticity ("the ties that ordinarily bind children" [271]), and evocations of American revolutionary sentiment ("we did more than Patrick Henry" [306]). Within this complicated narrative matrix, he embeds emotionally expressive passages so intense that they have been characterized as "purple prose" (Moses, "Writing" 75). Among these pivotal passages are his characterization of mournful slave songs (ch. 2), his lament for the abandonment of his grandmother (ch. 8), and his impassioned soliloquy on the bank of Chesapeake Bay (ch. 10).

Each of these passages constructs a persona that contrasts markedly with prevailing critical conceptions of Douglass's austere "manhood," for each evokes a powerful emotional response that blurs the boundaries between independent self and others. Instead of viewing Douglass as a separate person, the reader partakes of his pain, sharing "a direct, immediate, emotional message" that—in the nineteenth century—often had feminine connotations (Lehuu 86). According to Karen Sánchez-Eppler, such direct emotional appeal is a familiar device in sentimental fiction, in which reading is "a bodily act" that "radically contracts the distance between narrated events and the moment of their reading, as the feelings in the story are made tangibly present in the flesh of the reader" ("Bodily Bonds" 100). Re-creating the experience of listening to the slaves' mournful songs, Douglass resorts to the tangible appeal of tears:

> I have frequently found myself in tears while hearing them. The mere recurrence to those songs, even now, afflicts me; and while I am writing these lines, an expression of feeling has already found its way down my cheek.   (263)

The rhetorical efficacy of such moments is predicated on Douglass's conviction that his readers share his feeling heart. Within the *Narrative*, the epitome of such sympathetic responsiveness is Douglass's mistress, Sophia Auld, who—before her corruption—was "a pious, warm, and tender-hearted woman." But once she was trained "in the exercise of irresponsible power," her "tender heart became stone" (277). In Douglass's sentimental lexicon, a hard or stony heart cuts its possessor off from human sympathy, dehumanizing him or her to the level of a wild beast. For example, the overseer who beats Douglass's Aunt Hester displays an "iron heart" (258). One's "heart must be harder than stone," Douglass observes, to witness such abuse "unmoved" (276).

Douglass assumes that his readers' capacity to identify with and feel the pain of those in bondage will motivate their moral resistance to slavery. Just as his memory of the mournful slave songs continued to "deepen" his "hatred of slavery" and "quicken" his "sympathies for [his] brethren in bonds," his readers would follow a similar emotional trajectory:

> If any one wishes to be impressed with the soul-killing effects of slavery, let him go to Colonel Lloyd's plantation, and, on allowance-day, place himself in the deep pine woods, and there let him, in silence, analyze the sounds that shall pass through the chambers of his soul,—and if he is not thus impressed, it will only be because "there is no flesh in his obdurate heart."   (263)

In this sentimental model of response, Douglass's evocation of the pain endured by slaves resonates in the "chambers" of the reader's soul, until his or her "heart" is "impressed" (literally, pressed). Only those with "obdurate" (literally, hard) hearts could fail to receive the impress of Douglass's rhetoric; all others—he assumes—would be touched by his emotional appeal.

In antebellum America, the most enduring impressions were often evoked by the pervasive rituals and signifiers of mourning, which shaped responses to "life, death, family structure, social behavior and religion" (Pike and Armstrong 13). In a culture in which everyone mourned, it was not easy to define the barrier separating the grief and the pain of others from one's own sense of bereavement. It was difficult to resist tears that elicited patterns of "affect and identification" that crossed "gender, race, and class boundaries" (Samuels 6). The fluidity of mourning, as well as the overdetermination of the many signifiers of grief, prevented the easy containment of grieving within a specific set of cultural forms. In many instances, the rhetoric of antebellum social reform depended upon dramatizations of middle-class readers as prospective mourners, grieving for the losses suffered by the destitute, the imprisoned, the mentally ill, and the enslaved. Embodying the assumption that reform efforts could be effectively motivated through the transmission of sentiment, reform writers often resorted to familiar tropes of mourning.

In the *Narrative*, Douglass exploits the middle-class demand for sentimental pathos by displacing the prevalent signifiers of mourning from specific losses to a general sense of grievance. In the process, he shifts attention from individual victims to representative figures trapped in an unendurable bondage. Perhaps the most striking of such figures is found in Douglass's portrait of his suffering grandmother, who was abandoned in her old age. Douglass's densely textured lament functions as a sentimental tale embedded within his text:

> The hearth is desolate. The *children*, the unconscious *children*, who once sang and danced in her presence, are gone. She gropes her way, in the darkness of age, for a drink of water. Instead of the voices of her *children*, she hears by day the moans of the dove, and by night the screams of the hideous owl. All is gloom. The grave is at the door. And now, when weighed down by the pains and aches of old age, when the head inclines to the feet, when the beginning and ending of human existence meet, and helpless infancy and painful old age combine together—at this time, this most needful time, the time for the exercise of that tenderness and affection which *children* only can exercise towards a declining *parent*— my poor old *grandmother*, the devoted mother of twelve *children*, is left all alone, in yonder little hut, before a few dim embers. She stands—she sits—she staggers—she falls—she groans—she dies—and there are none of her *children* or *grandchildren* present, to wipe from her wrinkled brow the cold sweat of death, or to place beneath the sod her fallen remains.   (284; my emphasis)

In this passage, the language of loss and bereavement provides a powerful emotional charge intended to shock Douglass's readers out of their detached complacency. They are forced to care about Douglass's grandmother by a language that evokes a sentimentalized vision of shattered family ties. Significantly, Douglass dwells on the very terms of relationship that many critics have failed to see: *parent, grandmother, grandchildren,* and *children* (a word repeated six times). Evoking the lost world of "tenderness and affection," he measures the expense of its absence. Using a narrative mode most often associated with nineteenth-century women writers, he links his sorrow for his grandmother to a lament for all those still trapped in slavery.

This theme of mourning runs throughout Douglass's writing. In his "Letter to His Old Master," for example, he evokes "the wails of millions [that] pierce my heart" (*My Bondage* [Dover] 426). Similarly, the oration "What to the Slave Is the Fourth of July?" re-creates "the plaintive lament of a [. . .] woe-smitten people"; while the speech on "The Internal Slave Trade" mourns the "piteous cries" and "doleful wails" of those still trapped in slavery (*My Bondage* 442, 448). All these texts create images of Douglass as a mournful reformer who has generalized his own sense of pain (as an ex-slave) into a politicized grief for those still trapped in bondage.

Such politicized scenes of mourning were a staple for writers, such as Harriet Beecher Stowe, who have come to be identified with the politics of "sentimental power" (Tompkins). One of the most evocative mourning scenes occurs near the end of *Uncle Tom's Cabin* (serially published six years after Douglass's *Narrative*), where Stowe links the capacity to grieve for a dead child to a politicized mourning for those trapped in slavery:

> By the sick hour of your child; by those dying eyes, which you can never forget; by those last cries, that wrung your heart when you could neither help nor save; by the desolation of that empty cradle, that silent nursery,—I beseech you, pity those mothers that are constantly made childless by the American slave-trade! And say, mothers of America, is this a thing to be defended, sympathized with, passed over in silence?
>
> (514–15)

Using the most familiar and clichéd of situations, that of a mother grieving for her dead child, Stowe displaces personal grief from the private arena to the public context of racial oppression. This political move is made possible by the overdetermination of maternal mourning as a culturally familiar site that Stowe could tap as if it were universally available. Every reader of this passage, she assumes, knew what it meant to mourn.

But while Stowe's "sacred drama of redemption" (Tompkins 134) emphasized "salvation through motherly love" (125), Douglass constructed a different sentimental narrative. Like Stowe, he expanded personal grief into a public symbol of the human expense of slavery. But he linked this expression of grief to losses that he himself had experienced as a slave. In the process, Douglass becomes both the agent and the object of mourning. He generates a politicized awareness of the human expense of slavery at the same time that he counts himself as one of its victims. "My feet have been so cracked with the frost," he observes, "that the pen with which I am writing might be laid in the gashes" (271). By using his own life as the occasion for mourning, Douglass ran the risk of being objectified as a suffering victim. But at the other extreme, his generalization of pain into a shared suffering threatened to erase the specificity of his racialized body (Sánchez-Eppler, "Bodily Bonds" 114). This narrative ambiguity is inherent to sentimental narrative forms, which often depended upon a writer's autobiographical evocation of specific losses that could be generalized and shared. In order to move their readers, sentimental writers placed their dramatizations of grief within larger frameworks of political consciousness that maintained contact both with specific aspects of personal suffering and with general emblems of loss. However, it is an open question whether the sentimental rhetorical evocation of African American suffering in the nineteenth century crossed the color line without partially diminishing the anguish of slavery. Douglass, we might say, conveys the pain of tears but not of the lash.

One of the most evocative scenes of personal suffering is Douglass's impassioned lament on the bank of Chesapeake Bay. Having nearly been broken by the brutal Edward Covey, Douglass felt that "the dark night of slavery [had] closed in upon me," and he "sank down again, mourning over my wretched condition" (293). But he began to escape from the inarticulate abyss of sorrow, as he transformed his grief into a mourning that his readers could share. It is striking that he dramatizes his mourning in a familiar Christianized language that formed the bedrock of sentimental narrative forms. "I have often," he begins,

> in the deep stillness of a summer's *Sabbath*, stood all alone upon the lofty banks of that noble bay, and traced, with saddened heart and tearful eye, the countless number of sails moving off to the mighty ocean. The sight of these always affected me powerfully. My thoughts would compel utterance; and there, with no audience but the *Almighty*, I would pour out my *soul's complaint* [. . .].   (293; my emphasis)

The ensuing plea for divine deliverance ("O God, save me! God, deliver me!") repeats a phrase that occurs over two dozen times in the Book of Psalms, in passages such as "Deliver me from mine enemies, O my God" (Ps. 59) and "Deliver me, O LORD, from the evil man" (Ps. 140). Echoing the Israelites' lament for their captivity in Babylon, Douglass evokes a biblical narrative of captivity that is redeemed in the triumphant moment, after his battle with Covey, when he feels "a glorious resurrection from the tomb of slavery, to the heaven of freedom" (299). In this passage, the images of Israel's release from bondage and Christ's resurrection are superimposed. The transfiguration of one man (Douglass as suffering Christ) becomes the potential redemption of a people. But this image of triumph depends, for its effect, on the dark night of the soul that preceded it. Douglass's image of triumphant manhood, in other words, cannot be separated from its roots in pain; sentimental pathos is the obverse of his image of triumphant manhood.

Douglass's *Narrative*, William L. Andrews has argued, embodied a "radical stage in the process of self-authorization that distinguished black autobiography in the 1840s." For the first time, "the reader could be shown not just the incident or what the incident signified but how to *feel* about it" (Andrews, *To Tell* 247). Douglass's representation of feeling became a central aspect of the complex narrative persona that he constructed in his text. To understand this aspect of his literary performance, it is necessary to re-create the literary culture within which his text was received. Utilizing familiar sentimental literary forms, Douglass was able to evoke the reader's sympathetic tears. During the course of his *Narrative*, he employed the reader's interest and sympathy by depicting himself as a man of reason, moral principle, religious faith, and sentiment. As the various slaveholders become increasingly bestialized in his depiction, Douglass the narrator stands apart as a man readers can trust. And, ultimately, a large part of their trust depends on his capacity to elicit a mournful sympathy that they can at least partially share. We care about Frederick Douglass, because he shows us a face that we can recognize—a man of principle and deep feeling who understands the needs of the human heart.

Douglass's Natural Rights Constitutionalism
Gregg D. Crane

The question one faces in teaching Douglass has less to do with whether one will refer to the antebellum legal context than with how and in what detail one will present this background information.[1] Beginning class discussion with the prefatory material of either *Narrative of the Life of Frederick Douglass* (1845) or *My Bondage and My Freedom* (1855) requires at least some account of how antebellum Americans perceived the constitutional status of slavery. William Lloyd Garrison introduces Douglass's *Narrative* as a form of "testimony" that justifies a revolutionary break with an evil constitutional order (246, 251). James McCune Smith's introduction to *My Bondage and My Freedom*, in contrast, portrays Douglass's autobiography as personifying American republican ideals and justifying the preservation of the Union (*My Bondage* [Dover] xvii, xxv–xxvii).

To observe both the complex influence of American republican ideology on Douglass and his role in revising that ideology, my classes begin by reading the Declaration of Independence and the Constitution's preamble and Bill of Rights. I ask students what they think an "inalienable right" or a "self-evident truth" is. We talk about Jefferson's use of the language of consensus, the Declaration's tone of moral earnestness and its syllogistic structure—a pattern of argument favored by lawyers then and now. The class considers what the document claims to establish and the relation of the Declaration's egalitarianism to the institution of slavery, noting that language criticizing the crown as the instigator of slavery was deleted from the final version of the Declaration at the behest of southern states. I hand out passages from Jefferson's *Notes on the State of Virginia* proclaiming the injustice of slavery, the racial inferiority of African Americans, and the necessity of expelling free blacks (137–41, 163). I ask my students whether the moral consensus that gives rise to the noble egalitarian sentiments of the Declaration is implicitly predicated on the preservation of a racially, ethnically, and culturally homogeneous society.

Moving from the Declaration to the Constitution's preamble, students are often quick to comment on the relative emotional flatness of the Constitution's language, its greater specificity, and its more legalistic and less philosophical tone. They debate the degree to which either the Declaration of Independence or the Constitution founds American law on morality or the majority's political power. Although the Constitution clearly recognizes the legitimacy of legislative expressions of political majorities, including the Constitution itself, it also provides for limits on majoritarian will in the Bill of Rights and the division of governmental powers. As Jefferson put it, the American Revolution established not an "*elective despotism*" but a government "in which the power" was "so divided and balanced among several bodies of magistracy, as that no one could transcend their legal limits, without being effectually checked and restrained by the others" (*Notes* 120). I distribute James Madison's comments in Federalist number 51 on the threat of tyrannical majorities and his belief in a strong federal government and the diversity of the national citizenry as a check on the legislative oppression of minorities in less populous and less diverse states and regions (*Federalist Papers* 318–22). And we confront, as did the abolitionists, the Constitution's obvious failure to "secure the Blessings of Liberty" for the entire American population. Although the framers did not use the words *slave* and *slavery*, several provisions implicitly recognized the slave system (e.g., the Constitution's fugitive slave clause, which mandated the return of "Person[s] held to Service or Labour in one State"; the restriction on Congress's authority to prohibit participation in the international slave trade for twenty years from ratification; and the "three-fifths clause" under which each slave was counted as three-fifths of a human being for the purposes of establishing representation and direct taxation) (US Const., art. 4, sec. 2; art. 1, sec. 9; art. 1, sec. 2). Inquiring into the basis of American law requires a glance at the natural rights tradition that inspired the antislavery movement as well as the American Revolution.

The liberal version of natural rights theory expressed in the Declaration of Independence, the Constitution's preamble and Bill of Rights, and Douglass's narratives has its roots in the work of such thinkers as Hugo Grotius; John Locke; Anthony Ashley Cooper, the third earl of Shaftesbury; Francis Hutcheson; Joseph Butler; Adam Smith; Jean-Jacques Rousseau; and Montesquieu who variously sought to name the ethical principles that authorize legal systems and revolutions. In *Two Treatises of Government*, Locke describes the original equality of people and their fundamental rights to life, liberty, and property as discerned by the reflection of "right reason" on sense experience (271). According to Locke's philosophical heirs, Shaftesbury, Hutcheson, Butler, and Smith, our "moral sense" intuits the existence of fundamental legal rights as it does the difference between right and wrong. This moral sense differs from Locke's right reason in that it encompasses sympathetic feelings as well as critical judgment (see, e.g., Adam Smith 321–27). For theorists of the American Revolution, such as Richard Price, Thomas Paine, and Thomas Jefferson, one's moral sense could detect whether British rule impermissibly abridged the colonists' fundamental rights, and, for James Wilson and other framers, the Constitution drew its fundamental authorization from the independent moral sense of individual Americans (Richards, *Foundations*, 82–89, 138–39).

The liberal natural rights jurisprudence of Locke and his heirs countered a conservative and positivistic natural rights conception of law as the expression of the sovereign's power. Locke felt that this political philosophy boiled down to the assertions that "*all Government is absolute Monarchy*" and "*no Man is Born free*" (142). As Richard Tuck notes, "most strong rights theories have been explicitly authoritarian rather than liberal" (3). Numerous natural rights philosophers have been willing to endorse slavery in certain circumstances (Buckle 48–52, 82–83). In addition, even natural rights theories that conceive of law as morally grounded allow for power to play some role in creating rights. Grotius, for instance, thought that human beings perceive fundamental rights through "an intuitive judgment" that makes "known what things from their own nature are honorable or dishonorable," but he also described property rights as a consequence of the power to possess. He cited the classical example of the acquisition of theater seats: once the seats are claimed by physical possession, they become property. The agency and power of the occupant creates the cognizable legal relation denominated as a right (Tuck 61–62).

Chief Justice Roger B. Taney's *Dred Scott* decision offers an apt application of the more conservative and positivistic version of natural rights theory. In Taney's view, the primary qualification for citizenship status is the possession of power—a people who have been "subjugated by the dominant race" and "considered as a subordinate and inferior class of beings" cannot be "constituent members of this sovereignty" (*Dred Scott v. Sandford* 60 US [19 How.] 393, 404-05 [1857]). In a "supplement" that Taney drafted in response to public hostility to the *Dred Scott* opinion, he refers to the African race as "made subject" to "white dominion" by "the order of nature," justifying the legal condition of slaves in the diction of conservative natural rights theory (Tyler 579). The Southern pro-slavery apologist George Fitzhugh was among those who set the stage for Taney's use of the absolutist rhetoric of natural rights. In *Sociology for the South; or, The Failure of Free Society* (1854), Fitzhugh defends slavery as a naturally authoritarian scheme of social organization that, like the family or the beehive, appropriately reflects an inherent distribution of power and responsibility.

By contrast, liberal natural rights theorists rejected the idea that the authority of law is simply a matter of the allocation of power, with the weak properly and inevitably obeying the strong. In *The Analogy of Religion, Natural and Revealed, to the Constitution and Course of Nature* (1736), Butler distinguishes between religious commands that we obey because they are perceived to be right in themselves and those that we obey because a superior power, God, requires it (148). When moral and positive commands conflict so that "it is impossible to obey both," the moral command supersedes the positive injunction. Butler considered, as did the other liberal natural rights theorists, the very existence of a moral sense that discerns the dictates of virtue to be the best evidence of its preeminent authority. The truths comprehended by this faculty of moral cognition, "whether called conscience, moral reason, moral sense, or divine reason; whether considered as a sentiment of the understanding, or as a perception of the heart," make up the fundamental moral authority for "all civil constitutions" (148–50, 294).

With this jurisprudential background in mind, students readily perceive that Douglass describes his study of *The Columbian Orator* as inspiring a natural rights epiphany.[2] Before his careful examination of this popular reader, Douglass's innate moral sense had intuited the wrongness of slavery, but the jurisprudential import of these feelings remained mysterious and ephemeral:

"interesting thoughts of my own soul, frequently flashed through my mind, and died away for want of utterance." The natural rights rhetoric Douglass acquired from *The Columbian Orator* "enabled [him] to utter [his] thoughts, and to meet the arguments brought forward to sustain slavery" (*Narrative* 279). Learning how to express these intuitions in the rhetoric of natural rights reveals that Douglass's prelingual moral intuitions argue for his entitlement to the inherent rights of citizenship—the inherence of the rights and his entitlement to them is demonstrated by the innateness of his moral intuition of their existence and his humanity. In a circular pattern of prior intuitions and later articulations that Douglass uses in describing the sorrow songs, the inarticulate feelings of the moral sense both validate and are validated by a subsequent ability to name and explain those feelings through the acquisition of natural rights literacy.

Douglass contrasts the natural rights lessons of *The Columbian Orator* with the moral anarchy produced by the system of slavery, a form of government and social organization that hardens the heart and destroys the moral sense of the slaveholder. For example, the overseer Gore's flagrant murder of Denby goes unreported and unpunished because, in the slave system, the rule of law is homologous with the absolute power of the slaveholder. Douglass mentions this incident in both his antebellum narratives, but in *My Bondage and My Freedom* he adds the comment "*Everything must be absolute*" in slavery (121). This addition echoes Justice Thomas Ruffin's frank admission of the positivistic basis of the southern legal system in *State v. Mann* (1829). Douglass read the North Carolina case in *The Key to* Uncle Tom's Cabin (1853), a documentary indictment of slavery that Harriet Beecher Stowe produced to respond to criticism of her novel's accuracy. Like Denby's case, *Mann* provocatively demonstrated the utter failure of American law to check the will of the powerful by enforcing the natural rights limits recognized by the moral sense. *Mann* involved a female slave, Lydia, who was shot when she attempted to flee a beating. At the trial court level, John Mann, the defendant who had "hired" Lydia for one year, was found guilty of assault and battery. Ruffin reversed Mann's conviction on the basis that, in the system of slavery, "the power of the master must be absolute, to render the submission of the slave perfect" (Stowe, *Key* 146).

Ruffin was not blind to the force of a liberal natural rights argument: "I must freely confess my sense of the harshness of this proposition. [. . .] And as a principle of moral right, every person in his retirement must repudiate it." Yet Ruffin claimed that "in the actual condition of things, [the absolute power of the slaveholder] must be so" (*Key* 146). Ruffin's opinion thus removes moral intuition from the judicial process. In the "moral-formal dilemma" that Robert Cover discerns in American antebellum jurisprudence, a judge's moral opposition to slavery would often collide with his positivist approach to the law, which required him as a matter of professional duty merely to apply the declarations of proslavery legislatures (25–29).

Although Douglass's vision of natural rights literacy offers an alternative to the positivistic legal theory of Ruffin and Taney (e.g., the slave who wins freedom through his superior moral reasoning in *The Columbian Orator* [*Narrative* 278]), Douglass also describes physical resistance as a necessary component of his natural rights vision and suggests an equivalence between resistance "with words or blows" (Foner, *Life and Writings* 2: 405). Blurring the distinction between natural rights speech and action, Douglass contends that revolutionary violence is acceptable, in part, because it is an elemental form of natural rights communication. Violence for the outnumbered and disfranchised group is in Douglass's writing a kind of exigent speech. Douglass's use of force in his battle with Covey constitutes the final and ultimate statement of his humanity. As he puts the point in *My Bondage and My Freedom*: "A man, without force, is without the essential dignity of humanity" (246–47). Moral entitlements, human rights, the right to be recognized as a full member of the human community depend upon some degree of force. Thus Douglass's narratives contain a paradox of liberal natural rights theory—the moral norms that are supposed to ground law in something other than power are in turn dependent on the possession of power.

To frame class discussion of Douglass's shifting views of the Constitution, I describe the three primary variants of abolitionism in the 1840s and 1850s. The radical abolitionism of Lysander Spooner, William Goodell, and Alvan Stewart insisted that slavery was constitutionally illegitimate throughout the United States because it conflicted with the superior principles of the liberal natural rights tradition that were embedded in the Constitution. The radicals' view of the constitutional significance of natural rights principles could draw support from certain Supreme Court precedents. Justice Samuel Chase had referred to the authority of natural rights principles in *Calder v. Bull* (1798), and Chief Justice Marshall confirmed the suasive appeal of natural rights theory in *Fletcher v. Peck* (1810), where he voided a state statute, reasoning, in part, that it was contrary to "general principles which are common to our free institutions" (*Fletcher v. Peck* 10 US [6 Cranch.] 87, 139 [1810]). Moderate abolitionists, such as Salmon P. Chase and Charles Sumner, contended that slavery was a matter of local positive law and that the federal government could bar the extension of slavery into the territories where it had primary authority for establishment of local law. The moderates took a wither-on-the-vine approach, hoping that, shut off from the federal government's recognition and support, slavery would eventually fade away. Garrisonians considered slavery to be a sin that the Constitution had at best allowed and at worst fostered. Maintaining that the Constitution was fatally afflicted with the moral disease of slavery, Garrisonians called for its annulment, rejected political participation under its banner, and urged the dissolution of the Union (Wiecek 16–20).

Before Douglass converted to the radical form of abolitionism, he, like Garrison (and Justice Taney), read the historic failure of the Constitution "to protect the weak against the strong, [. . .] the few against the many" as dispositive evidence that the Constitution was proslavery (Foner, *Life and Writings* 1: 374). But as he became more independent of Garrison, more the advocate of abolition and less the mere witness against slavery, Douglass had to respond to the radical abolitionists' argument that, contrary to the Garrisonian position, the Constitution should be embraced as an egalitarian, antislavery charter. William Goodell contended, for instance, that a straightforward reading of the Constitution's preamble justified the eradication of slavery: "To promote the general welfare" could not be consonant with "crushing the laboring, the producing class, in half the States of the Republic," and securing "the blessings of Liberty" had to require the "overthrow" of "the deadly antagonist of liberty, to wit, slavery" (41). Arguing with the radical abolitionists when he was the editor of the *North Star* compelled Douglass "to re-think the whole subject, and to study, with some care, not only the just and proper rules of legal interpretation, but the origin, design, nature, rights, power, and duties of civil government." Eventually, Douglass came to agree that the Constitution could not have been devised to secure the blessings of liberty to all Americans and "have been designed at the same time to maintain and perpetuate a system of rapine and murder like slavery; especially, as not one word can be found in the constitution to authorize such a belief" (*My Bondage* 397). Because the Constitution was "in its letter and spirit, an anti-slavery instrument," dissolution of the Union was unnecessary and counterproductive and abstaining "from voting, was to refuse a legitimate and powerful means of abolishing slavery" (*My Bondage* 396).

Adopting Lysander Spooner's interpretive approach in *The Unconstitutionality of Slavery*, Douglass argued that "the language of the law must be construed strictly in favor of justice and liberty" and that "[w]here a law is susceptible of two meanings, the one making it accomplish an innocent meaning, and the other making it accomplish a wicked purpose, we must in all cases adopt that which makes it accomplish an innocent purpose" (Foner, *Life and Writings* 2: 476). As a radical abolitionist, Douglass agreed with William Howard Day, a delegate to the 1851 State Convention of Colored Citizens of Ohio, that proslavery interpretations of the Constitution like Garrison's and Justice Taney's mistook past "construction[s] of the Constitution of the United States" for "the Constitution itself" (Aptheker 1: 318). Instead of looking backward at how the Constitution and the Declaration of Independence had been read by the enemies of African American citizenship, Douglass looked forward to the type of republic foreshadowed by the framers' aspirational language of rights, equality, and self-government. The forward-looking perspective of Douglass and the radical abolitionists advocated a fluid Constitution that anticipated social change.

Douglass's conversion to radical abolitionism reflected his pragmatic approach to American legal theory and the antislavery cause. Douglass came to see that, in effect, Garrison's "No Union" argument abandoned the South and its slaves, protecting the legal and political autonomy of New England's white majority in a secessionist manner not unlike that described by Senator John C. Calhoun's concept of "concurrent majorities." While Garrison insisted on using natural rights principles to argue for the overturning of the American constitutional system, Douglass was willing to work with available legal doctrine, seeking to reclaim the Constitution and its tradition. And while Garrison took a primarily regionalist view of the slavery issue, Douglass strove to forge a national rights conscience that, as part of American constitutionalism, would protect the fundamental rights of present and future minorities.

Broadly speaking, Douglass's radical move in revising the rhetoric of the founding fathers was to reconceive the natural rights consensus validating revolutions and legal systems as the fluid, changing agreement of a racially heterogeneous society. In studying the legal aspects of Douglass's narratives, most students discover that their own ideas of citizenship and human rights bear a closer resemblance to those of Douglass than to those of the founding fathers, a discovery they share with constitutional scholars, such as David Richards and Judge Leon Higginbotham, who have noted the centrality of Douglass's jurisprudence to current conceptions of the Constitution (Richards, *Conscience* 257; *Commonwealth of Pa. v. Local U. No. 542 Int. U. of Op. Eng.*, 347 F. Supp. 268, 270–71 [1972]).

NOTES

[1]The manner in which one presents the jurisprudential background to Douglass's antebellum narratives clearly depends on the class one is teaching. In survey courses, I am often limited to lecturing on the legal background and conducting limited class discussion on brief excerpts of the Constitution, the Fugitive Slave Act of 1850, and certain important legal decisions (e.g., *State v. Mann*, 13 NC 229 [1829]; *Prigg v. Pennsylvania*, 41 US [16 Pet.] 539 [1842]; *Roberts v. City of Boston*, 5 Cushing 198 [Mass. 1849]; and *Dred Scott v. Sandford*, 60 US [19 How.] 393 [1857]). When the focus of the course is narrower, I give students more of this collateral material to read and discuss. We spend time talking about how to find and analyze legal material. For certain of my classes, I arrange an orientation at the local law library, and I take the students step by step through the process of using legal indexes to find cases and statutes. Morris Cohen's *Legal Research in a Nutshell* offers a clear introduction to the structure of American law and how to find relevant case decisions and statutes. In addition, there is a wealth of secondary material to help students and teachers working with the political, legal, and philosophical context for the slavery debate. Here are just a few suggestions. Helen Catterall's five-volume compilation *Judicial Cases concerning American Slavery and the Negro* is an excellent state by state survey of cases addressing race and slavery. Certain scholarly works serve as useful guides to relevant background material, such as David Richards's *Foundations of American Constitutionalism* and *Conscience and the Constitution: History, Theory, and Law of the Reconstruction Amendments*, William Wiecek's *The Sources of Antislavery Constitutionalism in America*, Don Fehrenbacher's *The Dred Scott Case, Its Significance in American Law and Politics*, Robert Cover's *Justice Accused: Antislavery and the Judicial Process*; Mark Tushnet's

The American Law of Slavery, 1810–1860: Considerations of Humanity and Interest.
Eric Sundquist's *To Wake the Nations: Race in the Making of American Literature* and
Brook Thomas's *Cross-Examinations of Law and Literature: Cooper, Hawthorne,
Stowe, and Melville* provide fine models for relating the historical and legal material to
literature.

[2]Students often want to know how, besides by reading *The Columbian Orator*, Douglass obtained his sense of natural rights jurisprudence. I tell them that he acquired it
much the way we do. He debated the meaning of the Declaration of Independence and
the Constitution. He examined abolitionist arguments saturated with the themes and
figures of the natural rights tradition. He read contemporary case law that spelled out
the difference between power-based and morality-based models of law. Before writing
the second version of his autobiography, which embraces the Constitution as an antislavery document, he read Stowe's *Uncle Tom's Cabin*, which is deeply influenced by
the liberal natural rights tradition of Butler, Hutcheson, and Shaftesbury. And on specific points, such as property rights, Douglass's political thought frequently reflects his
close study of the principles set forth in Locke's *Two Treatises of Government* (*Douglass
Papers* 2: 165).

Shattering Kidnapper's Heavenly Union: Interargumentation in Douglass's Oratory and *Narrative*

Keith D. Miller and Ruth Ellen Kocher

When Frederick Douglass escaped from slavery in 1841, he became a popular abolitionist orator, electrifying Northern audiences with highly provocative denunciations of slavery. Responding to Douglass's attacks, white Southerners called him a liar, claiming that he knew nothing about slavery because he had never been a slave. As Douglass explained, "[T]his doubt being used to injure the anti-slavery cause, I was induced to set the matter at rest by publishing the narrative of my life" ("I Am Here" 40). Douglass's *Narrative* of 1845 established his status as a fugitive slave by specifying his personal history with various masters and supervisors in Maryland.

While the *Narrative* proved to everyone's satisfaction that Douglass had indeed been a slave, its publication precipitated another problem. Because the *Narrative* gave the name of the most recent "owner" from whom Douglass had absconded, that disclosure exposed him to possible recapture by that owner, who was legally entitled to his human "property." Seeking to elude possible slave catchers, Douglass fled the United States for the British Isles. As he explained to an Irish audience, "[I]t was thought better for me to get out of the way lest my master might use some stratagem to get me back into his clutches. I am here then in order to avoid the scent of the blood hounds of America [. . .]" ("I Am Here" 40).

Douglass returned to the United States after his supporters had purchased his freedom from his slave master. He resumed his oratorical career, hurling lightning bolts from one platform after another as he delivered a seemingly endless marathon of speeches. Beginning in 1847, he also published and edited the *North Star*, a popular abolitionist newspaper.

Narrative, then, is far more than a literary text that invites readers to explore its omissions, paradoxes, fissures, and ironies. It served as an incident in Douglass's antislavery crusade, a text that he produced to validate his ethos as an orator, and an interruption in his river of speeches. Like his hundreds of abolitionist addresses, his abolitionist newspaper, and his abolitionist novella of 1853, the *Narrative* existed for one major purpose: to convince Americans to dismantle slavery as soon as possible. Douglass's text exemplifies Walter Fisher's contention that narration can offer arguments at least as effective as rational appeals.

In appealing for abolition, Douglass constructed a large, extended system of argumentation—call it interargumentation—flexible enough to employ when speaking in countless lecture halls and when writing an autobiography. Thus, in approaching the *Narrative*, teachers and students must consider its resplendent place within Douglass's larger rhetorical tapestry and its interargumentative relation to the rest of that tapestry.

Henry Louis Gates, Jr., convincingly argues that Douglass arranges the first chapter of the *Narrative* through a fairly elaborate series of binary oppositions that he then dismantles (*Figures* 80–97). William L. Andrews notes that Douglass organizes the remainder of the *Narrative* through more binaries that remain stable (*To Tell* 123–38). Douglass relied on this structural vehicle because, as Fredric Jameson explains, binary opposition "generates an order out of random data" and can function as a "deciphering device" to help the mind "perceive difference and identity" as it confronts "a mass of apparently homogeneous data" (113, 117).

But Douglass does not simply deconstruct some binaries and pile up others. Rather, he generates interargumentative order out of data unfamiliar to Northerners by arranging many speeches and the *Narrative* according to the same commanding binary: True Christianity / False Christianity. He constantly pits True Christianity, which he explicitly embraces, against the False Christianity of racism and slavery.

Douglass wielded his commanding binary in a number of the extant speeches he delivered before the publication of the *Narrative*. For example, in "American Prejudice and Southern Religion" and "The Church Is the Bulwark of Slavery," he blasted Northern churches that defiled true Christianity by exercising racial discrimination during the Holy Eucharist. The celebration of the Lord's Supper was a sacred experience while racist violations were despicable manifestations of false Christianity. In "The Southern Style of Preaching to Slaves," he again decried false Christianity as he mockingly imitated slaveholders' sermons to slaves, lampooning slave masters' self-serving perversion of the Golden Rule.

In "Southern Slavery and Northern Religion," Douglass further exemplified the falsely Christian white South by relating his and other children's experiences that he would later include in the *Narrative*: the separation of children from their mothers; Douglass's and other children's eating from a trough; and the cruel abandonment of his aged and enfeebled grandmother by her slaveholder. In "My Slave Experience" he added accounts of cruel whippings and the story of Demby, a slave shot to death for refusing to submit to the lash—all of which would appear in the *Narrative*.

In long polemical passages that Douglass used as a dress rehearsal for later orations, the appendix of the *Narrative* instantiates and explains the commanding binary:

> [F]or, between the Christianity of this land and the Christianity of Christ, I recognize the widest possible difference—so wide, that to receive the one as good, pure, and holy, is of necessity to reject the other as bad, corrupt, and wicked. To be the friend of the one, is of necessity to be the enemy of the other. I love the pure, peaceable, and impartial Christianity of Christ: I therefore hate the corrupt, slaveholding, women-whipping,

cradle-plundering, partial and hypocritical Christianity of this land. [. . .] The man who wields the blood-clotted cowskin [whip] during the week fills the pulpit on Sunday [. . .]. We have men sold to build churches, women sold to support the gospel, and babes sold to purchase Bibles [. . .].   (326–27)

In the appendix, Douglass also quotes lines that satirize slave masters' Christianity as "Kidnapper's heavenly union" (330).

Before reaching the appendix, Douglass skillfully weaves his governing binary into the body of the *Narrative*. One of his obvious strategies is to exemplify False Christianity by portraying sadistic slaveholders who served either as pastors or as prominent lay Christians. He reports that the church leaders Wright Fairbanks and Garrison West used force to disband his Sabbath school (288). The Reverend Daniel Weeden enjoyed whipping his slaves. Embracing the lash and Christianity with equal relish, the Reverend Rigby Hopkins, in Douglass's words, "could always find some excuse for whipping a slave" while "there was not a man any where round, who made higher professions of religion, or was more active in revivals [. . .]" (302, 303). After converting to Christianity at a camp meeting, Thomas Auld behaved more brutally toward Douglass and other slaves than he had previously (287). By depicting the unreligious William Freeland as his least objectionable supervisor, Douglass in effect argues that False Christianity is far worse than no religion at all (301).

The most despicable character in the *Narrative* is Edward Covey, "a class-leader in the Methodist church" who "sometimes deceived himself into the solemn belief, that he was a sincere worshipper of the most high God" (289, 292). The slaves, however, dubbed him "'the snake,'" for he would "crawl" around or remain "coiled up in the corner of the wood-fence" and surprise anyone unfortunate enough to pause briefly while working (291–92). As the perfect embodiment of False Christianity, Covey inverts all values, including those of the natural world: "The longest days were too short for him and the shortest nights too long for him" (293). The climax of the *Narrative* occurs when Douglass refuses to submit to Covey's whip and outwrestles the Satanic, snakelike overseer. In the *Narrative* all these examples are in contrast to Douglass's stated devotion to True Christianity and grateful references to Providence and the Almighty.

Structuring the *Narrative* through his chief binary is a brilliant strategy that enables Douglass to present himself simultaneously as an abolitionist and a radical church reformer. Like his earlier orations, the *Narrative* implicitly argues that not only do slaveholders systematically brutalize the workers who are building the South, they also invert true Christianity. Instead of simply ignoring Christmas, slave masters desecrate the hallowed day by encouraging slaves to drink excessively—a temptation to which many slaves unfortunately succumb, thereby helping to complete the inversion (299–300). Slaves again manifest their complicity by boasting to one another about their "owners," whom they actually disdain. Emancipation is necessary not only to relieve the degradation and suffering of slaves but also to repeal the Southern inversion of True Christianity and thereby to save the white church, which is deeply implicated in slavery.

Why did Douglass extend in the *Narrative* the main binary that he had used in addresses? He did so to offer a perspective by incongruity that would shatter Northerners' piety.

Kenneth Burke declares that a "perspective by incongruity" violates "piety" or *"the sense of what properly goes with what"* (*Permanence* 74). Although "piety" usually denotes religious devotion, Burke uses it to indicate any powerful allegiance. Similarly, the Protestant theologian Paul Tillich defines faith as "ultimate concern" and argues that humans can vest their "ultimate concern" in such seemingly secular "gods" as "the nation" and "social success and economic power" (1–3). He explains that no matter how secular an ultimate concern might become, as long as people cling to it doggedly they are devoutly religious. In his words, "Idolatrous faith is still faith" (16). Explicating Burke, Julia Allen and Lester Faigley analyze the power of a perspective by incongruity to threaten piously held convictions:

> By juxtaposing incongruous ideas, Burke says, we "shatter pieties." In other words, by juxtaposing one ideological correctness together with another, of a different ideological stripe, the two call each other into question [. . . and] the piety will thus be "shattered." (162)

Burke claims enormous power for such rhetorical juxtapositioning by naming it "atom-cracking" (*Attitudes* 308).

In the *Narrative* Douglass juxtaposes Christianity—the great religion of Victorian America—and slavery, an institution that had long been sanctioned in the South and accepted by the North. He crashes together the ideological correctness of True Christianity and the presumed naturalness of slavery, putting audiences, who accepted Christianity as ultimate truth, in the position of having to reject slavery as its opposite. Whether Douglass in private subscribed to Christianity or (as Donald Gibson argues ["Faith"]) rejected it matters less than his spectacular rhetorical ability to marshal Christianity as a vehicle for shattering piety in his attack on bondage.

In teaching the *Narrative*, we locate it within Douglass's rhetorical tapestry. Students examine literary dimensions as part of Douglass's narrative argument, understand that narrative argument as part of his interargumentation, and visualize that interargumentation as a major contribution to the entire abolitionist project.

Following this approach, students can explore the literary ironies, fissures, contradictions, and omissions that Gates, Andrews, Gibson, David Van Leer, and others have spotted in the *Narrative*. We ask students whether—and in what way—the anomalies and destabilizing tendencies noted by recent critics advance or retard Douglass's polemic and whether they would have mattered to Douglass or his nineteenth-century audiences.

Our approach encourages students to consider what Deborah McDowell has illuminated: Douglass's reinscription of patriarchal authority, which appears to contradict his antebellum political support for women's rights. We ask students about Douglass's decision to shatter the piety of slavery while reinforcing the piety of the patriarchy. Do reformers succeed by shattering one piety at a time? Or do they need to assault racial and sexual oppression simultaneously? Could or should a nineteenth-century reformer have done so? How many—and which—fundamental social assumptions can reformers expect moderate audiences to reexamine at one time? We also ask students to consider whether Douglass was trying to cleanse Christianity in a manner similar to that of Martin Luther, as we contend, or whether he hated and rejected that religion, as Gibson claims ("Faith"), or indicted it, as SallyAnn Ferguson argues.

In addition, we note that the interargumentative binaries that structure Douglass's pre-*Narrative* speeches and his *Narrative* demand resolution; for, as Claude Lévi-Strauss maintains, "mythical thought always progresses from the awareness of oppositions toward their resolution" (819). Unlike the storytellers whose work Lévi-Strauss investigates, however, Douglass could not possibly resolve his binary tensions as long as slavery continued to thrive. The structure of the *Narrative* remained incomplete because it depended on the "text" of national life.

After the *Narrative* appeared, Douglass sustained the binary tensions in his interargumentative tapestry even as he demanded their resolution. For example, in a February 1846 address in Scotland, he dramatically opposed slavery to Christianity as he urged the Free Church of Scotland to sever its ties with its affiliated American slaveholders:

> I [maintain] that man-stealing is incompatible with Christianity—that slaveholding and true religion are at war with each other—and that a Free Church should have no fellowship with a slave church—that as light can have no union with darkness, Christ has no concord with Beelzebub [. . .] and no man can serve two masters,—so I maintain that freedom cannot rightfully be blended with slavery.   ("Free Church" 159)

Five weeks later, in another jeremiad delivered in Scotland, he tightened the lines to include virtually no explanation apart from the binaries:

> 'Tis the *Free* Church of Scotland, what free church and slave church opposites!—light and darkness, liberty and slavery, freedom and oppression, Bibles and thumbscrews, exhortations, and horsewhips, all linked and interlinked.   ("Free States" 188)

Although these binaries were "all linked and interlinked" by slaveholders, such linkage represented the yoking of metaphysical opposites. Douglass shattered the piety of slavery by explaining that slave masters violated the nature of the universe.

Following the horrific 1857 *Dred Scott* decision of the United States Supreme Court, Douglass reviled the Court's decision as "an open, glaring, and scandalous tissue of lies" ("Dred Scott" 167). Recapitulating familiar incongruities, he assaulted slavery by invoking the Bible. He also generated a new binary, false resolution / true resolution, to ridicule the strenuous efforts to guarantee the permanence of slavery:

> Loud and exultingly have we been told that the slavery question is settled, and settled forever. You remember it was settled thirty-seven years ago, when Missouri was admitted into the Union with a slaveholding constitution. [. . .] Just fifteen years afterwards, it was settled again by voting down the right of petition, and gagging down free discussion in Congress. Ten years after this, it was settled again by the annexation of Texas . [. . .] In 1850 it was again settled. This was called a final settlement. [. . .] Four years after this settlement, the whole question was once more settled, and settled by a settlement which unsettled all the former settlements. The fact is, the more the question has been settled, the more it has needed settling. (166–67)

He argued that only one true resolution of slavery was possible—abolition. Other resolutions, including the newest "settlement," were false and would fail, just as the Missouri Compromise and subsequent false resolutions had failed. The failures were inevitable, despite brilliant leadership: "Clay, Calhoun, and Webster each tried his hand at suppressing the agitation [against slavery], and they went to their graves disappointed and defeated" (166).

In the same address he coined another new binary, past ignorance / present awareness, to celebrate abolitionists' success in shattering piety and to herald a massive, positive movement toward true resolution. He insisted that, despite the recent "hell-black judgment of the Supreme Court" (168), a gargantuan change was well under way:

> [Abolitionism] started small, and was without capital either in men or money. [. . .] There was ignorance to be enlightened, error to be combatted, conscience to be awakened, prejudice to be overcome, apathy to be aroused, the right of speech to be secured, mob violence to be subdued, and a deep, radical change to be inwrought in the mind and heart of the whole nation. This great work, under God, has gone on, and gone on gloriously. (165)

He elaborated:

> Politicians who cursed [abolitionism] now defend it; ministers, once dumb, now speak in its praise; and presses, which once flamed with hot denunciations against it, now surround the sacred cause as by a wall of living fire. (166)

Varying his well-tested, commanding binary and explaining the inevitable true resolution, Douglass claimed that bondage affronted God: "The Supreme Court of the United States is not the only power in this world. It is very great, but the Supreme Court of the Almighty is greater" (167). Chief Justice Taney "cannot reverse the decision of the Most High," for "God will be true though every man be a liar" (167, 168). Indeed the false resolution of the Supreme Court could paradoxically usher in True Christianity; for, in the *Dred Scott* case, the Court might be forging "one necessary link in the chain of events preparatory to the downfall and complete overthrow of the whole slave system" (168–69).

As symbolic action, Douglass's orations and his *Narrative* obviously served as earlier links in that same chain of events. But despite the progress toward abolition, Douglass's interargumentative rhetoric by incongruity—including his speeches and the *Narrative*—still remained incomplete and unresolved. He could not possibly ease his interargumentative tensions, moving from an awareness of oppositions toward their resolution, until slavery ended.

But in February 1863 Douglass responded to the Emancipation Proclamation by deeming it "the greatest event of our nation's history" ("Proclamation" 549). For anyone, saluting Lincoln's edict meant saluting the end of slavery. For Douglass, applauding the edict also meant sewing the last stitch of his extended tapestry and, *finally*, resolving the binary tensions of his interargumentation. Only by publicly applauding Lincoln's act could Douglass note the end of the kidnapper's heavenly union and thereby complete his interargumentative structure and conclude his *Narrative*.

A Labor Studies Approach to Douglass's *Narrative*
Laura Hapke

> We were worked in all weathers. . . . [I]t was never too
> hot or too cold; it could never rain, blow, hail, or snow,
> too hard for us to work in the field. Work, work, work,
> was scarcely more the order of the day than of the night.

> Until a very little while after I went there [to the
> Baltimore shipyard], white and black ship-carpenters
> worked side by side, and no one seemed to see any
> impropriety in it. [. . . Unlike myself,] [m]any of the
> black carpenters were freemen. Things seemed to be
> going on very well. All at once, the white carpenters
> knocked off, and said they would not work with free
> colored workmen.

By 1845, when *Narrative of the Life of Frederick Douglass* appeared, foes of
the oppressive new factory system were already invoking the phrase "white
slavery" to compare it with the South's black-fueled plantations, foundries, and
mills. And it was the slave's unwilling servitude that Frederick Douglass captured so well in the first epigraph. Yet the second epigraph captures another
painful labor truth. Fearful of the de-skilling that a burgeoning technology and
a cheap, nonwhite labor supply might produce, the fledgling Euramerican
labor movement had declared its separateness from black toil. White working-
class identity was instead anchored in the "honorable trades" like carpentry and
shipbuilding. The dignity of labor was thus erased from "nigger work," a widely

used racist phrase, or from what in more enlightened labor quarters was viewed as the economic dehumanization of the Southern system.[1]

Ever alert to the racial tensions of the labor movement, Douglass provides an astute analysis of the Baltimore shipyard where his avaricious owner, Master Hugh, had apprenticed him. There slave and free, apprentice and journeyman, black and white, plied the same skilled trade. In an allegory of labor relations before (and, many argue, after) the CIO era, the same white workingmen who permitted transient interracial alliances repudiated them for fear that "free colored carpenters [. . .] would soon take the trade into their own hands" (312). Thus the cruelty that Douglass suffered at their hands was both real and prophetic. As slave, he embodied antebellum labor's deepest fears; as imported black construction worker, he was the first of the hated scabs of the strike-torn industrial decades to come.

On one level, the Baltimore sections of Douglass's *Narrative* highlight the troubled race relations that prompted Douglass, many years after he had risen to prominence, to remind his son that it was easier for a black man to become a lawyer than to enter the skilled trades, all the while exhorting African Americans to "learn trades or starve!" (Foner and Lewis 118). Thus at the urban university where I teach required composition, elective literature, and interdisciplinary literature-history undergraduate courses on narrative representations of the American worker, I first contextualize Douglass's forced-work narrative within what soon became the northern black proletarian (and southern rural peonage) experience. (W. E. B. Du Bois charted the disfranchisement of the South's black proletariat in his classic book *Black Reconstruction*.) I also contend that the Douglass work, though not customarily taught as a (pro)labor text, is a field-as-factory and skilled-work tale of extraordinary richness. It details not only the cruel conditions of slave employment but also the work culture—from covert resistance to escapist behavior on rare holidays—that evolved in response to it. As such, it is an excellent introduction to other radical labor literature and to a social protest tradition that both encompasses and transcends the experiences of oppressed minorities.

Before elaborating on Douglass's narrative links to the United States working class, however, I take my students through a series of decoding exercises centered on his elegant prose. Most undergraduates at my university plan business or computer science careers. Many have difficulty focusing on word choice, connotation, and the like, and literature courses take them into unfamiliar linguistic territory, despite years of high school classes. For all the beauty of Douglass's language, it is formal and his diction, by modern narrative standards, elaborate. To be reasonably sure that these undergraduate readers know what they are reading, for the first week I ask them to write paraphrases of key passages from the text, both ones I have selected and ones they have chosen, first in standard English, then in a more colloquial way. Such exercises not only strengthen students' abilities to concentrate on Douglass's sentence structure but also help students hone the paraphrase skills they will need for their research essay on the *Narrative* later in the semester. I ask whether a modern version of the writing loses in translation. Many agree that it does. I then ask whether a slang version of his ideas makes them more accessible; a few assent but most come to prefer Douglass's own style.

The polished style, of course, raises other questions about Douglass. In the text as a whole, I stress, Douglass establishes himself as a vital part of a generation of American authors concerned with manual work: the urban Gothic novelist George Lippard and the American Renaissance triad of Melville, Emerson, and Thoreau. More than any of his contemporaries, Douglass is as much the great man as he is the eyewitness historian of work. I then divide my students into groups to consider whether Douglass's "educated" language and the class status it suggests isolate him from his earlier selves as a field slave, a slave carpenter, and a northern menial. Or is his language a tribute to what working people can achieve through self-elevation? On a wider level, must workers sound "dumb"? Can one work with one's hands and write with them too? Questionnaires on the text distributed at semester's end have revealed over the years a variety of student reactions to the Douglass prose style. Students have characterized his diction as "amazing," "difficult," and "unrealistic." However they view his language by mastering it they are implicitly engaging themselves with the language of an early classic of United States work literature. They are now as ready to read a Melvillian discussion of whalers or a Thoreauvian passage on an Irish railway worker as to appreciate the deliberate simplicity of Langston Hughes's poem "Song of a Negro Wash-Woman" (1925), Zora Neale Hurston's allied short story "Sweat" (1926), or Mike Gold's Lower East Side classic *Jews without Money* (1930).

My preference, though, is to connect Douglass's narrative to twentieth-century texts by worker writers. To that end, I stress that, despite fictional elements, the *Narrative* is not a work of fiction but that it is one of the best blue-collar texts of the modern era, for it portrays a worker protagonist as he moves from economic oppression to self-definition. My classroom discussions, while beginning with the *Narrative*'s impassioned preflight sections, move quickly to Douglass in his noble fugitive persona. In that guise, he grapples prophetically with what the dignity of labor means to a black man who, after migrating to the "free" North, cannot secure a job worthy of his skills. "[B]ut such was the strength of prejudice against color, among the white calkers," he writes in the closing pages, "that [. . .] of course I could get no employment" (325). How, I ask, is his description altered by the phrase "of course"? Is it bitter or pragmatic? By modern standards, is he angry or not?

Querying Douglass's use of "of course" leads to discussions of tone and prepares for the semester's later texts on job discrimination by classic African American authors. The path can also lead to the hidden injuries of class, to use the title of Richard Sennett and Jonathan Cobb's important book. Even without a knowledge of proletarian fiction (largely by white authors), many of my students, who are first-generation college entrants from working-class homes and no strangers to such hurts, are able to enter into a carefully probing discussion of elitism in American institutions and can offer a host of stories. (The daughter of a pipefitter, I throw in a few of my own as well.) The larger point is that whether focusing on key turns of phrase, on crucial scenes, or on whole chapters, students can begin to see how the *Narrative*, as the precursor of black proletarianism, prefigures many later social protest texts. Syllabi thus might follow the Douglass text with a series of readings from novels such as Hughes's autobiographical *Not without Laughter*, William Attaway's *Blood on the Forge*, and the Everglades agrighetto sections of Hurston's romantic scrutiny of black rural sexual politics, *Their Eyes Were Watching God*.

Attaway's newly resurrected novel, set in the early decades of the great migration but speaking to the author's own hardscrabble 1930s era as well, is particularly instructive. Updating the Douglass transit, it moves a trio of grossly exploited sharecropping brothers, Melody, Chinatown, and Big Mat, from southern economic servitude to the modern industrial city of big steel's Pittsburgh. Like the newly escaped Douglass, the brothers are hired for menial labor, which they saw as potentially offering the same satisfaction that Douglass expressed when he called his first job as a free man "new, dirty, and hard work [, . . . the] first work, the reward of which was to be entirely my own" (324–25). Yet as fodder for the industrial mills, the brothers are cut off from the very mobility achieved by their exceptionally talented antebellum predecessor. Unprepared for both the physical constrictions of the hellish factory and the few freedoms their wages can buy, they experience new forms of oppression. They fall victim to industrial accidents, manipulation by union-busting steel mill management, and disorientation in a titularly free North that urges them to consume but not to reflect.

Conscripted and taken north by unscrupulous labor agents, the brothers struggle to learn how they must behave and what work they are expected to do. Walking to their jobs at the huge Bessemer mills, they react to the drab immigrant town near the foundries, staring and being stared at by the Slavic workmen whose jobs they will share: "Boy, this here North don't seem like nothin' to me," complained Chinatown. "All this smoke and stuff in the air! How a man gonna breathe?"(68). Such passages raise important questions about continuities and discontinuities between Attaway's and Douglass's work environments.

Students can recognize that the Attaway novel, bleak as it is, extends the Douglass narrative's critique of how free black labor was treated. Supplying further background from classic labor (and joblessness) histories such as Gilbert Osofsky's *Harlem: The Making of a Black Ghetto: Negro New York, 1890–1930*, Richard L. Rowan's *The Negro in the Steel Industry*, and updated texts, particularly the sterling work of Jacqueline Jones, instructors can suggest paper topics that use texts by Attaway and others to probe Douglass's guardedly hopeful abolitionist conclusion. To further layer the assignment, I suggest news articles about inner-city unemployment, as well as William Julius Wilson's important book on the disappearance of jobs in America's ghettos.

Later in the semester, the instructor can widen the significance of Douglass's narrative to study the nonblack social protest writer's quest for self in texts such as Jack Conroy's basic-industry picaresque novel *The Disinherited* and John Steinbeck's Okie epic *The Grapes of Wrath*. Depression-era fiction, as a number of capable modern interpreters have pointed out, provides a bildungsroman framework for the protagonist's discovery that collective action is needed for social change (Foley 284–85). Thus the radical novelist privileges a spokesman for laboring people, whether Conroy's Larry Donovan or Steinbeck's Tom Joad, even as that hero urges group effort. The point can be made that Douglass heralds all these labor classics in his authorial struggle to balance Franklinesque individualism and worker solidarity; succeeding by one's own efforts and rising with one's class; spirited defense of oppressed laboring people and wary hope for the fruits of the American Dream. The instructor who keeps a clippings file can bring in information on the woes of working-class people, whether Detroit teamsters, Latino garment workers in California, or the nine thousand people who lined up in predawn winter Chicago for five hundred hotel jobs.[2]

In creating paper topics to parallel the semester's readings, the instructor might begin with contrasts between Douglass's passionately detailed discussions of black labor exploitation, particularly those in his tenth chapter, and more ambivalent period descriptions of the (white) work experience. Some semesters I assign selections from "Bartleby the Scrivener" or *Redburn* by the onetime clerk and sailor Herman Melville. Both are brilliant but elitist texts in which clerks and sailors variously fail the test of gentrification. (Melville's alter ego Wellingborough Redburn asks himself how he can endure a voyage with deckhands who are not gentlemen.) By suggesting that students distinguish between Melville and Douglass, I have received impressive essays that compare Melville's defense of the WASP gentleman with Douglass's defense of the natural gentleman. I have also received cogent essays on the differences between the two authors' approaches to mind-numbing work, a topic that can be enlarged to include students' own anecdotes about underpaid or demeaning part-time jobs.

I also assign papers comparing representations of enslavement in Douglass with those in other important "slave" texts, such as Martin R. Delany's *Blake* and Harriet Wilson's *Our Nig*. The Delany novel is a good counterpoint to the *Narrative*. It features a Nat Turner figure of extraordinary personal power, raising him to godlike proportions. Yet by so doing, it implicitly deemphasizes the very toil that Douglass delineates. Wilson's novella, set in the "free North" and dramatizing the life of an indentured servant who finally secures her liberty, poses urgent questions about the gendered nature of African American enslavement, filling in descriptive gaps left in ex-slave narratives by males.

Late in the semester, sometimes after a series of texts by authors as diverse as Stephen Crane, Upton Sinclair, Sandra Cisneros, and Tillie Olsen, I return to Douglass as a touchstone for the new black autobiographers, who are in a sense heirs to a slave narrative tradition. Excellent in this regard are Ruthie

Bolton's account of her abusive southern father, *Gal*, and Nathan McCall's troubling prison memoir *Makes Me Wanna Holler*. Both include extensive sections on the workers who move from the job place to criminal activity and back. Some instructors might wish to assign the inner-city naturalist Richard Price's explosive Newark housing-projects novel, *Clockers*, profane as it is. I ask students to consider what Douglass might say of the drug-trade labor environment and remind them that, from the 1960s onward, black residents in public housing developments dubbed them "plantations."

Particularly in interdisciplinary courses, research papers can use passages from the Douglass text to contextualize subsequent black labor history. Here individual conferences with students are necessary to structure the assignment: an instructor might suggest tracing the idea of the black artisan in Douglass's text in discussions of postbellum work. Of crucial importance in shaping such an assignment are texts like those by John Hope Franklin and Alfred A. Moss, Jr., *From Slavery to Freedom: A History of African Americans*, and one edited by Philip S. Foner and Ronald L. Lewis, *Black Workers: A Documentary History from Colonial Times to the Present*. From the grandfather of the new social historians, Herbert Gutman, instructors can assign essays on the use of black strikebreakers in 1870s Ohio or ask students to research strikebreakers' deployment in the great steel strike of 1919, in which the Carnegie management successfully drove racial wedges between white and black workers. Perhaps honors-level students can be asked to make connections between Douglass's text and African American labor landmarks such as the work stoppages in the Reconstruction South, the rise of the Brotherhood of Sleeping Car Porters, the Harlem food boycott of 1934, and the Memphis sanitation workers' strike of 1968.

Whether in a close reading of a passage on Covey's whipping of Douglass, a thematic yoking of the *Narrative* and an Attaway or Conroy novel, or a brief research paper comparing and contrasting Douglass's early experiences as a free man and those of African American domestic service in the North of the great migration, a labor studies approach to the Douglass text illuminates rather than competes with the traditional emphasis on its creator's search for a dignified racial identity. Instructors who wish to focus on racial aspects of Douglass's working-class consciousness will of course modify the suggestions given here, deemphasizing the links I suggest between the *Narrative* and the radical fiction of the 1930s, in which black working people do not act in militant ways. (Partial exceptions are Richard Wright's *Native Son*—at least if read allegorically—and Arna Bontemps's historical novel *Black Thunder*.) Still, my approach can widen the American literary discourse of race to include class without scanting the history of racial conflicts among working people. Above all, it can interest students in a revisionist reading of Frederick Douglass as one whose exemplary "representative man" need not be opposed to the ordinary working stiff.

NOTES

[1]Ironically it is two Irish dockworkers, members of the *unskilled* trades, who "advised [Douglass] to run away to the North" (280).

For the literature instructor unfamiliar with the race politics of antebellum labor, see, for instance, Lott 155, 202; Laurie 77–78; and essays by various hands in Newton and Lewis. An excellent general discussion of slave labor from a labor studies perspective is in Levine et al., ch. 9.

[2]See, for example, "Scattered Violence," "Los Angeles Sweatshops," and "Refugees from Recession." For prolabor reportage, see periodicals such as *Labor Notes*, published monthly by the Labor Education and Research Project and listed in the Alternative Press Index.

"Trust No Man!" But What about a Woman?
Ellen Craft and a Genealogical Model for
Teaching Douglass's *Narrative*
Barbara McCaskill

In the first decades of the nineteenth century, American audiences swarmed to purchase seats on the ever-popular lyceum circuit. For spartan or opulent billing, its speakers pontificated on every conceivable topic, from the music of the spheres to the mating calls of spotted geese to the Second Coming. It would seem that the lecture podium perfectly advanced, transposed, and synthesized competing Victorian fantasies of the Yankee hero both as a kind of Davey Crockett, Daniel Boone homespun pioneer and as a cosmopolitan, Jefferson-like or Franklinesque savant.

Yankee heroines, however, proved routine bystanders in this picture. The fantasy that eluded them was the feminist dream of a promiscuous lyceum: one that admitted both genders without attaching the automatic penalty either of "unsexing" or of dismissing as lesbian, spinsterish, degraded, uppity, or loose those women who seized agency there as speakers and spectators. Though writing rather than speaking, Harriet Jacobs alludes to this wish that talent finally, permanently, would supersede gender when in her narrative's preface she frets, "I trust my motives [to free the slaves] will excuse what might otherwise seem presumptuous" (*Incidents*, ed. Gates, 335).

Would Jacobs have remained so self-effacing to her readers, praying publicly to be "more competent to the task [of writing]" (335), had she known that, in the decades of the present so-called woman's century, the lyceum's limitations linger? Regardless of the panoply of signal texts on the fugitive narrative tradition (some of which are Foster, *Witnessing Slavery*; Sekora and Turner, *The Art of the Slave Narrative*; Davis and Gates, *The Slave's Narrative*; Andrews, *To Tell a Free Story*; McDowell and Rampersad, *Slavery and the Literary Imagination*), most students in my late-twentieth-century classrooms have never studied Douglass's *Narrative* in relation to those of ex-slave women. Or if they have, they often bear out, as Deborah McDowell observes in her essay "In the First Place," that our Douglass pedagogy relies on a politics of gender that, by constructing "Douglass as 'the first,' as 'representative man,' as the part that stands for the whole," depends on black women's objectification, subordination, rejection, or, once again, exclusion (56).

Instead of an African American literary tradition that operates "within the logic of first and second," McDowell calls for a "genealogical" model that emphasizes "the process of cultural production involved in making Douglass and Wheatley, or, for that matter, any 'first' or 'prior' figure, and the uses to which that production has been put" (57). Teaching the making of the Georgia fugitive Ellen Craft, I propose, can shift students' perspectives on early African

American literature from a hierarchical ordering based on chronology, genre, and gender to a more ideologically sensitive, less discursively polarized, genealogical endeavor.

When I walk into the classroom to teach Douglass's *Narrative*, I enter supported by nine years' full-time experience at large, predominately white public universities, where I have taught undergraduate and graduate classes in African American, multicultural American, and canonical white American literature. I am typically walking into an undergraduate classroom composed of twenty-five freshmen and sophomores or thirty-five juniors and seniors or ten freshmen in the honors program. In an average class there are two African American students; in some classes there are one or two students of Latina or Latino or biracial or Native American descent. Two or three class members may be nontraditional students, old enough to be parents of their classmates, who return to culminate long dreams of graduating from college, to train in different professions, or to vouchsafe job security in an increasingly competitive, volatile, downsized workforce. In my graduate seminars, which average fifteen students, the racial and ethnic backgrounds are more diverse.

Whenever I teach the *Narrative*, in keeping with the genealogical model's de-hierarchization of chronology, I begin with Douglass's conclusion: "The motto which I adopted when I started from slavery was this—'Trust no man!' I saw in every white man an enemy, and in almost every colored man cause for distrust" (320). His words warn his readers of the visceral situations—friendlessness, fright, homelessness, hunger—that track a fugitive's flight from the South to the North. Symbolically his catalog of paradoxes—"in the midst of plenty, yet suffering the terrible gnawings of hunger,—in the midst of houses, yet having no home,—among fellow men, yet feeling as if in the midst of wild beasts" (320)—alludes both to the so-called society that defines its darker colleagues as "savage" and to those so-called savages like Douglass himself who manage to ascend the summits of civilization. And at the moment he warns his readers to "Trust no man!" Douglass trusts them to trust him to be entrusted to represent, both as white America's nemesis and white America's friend, as exile and national, as idiot and intellect, the slave he has been and the man he has become. "Trust no man!" Douglass warns, even as he writes himself "first" to be trusted least *and* most.

But, I ask my students, what about a woman? In relation to Douglass and his *Narrative*, the Clinton, Georgia, fugitive Ellen Craft and the themes of her thrilling story have been sidelined to what McDowell has called "prior" status. In my research on Craft, I have documented that her story was "widely retold" in nineteenth-century abolition literature, by her husband William; by the *Liberator* editor William Lloyd Garrison; by the novelist Lydia Maria Child; by the Underground Railroad conductor William Still; by the novelist and biographer William Wells Brown and by his daughter Josephine Brown; and by the Civil War hero Colonel Thomas Wentworth Higginson. It was retold again in the twentieth century "by such [. . .] historians as R. J. M. Blackett, Ruth Loewenberg and Peter Bogin, Clare Midgeley, Peter Ripley, and Dorothy

Sterling" (McCaskill, "Designs on the Sign of Race" 28–29; "A Stamp on the Envelope"; and "Yours Very Truly"). Very fair-skinned, Craft escaped bondage in December 1848 disguised as a Southern slaveholder, her dark-skinned husband masquerading as her valet. Both arrived free in Philadelphia on Christmas Day. After a hair's-breadth escape to England in 1851 from agents of the Fugitive Slave Act of 1850, the Crafts settled abroad for nearly two decades before returning to a post-Reconstruction Georgia.

By what process, my students ask, did such romance—bittersweet, daring, real—become footnoted to Douglass's narrative and those of other males in the fugitive narrative tradition? The answer, as McDowell pursues, "hinge[s] on a declaration of priority or subordination critiqued in the writing of so many black women" (57). By investigating the criteria of chronology, gender, and genre as crucial for hierarchized literary assessments, I lead my students to understand how a Craft is diminished and a Douglass raised.

First, chronology makes Craft less important. The book she wrote with her husband, *Running a Thousand Miles to Freedom*, was published in England fifteen years after Douglass' own 1845 triumph, eight years after the inaugural serialization of Stowe's international blockbuster *Uncle Tom's Cabin* (1852). The titanic, transatlantic marketing of Douglass's *Narrative* alone easily eclipses the single edition of *Running*. The *Narrative*, as Henry Louis Gates, Jr., tells us, "sold 5,000 copies in the first four months of publication; between 1845 and 1847, it sold 11,000 copies; in Great Britain, nine editions were printed in these two years; and by 1860, 30,000 copies had sold" (*Classic Slave Narratives* xi). William L. Andrews says that the *Narrative* was also published in "a French and Dutch translation in the first three years of its existence" (*Three Classic Novels* 11). Since all this hoopla was overlayed by the imminence of war, *Running* could be relegated as a curt coda to the fifteen-year "culmination" of African American autobiography marked by Douglass's second autobiography, the 1855 *My Bondage and My Freedom*, Harriet Jacobs's 1861 *Incidents in the Life of a Slave Girl*, and J. D. Green's 1864 *Narrative* (Andrews, *To Tell* 205–63). That what is presented as a cowritten narrative reads like one exclusively written by William also does not do much to vindicate claims for the "firstness" of Craft's story.

If, in the fugitive narrative tradition, the genre defines the tale as much as the tale defines the genre, then genre, too, lessens Craft's standing. As Gates writes in his introduction to *Classic Slave Narratives*:

> In the long history of human bondage, it was only the black slaves in the United States who—once secure and free in the North, and with the generous encouragement and assistance of northern abolitionists—created a *genre* of literature that at once testified against their captors and bore witness to the urge of every black slave to be free and literate.   (ix)

Craft, however, is one who is witnessed to more than one who witnesses. She is sketched in William L. Still's *Underground Rail Road* (1872) masquerading in her male disguise; she is bundled in a woman's bonnet and basque—adjacent to a cameo of William—on *Running*'s frontispiece; she alternates pants and petticoats in the pages of the antebellum British and American press. In other words, scholars of the literature of abolition are more likely to appreciate Craft as a gender-bending visual image than as a genre-building fugitive writer.

And gender is the coup de grace that would banish Craft altogether from the files of fugitive firsts. Even when we think we apprehend her voice, it is not in a separately published, book-length, first person, male ex-slave's autobiography, where, as John Blassingame notes, "more clearly than in any other source, we learn what went on in the minds of black men" (qtd. in Carby, "Hear" 64). Rather, Craft writes in that quintessentially feminine, questionably literary, quite "prior" form: the letter. In an 1852 letter widely republished in the transatlantic abolitionist press (*Liberator, Pennsylvania Freeman, National Anti-slavery Standard, Anti-slavery Advocate*), Craft remonstrates against the "strange report" and "absurd calumny" that she desires to abandon English liberty "in the hands of an American gentleman in London, on condition that he would take [her] back to the family who held [her] as a slave in Georgia."

Her letter reads as an androcentric one—that is, as one contained by and affirming patriarchy—because of its confessional, rather than imperative, tone, its subject of (the absence of) male protection, and its reinscription of male authority when Garrison frames her words by reminding *Liberator* subscribers that Craft remains married and recently has given birth to a son. As my students are quick to see, Craft's feminine circumspection and demurral contrast with such adjectives as "powerful," "godlike," "commanding," and "self-emancipated," with which Garrison endows to Douglass's masculine voice (Gates, *Classic Slave Narratives* 245, 246). The hyperinflation of Craft's femininity in both the content and the placement of her letter anticipates what I share with my students as William's muzzling of her voice and pedestaling of her body in their book-length narrative.

> For practical purposes [in *Running a Thousand Miles*] Craft utters little so as not to draw suspicion to their escape. For ideological reasons, a "nervous and timid" Craft "shrinks" at tense moments or bursts into "violent sobs"; and, as William writes of his wife, ever the true woman, "at first she shrank from the idea" of escaping disguised as a man, even if that masculine masquerade was the only way of manumitting herself.
>
> (54, quoting from *Running* 287, 293, 316)

After leading my students in our confident claims of Craft as a "prior" to Douglass's "first," I trouble the waters. For, if Douglass uncovers "how a man was made a slave" and "how a slave was made a man" (294), then Craft whirls just as dervishly to claim how a woman is made a slave, how a slave is made a woman, and how a woman is made a man made woman, assertive and free. Attired as her would-be slaveholding rapist, she alludes to the ownership of property and person that slaveholding white men in the South tag themselves as exclusively entitled to. At the same time, frozen in this picture in her *flight* from these paltry pharaohs and their rotting earthly paradise, she severs her affiliations with them and serves them notice of this black woman's superior claims to slyness, snap, and sangfroid. She very well might have sat—corseted, skirted, and silent—in a "lady's chair" on the dais when her husband, William Wells Brown, and other male fugitives spoke from the speaker's platform, passionately and eloquently, on behalf of "the four millions of the enslaved."

Yet, her sex disguised, she stands as a feminized High John the Conqueror. To worried white audiences, she transmits the trickster message that the slave whom Massa and Missus cannot trust may yet be an equally intractable ward to even her sympathetic abolitionist-feminist guardians. To bemused black audiences, she stands as a testament to the myriads of African American women, including the women called the Moses of her people, Harriet Tubman herself, who sought out the "shame" of male attire to liberate themselves and their people and often, ironically, to entitle themselves to the freedoms and demands of middle-class white femininity that enslavement denied them. From an ostensibly trivial, "prior" figure thus emerges one who meant different things to different constituencies and who perhaps still points to competing groups who would highlight or mute her story, who would make it matter—or make it disappear.

In other words, by making plain, and then problematizing, our assumptions of "first" and "prior," we can shift the conversation of the fugitive narrative tradition to a genealogical model that enables students to see how ideologies of femininity and masculinity have assisted in producing these texts, to see who has determined the ideologies that produce them, and to understand why, in the first place, these texts must be produced. In my research on Craft, I have used a reassessment of her narrative, letter, and engravings as "prior" as a launching point for this process. First, I have traced how Craft was appropriated by black and white abolitionists as a symbol of the indeterminacy of constructions of gender and race, only to be completely subsumed in essentialized blackness and essentialized femininity, respectively, in the two postbellum versions of William Wells Brown's *Clotel* and in Lydia Maria Child's writings for the newly freed slaves (*Freedmen's Book*). Then, I have discussed the social functions that these various depictions of Craft served in abolition, uplift, and suffrage ("Designs" 23–119).

Similarly, perhaps we can ask our students, outside "the logic of first and second" (McDowell 57), why the current resurrection of scholarly interest in even illiterate and muted slave women like Craft, Harriet Tubman, Sally Hemings, and Sojourner Truth and in such spiritual autobiographers as Julia A. J. Foote and Jarena Lee has not been accompanied by a parallel explosion of interest in a wider range of male fugitive narrators? Why, in the face of this burgeoning female presence and the ever-growing leverage that African American publishers, booksellers, librarians, and distributors have in the industry, does Douglass's

sacrosanctity as *the* male slave's experience remain? Do African American literature and letters in a predominately white, patriarchal academy safeguard
influence, visibility, tenure, and respect by still making Douglass's masculine
word the altar and the sine qua non of its titulary temples?

Or, perhaps, rather than the same old–same old, Douglass's serene with-
standing of the winds of ideological whimsy may signify a crisis of identity.
Where black identity is challenged to redefine itself in relation to such categories as "biracial," "mixed-race," and "mixed marriage," where black masculinity must reassess itself in the light of Dennis Rodman's and Ru Paul's switches
to urban adventures in drag, where black femininity (after Lani Guinier, Joycelyn Elder, Hazel O'Leary, and Anita Hill) has had to hoist its collective slip and
honor its collective name, perhaps the image of Douglass as the black race's race
man is—like collards (not kale), grits (not oatmeal), butter beans (if cooked
right, no translation), and going down home (South) for the holidays—the ideological equivalent of a shared port in a storm. Perhaps blacks beatify Douglass
in self-defense. After all, historically, to defend ourselves from pillorying by the
multiple, manifold hubris and hate without, we have defined ourselves as consonant from within. Gates implies that this idea of the collective is fundamental
to the process of producing early African American autobiography:

> The black slave's narrative came to be a communal utterance, a collective
> tale, rather than merely an individual's autobiography. Each slave author,
> in writing about his or her personal life's experiences, simultaneously
> wrote on behalf of the millions of silent slaves still held captive through-
> out the South. Each author, then, knew that *all* black slaves would be
> judged—on their character, integrity, intelligence, manners and morals,
> and their claims to warrant emancipation—on this published evidence
> provided by one of their number. The slave authors therefore had to sat-
> isfy the dual expectations of shaping the random events of their lives into
> a meaningful and compelling pattern, while also making the narrative of
> their odyssey from slavery to freedom an emblem of every black person's
> potential for higher education and the desire to be free.
>
> (*Classic Slave Narratives* x)

Buried in our collective African American consciousness may be the memory
that, at one point, parts did emblematize the whole. Do many of us want to res-
urrect it? In other words, perhaps we African American people maintain the
"overpowering influence and cultural authority" (McDowell 57) of Douglass in
the male slave narrative pantheon, for familiarity, reassurance, inspiration—
hope!—from the stories of his continual self-fabrications.

Though the lyceum circuit has long since vanished, the legacy of its earliest
distinguished nineteenth-century African American women orators such as
Maria Stewart and Sojourner Truth has made an indelible mark on African
American literature and letters. No longer typecast Ellen Crafts, doomed to

recede into hearth and home as subordinates to a husband's success and authority, African American women writers stand alongside the male descendants of Douglass on *New York Times* best-seller lists, on college and university library inventories. Just as they can learn to reread Douglass, Craft, and other fugitive writers genealogically, my students, and yours, I hope, can also apply this demeanor to the current "renaissance."

Incidents in the Life of Frederick Douglass

Elizabeth Schultz

In the fall of 1969, I taught *Narrative of the Life of Frederick Douglass, an American Slave* for the first time. Clear in my memory and the memories of many of my students that semester were images of Watts, Detroit, and Newark burning; of Martin Luther King crumpling on a Memphis motel balcony; of black power and Black Panther defiance. My class, the first ever offered on African American literature at the University of Kansas, attracted more than one hundred undergraduates. Black and white, from urban and rural backgrounds, conservative and radical in political beliefs, my students were all desperate to find a context for understanding the incendiary events of those times. Since then, I have continued to teach Douglass's *Narrative* in a range of undergraduate classes, including a survey of antebellum American literature, a course in African American autobiography, and, most recently, a freshman honors course titled African American Narrative. Douglass's *Narrative* continues to provide an analogue for understanding the events of contemporary times. As Deborah E. McDowell notes, the *Narrative* "has been remarkably adaptable [. . .] to what Houston Baker has described as the 'generational shifts' in the interpretation of Afro-American literature" (38). In the years since 1969, my interpretation of the *Narrative* has shifted from a liberal androcentric approach to an approach including cultural studies, from an emphasis on my students' contemporary context to an emphasis that also embraces antebellum American culture.

My strategy in those early classes was to consider Douglass's description of himself as a representative American slave. His generalizations of his experiences were interpreted as the basis for his demanding freedom for all slaves. Thus we examined those sections and passages of the *Narrative* in which Douglass, as "a witness and a participant" (258), describes the lives of slaves collectively, especially as he had known them on Colonel Edward Lloyd's plantation. We noted that from the beginning Douglass tended to relate his personal experience to that of all slaves. In the narrative's first paragraph, he connects his personal and painful lack of knowledge regarding his birthdate with his realization that he cannot "remember to have ever met a slave who could tell of his birthday" (255).

The *Narrative* documented for us the impact of an unjust economic and legal system on human beings. We observed Douglass's detailed descriptions of individual situations, which reveal slavery's physical as well as psychological cruelty. In particular we noted his descriptions of a morally and epistemologically bewildering culture, one in which songs are not joyous, a person's feeling of power comes only from the perceived power of his or her master, delusions of freedom through inebriation strengthen bondage, the most devout Christians are the most brutalizing, human beings are sold as commodities. Examining these dreadful and degrading conditions, we realized that the overseers—Gore and Severe—could be understood allegorically and that Douglass himself, the representative slave, could be interpreted as the representative human being.

I thus directed my students to consider his *Narrative* as a bildungsroman, the story of a young man's coming-of-age through formalized rites of passage, which culminated in his attaining his identity and his freedom. To reinforce the important correlation between freedom and identity, I cited Ralph Ellison's well-known passage, "When I discover who I am, I'll be free" (*Invisible Man* 243). I encouraged my students to examine the sequence of events structuring the *Narrative*, reading it not as an individual's story but in relation to patterns of socialization identified by Carl Jung and Erik Erikson as applicable to generic human behavior. The students noted that throughout the *Narrative* Douglass marks the rites of passage as explicit metaphorical "gateways" with "pathways" leading from them. The first occurs at the conclusion of chapter 1, in which the boy Douglass witnesses the beating of his aunt, an experience that he sees as "the blood-stained gate, the entrance to the hell of slavery" (258). From this knowledge of slavery's infernal character, Douglass advances to a perception of more hopeful possibilities: on his arrival in Baltimore, he expresses his delight at seeing the kindly face of his new mistress, Sophia Auld, "brightening up my pathway with the light of happiness," and he attributes his going to live in Baltimore as opening "the gateway, to all my subsequent prosperity" (273). In Baltimore Douglass learns to read and write, thereby liberating his mind and spirit from slavery's moral and epistemological confusion. With his new knowledge, Douglass "understood the pathway from slavery to freedom," slavery's conspiracy to make him "a beast" rather than "a man" (275, 279).

With intellectual and spiritual freedom, Douglass must now attain physical freedom. His successful fight with the notorious slave breaker Covey proves "the turning-point in my career as a slave." At this critical crossroads on "the pathway from slavery to freedom," Douglass affirms "a sense of my own manhood" and asserts he will no longer be "a slave in fact" (298, 299). Eager to reinforce this sense of himself, Douglass seeks to share it with a community and to educate his fellow-slaves, using his self-knowledge to plan an escape to freedom with them. Imagining this escape, however, is terrifying: "Our path was beset with the greatest obstacles; and if we succeeded in gaining the end of it, our right to be free was yet questionable—we were yet liable to be returned to bondage. [. . .] At every gate through which we were to pass, we saw a watchman—at every ferry a guard—on every bridge a sentinel—and in every wood a patrol" (306). Although betrayal—an obstacle unanticipated and more horrifying than any imagined—ends Douglass's first attempt to escape bondage, he perseveres on the path to self-knowledge and freedom.

He next learns a trade, which allows him to become partially self-supporting and to feel that his "pathway became much more smooth than before" (314). However, Douglass remains constantly vigilant, refusing to be lulled into bestial contentment and determining to claim the full income from his work. In the 1845 *Narrative* Douglass suppresses the details of his eventual journey to the North, thus purposefully depriving the slaveholder of any "light by which he can trace the footprints of our flying brother" (316) and thus excluding the story of his successful escape to the North from his text. As a consequence, the metaphorical path, spelled out gate-by-gate and step-by-step and undertaken during his years of psychological and physical oppression, appears finally more momentous and memorable than the actual geographical journey. In the *Narrative*'s conclusion, as Douglass creates his own name and testifies in public regarding his experiences as a slave, he is united with society and gives voice to both his identity and his freedom.

Teaching the *Narrative* in recent years to a large undergraduate American literature survey class, composed largely of white students, has made me aware that in creating himself as representative slave and human being, Douglass was also creating himself as representative American man and, hence, as prospective American citizen. Both of these self-generative processes we interpret in relation to Douglass's acknowledgment of his story's role in the abolitionist movement and to his desire to appeal to his nineteenth-century readers, primarily educated middle-class, white Northerners. We discuss how Douglass, in order to convince this audience, relies on master narratives well known to antebellum readers, an argument made by several recent critics of the *Narrative*. William L. Andrews in *To Tell a Free Story*, for example, identifies Douglass's strategical pairing of two master narratives—the success story and the spiritual autobiography (130) by such writers as Benjamin Franklin and Jonathan Edwards respectively. Douglass can also be interpreted as responding to two popular contemporary texts—"Self-Reliance," by Ralph Waldo Emerson, and *Two Years before the Mast*, by Richard Henry Dana, Jr.—both written in 1840 and both projecting a robust, individualistic masculinity. To examine the *Narrative* in the context of nineteenth-century American culture is to consider it, as Russell J. Reising does, as "perhaps the first literary, political, and epistemological extension of ideas advanced in Emerson's major essays." Reising persuasively observes that although "Douglass anticipates the themes of isolation, orphanage, and alienation that pervade so many texts of the American Renaissance[, . . .] this is the point from which he begins to construct an identity, not an existential given" (257). To examine the *Narrative* in the context of nineteenth-century American culture is also to insist on the importance of gender in Douglass's self-creation.

We pay close attention to Douglass's detailed account of Demby, the slave who refuses to allow himself to be whipped and is murdered in view of many others but whose murderer is never brought to trial. In telling Demby's story, Douglass not only demonstrates slavery's reduction of a man to nothing but also anticipates his own refusal to submit to a slave breaker's demands and to allow slavery to eradicate him. Although Demby's "mangled body sank out of sight" (268) into the creek where he was shot and although no judicial notice of his death is taken, Douglass's account of this episode guarantees that Demby's name and heroic stance are not erased from historical memory. Thus despite slavery's attempt to annihilate the existence of the individual, the individual does prevail as Douglass himself insists, from the very title of his narrative, in which he names himself as both individual and American, to its conclusion.

At the end of the *Narrative*'s fifth chapter, writing of his conviction that he had a special providential blessing, Douglass explicitly embraces the Emersonian imperative "Trust thyself": "I should be false to the earliest sentiments of my soul, if I suppressed [my] opinion. I prefer to be true to myself, even at the hazard of incurring the ridicule of others, rather than to be false, and incur my own abhorrence" (273). According to Andrews, Douglass here "announces that truth to the self takes priority over what the white reader may think is either probable or politic to introduce into discourse"(*To Tell* 103). Instead of being alarmed by the boldness of Douglass's assertion, his white readership, familiar with Emersonian self-confidence, might well be prepared to respect the man who actively expresses it.

On the one hand, Douglass's descriptions of slavery throughout the *Narrative*, intensify Emerson's testimony that "[s]ociety everywhere is in conspiracy against the manhood of every one of its members" (*Essays* 29), although slavery, an economic and legal system, renders the shackles of conformity and consistency more durable than any social system Emerson imagines. On the other hand, Douglass's descriptions of his individual actions in response to the conspiracy of slavery reveal his Emersonian determination to express his independence. His ingenious methods of teaching himself to read and write introduce readers to the linked traits of self-reliance and self-determination.

Although Douglass is able to address a crowd at the *Narrative*'s conclusion, in the only example of his spoken rhetoric in the text he delivers a soliloquy standing alone on the banks of the Chesapeake "with no audience but the Almighty" (293). His implicit audience, however, is both the sentimental reader to whom he appeals in referring to his "saddened heart and tearful eye" (293)[1] and the romantic reader to whom he appeals through an elaborate association of ships with freedom. During the 1840s, numbers of young white, middle-class men, such as Richard Henry Dana, Jr., and Herman Melville, went to sea. Although they may have eventually discovered life aboard ship to be oppressive, many set out convinced that the sea offered them adventure and liberation from the land's responsibilities and restrictions, providing the basis for the romantic trope that Douglass draws on in his soliloquy.

Initially the ships appear to Douglass as "so many shrouded ghosts, to terrify and torment me with thoughts of my wretched condition" (293). However, his terror and torment are mitigated as he expresses his rage, grief, and envy, personifying the ships in the second person in his address and speaking directly through them to those idealized and privileged young white men who are free to go to sea as a lark:

> You are loosed from your moorings, and are free; I am fast in my chains, and am a slave! You move merrily before the gentle gale, and I sadly

before the bloody whip! You are freedom's swift-winged angels, that fly
around the world; I am confined in bands of iron! [. . .] The glad ship is
gone; [. . .] I am left in the hottest hell of unending slavery.   (293-94)

In later passages, Douglass implicitly associates himself with gallant American
seamen through his antipathy to the scurrilous behavior of pirates on the high
seas (310, 315). Midway in the soliloquy on the Chesapeake, he shifts dramatically from the second person to increased references to the first person, defin-
itively identifying himself with the nineteenth-century ideal of manhood as
self-determining, energetic, enterprising, and courageous:

I will run away. I will not stand it. Get caught, or get clear, I'll try it. I had
as well die with ague as the fever. I have only one life to lose. I had as
well be killed running as die standing. [. . .] Let but the first opportunity
offer, and, come what will, I am off.   (294)

His proclamation "I have only one life to lose" would have been easily recognized by his readers as a revision of the proclamation delivered by the revolutionary patriot Nathan Hale before his 1775 execution by the British: "I only
regret that I have but one life to lose for my country." Douglass concludes his
address by rationalizing his endurance and appealing specifically to his male
readers, aligning himself with their remembered experience of boyhood:
"Besides, I am but a boy, and all boys are bound to some one" (294).

Throughout the *Narrative*, in equating slavery with bestiality and freedom
with manhood, Douglass reinscribes the nineteenth-century ideal of manhood
as endorsed by Emerson. This is notable in his description of his fight with
Covey and in his commitment to his fellow slaves. Under Covey's lash, Douglass finds that "[m]y natural elasticity was crushed, my intellect languished, the
disposition to read departed, the cheerful spark that lingered about my eye
died; the dark night of slavery closed in upon me; and behold a man transformed into a brute!" (293). If by referring to his "natural elasticity," "intellect,"
and "disposition to read," Douglass explicitly ascribes to himself the characteristics of manhood, by referring to the dimming of "the cheerful spark" he
implicitly suggests that he sees himself as he wants others to see him.[2] In antic-
ipation of his description of his victory over Covey, Douglass again uses the
second person, this time addressing his readers directly: "You have seen how a
man was made a slave; you shall see how a slave was made a man" (294). The
fight itself epitomizes the actions of the self-determining, energetic, enterprising, courageous, and independent man: "It [. . .] revived within me a sense of
my own manhood. It recalled the departed self-confidence, and inspired me
again with a determination to be free" (298). Douglass reinforces this image of
his self-reliance by explicitly informing his readers that his victory was dependent on neither Sandy's root nor the help of others. Calling his fight a "battle"
(298), he further places himself in the tradition of American military heroes.

Aware of the painful contradiction that he was "fast approaching manhood" and was still a slave, Douglass takes up Emersonian doctrine to engender a like sense in a group of his fellow slaves: "I talked to them of our want of manhood, if we submitted to our enslavement without at least one noble effort to be free" (305). He brings his ingenuity to devise a plan of escape and his "life-giving determination" to persuade his fellow slaves of the necessity of freedom. Continuing to inscribe himself in relation to the American heroic tradition, he writes of this endeavor, indicating that their devotion to freedom exceeded the patriots':

> In coming to a fixed determination to run away, we did more than Patrick Henry, when he resolved upon liberty or death. With us it was a doubtful liberty at most, and almost certain death if we failed. For my part, I should prefer death to hopeless bondage.   (306)

However, following the group's betrayal in their escape plans and their resulting incarceration, Douglass implies that, despite his love and respect for these men, he can rely only on himself if he is to be free. He makes his subsequent escape plans by himself. In reading the *Narrative*'s concluding chapter, however, my students begin to identify what it cost Douglass to construct a character based on a model of heroic male individualism. They sympathize with the anguish he feels in acting alone, his sorrow at leaving friends in Baltimore as well as his "feeling of great insecurity and loneliness" (320) on arriving in New York. They are also surprised in this chapter by his suddenly mentioning his marriage to Anna Murray and shocked by his omitting information regarding his escape and his wife's assistance, putatively to protect those who helped him but possibly to represent himself to his white readers as an independent agent.

In this final chapter, Douglass further problematizes the model of heroic individualism. Inverting Emerson's imperative "Trust thyself," he necessarily adopts the motto "Trust no man" (320) to facilitate his escape. His inversion reveals the perils of extreme isolation and individualism, for a distrust of others, whether whites or blacks, Douglass terms "a most painful situation." Throughout the *Narrative*, Douglass seeks to prove he can live up to, indeed surpass, his readers' expectations for manhood and citizenship. But for the *Narrative* to gain the abolitionists' support and to serve the cause of freedom for his fellow slaves, he finally must also bring his white reader to participate imaginatively in the terror experienced by the fugitive slave. As a consequence, he repeatedly demands in his conclusion that this reader identify against himself (Fetterley xii) and "place himself in my situation" (320). My students thus perceive that Douglass's difficult task, given his dual purpose of liberating both himself and his fellow slaves, necessitates, paradoxically, his using the Emersonian model of the independent, individual male while simultaneously compromising that independence and individuality to establish community with both black slaves and white abolitionists.

In the syllabus for my American literature survey class, *Narrative of the Life of Frederick Douglass, an American Slave* is followed by Harriet Jacobs's *Incidents in the Life of a Slave Girl* (1861). Comparison of the two narratives illuminates not only the role of gender in shaping the experiences of men and women during slavery but also the role gender has in shaping the personae Douglass and Jacobs create as they respond to the expectations of their nineteenth-century readers. By considering the differences in the titles of the two works, my students begin to recognize that Douglass, boldly naming himself and proposing a comprehensive, linear text, addresses his audience with masculine authority, whereas Jacobs introduces the subject of her text to her audience with more feminine caution. Her caution, apparent in her preface and throughout her text, is reflected initially in her designation of her narrative as "incidents" and in her projection of herself as "a slave girl." Further discussion of the differences between the two works, however, leads my students to see that whereas Jacobs's gender circumscribes her more severely than Douglass's does him, she succeeds in radically subverting and defying both racial and gender categorizations.

Although Douglass may problematize conventional attitudes toward masculinity, he nonetheless minimizes references to family and domesticity in telling his story and the story of his fellow slaves. In addition, as McDowell argues, with the exception of his representations of his mother and grandmother, he selectively describes slave women, exaggerating their position "almost totally as physical bodies, as sexual victims" (48). In considering Douglass's representation and omission of women, my students come to understand that Douglass's *Narrative* is, in fact, also a series of incidents, which, through careful manipulation of information and rhetoric, nonetheless projects an impressive and memorable portrait of an American man's heroic struggle to shape his life.

Recently, in my freshman honors class on the African American narrative, my students have been impressed by the impact this portrait has had on twentieth-century black writers, who have explicitly drawn on it in constructing their own views of the heroic black man. In Ralph Ellison's *Invisible Man* (1952), the protagonist learns from Brother Tarp that the search for freedom demands courage, perseverance, and action. Tarp bequeaths him a portrait of Douglass as well as the leg iron Tarp had filed off when he escaped from nineteen years of slavery on a southern chain gang. In *The Autobiography of Miss Jane Pittman* (1971), Ernest Gaines's Ned acknowledges his debt to Douglass by taking Douglass's name and by returning to Louisiana to devote himself to the former slaves who had nurtured him during the chaotic days following emancipation. Although Ned Douglass is martyred in Gaines's novel, he leaves a legacy, as did his precursor, through his educational concerns and his powerful speeches. Paraphrasing Douglass, Ned encourages his people to recognize themselves both as Americans and as men: "Don't run and do fight. [. . .] The black man or white man who tell you to stay in a corner want to keep your mind in a corner too. [. . .] [I]f you must die, let me ask you this: wouldn't you rather die saying I'm a man than to die saying I'm a contented slave?" (110–11). Thus modern writers and contemporary readers, in their interpretations of the incidents in the *Narrative*, continue to find meaning in Douglass's heroic struggle to know himself, to attain his freedom, and to serve his fellows.

NOTES

[1]Douglass's familiarity with sentimental rhetoric is apparent in his poignant description of his grandmother's treatment (284). See Steele's essay in this volume.

[2]In describing his condition at the time of his fight with Covey, Douglass can also be seen constructing a particular physical image, with sentimental implications, for his reader: "I then presented an appearance enough to affect any but a heart of iron" (296).

Qualified Knowledge:
Douglass and Harriet Jacobs

John Ernest

One problem the teacher of Douglass's *Narrative* faces is, perhaps paradoxically, that many students are all too ready to believe that they can understand both the book and its world. Students often bring to the classroom a set framework for understanding and responding to slave narratives and a small and very general body of knowledge about slavery that they apply directly to individual narratives. This, at least, has been my experience not only with the predominately white students at the University of New Hampshire but also with the more diverse community at Florida International University in Miami. At both universities I have been blessed with excellent students who brought to the course various levels of academic training but genuine interest in the subject. Almost all my students have recognized the power of Douglass's *Narrative* and the seriousness of our collective attempt to arrive at a just understanding of an important text. But this very recognition, this seriousness, can make it difficult for me to draw students into a deep engagement with the text itself.

One of my white male students, for example, spoke out during a discussion of Harriet Jacobs's *Incidents in the Life of a Slave Girl* to question the terms of our discussion. In another course, he had been introduced to the Middle Passage and had seen pictures and read descriptions of Africans treated as cargo; he described, in graphic language, dehumanizing and immoral violations of humanity and expressed outrage that we would even try to treat this book as a literary text. He spoke with passionate disdain for what seemed to him the dry academic exercise of drawing out Jacobs's argument, thinking about her style, and following patterns (literary and ideological) that emerge in the process of narration. Certainly, I was troubled to discover that I had not succeeded in presenting literary study as something more than a dry academic exercise. But what struck me also about this statement was that we had not, in fact, approached this or other texts in the class as *mere* literary texts; we had considered each text as a way of reading both past and present, a way of reading the world, and we had faced rather directly—and were continuing to do so—the moral implications of *Incidents* and other texts for readers black and white, male and female.

My student's comments in some ways reminded me of the opening sentence of the 1855 preface to Frederick Douglass's *My Bondage and My Freedom*, in which the editor asserts, "If the volume now presented to the public were a mere work of ART, the history of its misfortune might be written in two very simple words—TOO LATE." My student also echoed the editor's assertion that the reader of *My Bondage and My Freedom* "is not invited to a work of ART, but to a work of FACTS—Facts, terrible and almost incredible, it may be—yet FACTS, nevertheless" (*Autobiographies* 105). What troubled me then, and troubles me still, is the ease with which one can claim authority over facts and then use that authority to effectively silence the text—for neither Jacobs nor Douglass had experienced the Middle Passage. Instead, they devote themselves in their narratives to what can be for contemporary readers intimately threatening visions of systemic moral violations, of a culture capable of rendering invisible what Jacobs terms the "all-pervading corruption" (*Incidents* [Gates] 382) that stretches beyond the South to the North and beyond the North of the nineteenth century to the United States of the twentieth.

At times, the role played by slave narratives in classrooms comes discomfortingly close to the so-called Negro exhibit: the moment at abolitionist meetings when "the fugitive slave turned his back to the audience and displayed his wounds and scars from floggings at the stake of slavery" (Baker, *Workings* 13). After spending a few classes working through the intricate arguments of, say, Ralph Waldo Emerson or Margaret Fuller, teachers might well present Douglass's *Narrative* as a book that speaks for itself. The teacher and the class express horror at the textual wounds on display—and then might go on to explore the symbolism of Melville's white whale for a few weeks. Too often students troubled by Douglass's powerful introduction to the horrors of the nineteenth-century culture of slavery don't read the text so much as take an opportunity to reaffirm their ethical self-images. They appropriately denounce wrongs and celebrate Douglass's strength; but because of this appreciation for Douglass's subject, many students may feel that any attempt to read the *Narrative* as a literary achievement is not only irrelevant but even ethically wrong. In their zeal to, in effect, defend this text from careful literary study, students turn Douglass's *Narrative* and other slave narratives into objects of knowledge rather than speaking subjects capable of teaching. What Frances Smith Foster has presented as the nineteenth-century reception of African American antislavery writing still applies today: "While white abolitionists were eager to privilege the authenticity of black writers' descriptions of slavery, it was only insofar as their descriptions confirmed what white readers had already accepted as true" (*Written by Herself* 82). Understood before it is read, the *Narrative* itself, like the fugitive slave on display, is left with its back to the crowd, unable to speak, to teach, to claim authority over the task of understanding.

We need to teach ourselves, in other words, not to hear what we expect to hear but rather to listen to what Douglass has to say; and we can learn this lesson best by introducing other voices into the syllabus—particularly, in my view, that of Harriet A. Jacobs's in *Incidents in the Life of a Slave Girl* (1861). As virtually all commentators on *Incidents* have noted, the story of Jacobs's pseudonymous Linda Brent is a story that challenges conventional understandings of "the slave narrative," narratives by men that mythologize, as Valerie Smith argues, "rugged individuality, physical strength, and geographical mobility" and thereby "enshrine cultural definitions of masculinity" (*Self-Discovery* 34). And the cornerstone of that shrine is the most famous narrative of all. Deborah E. McDowell offers perhaps the most focused of many challenges to the status of

Douglass's 1845 *Narrative* as the representative African American text of the nineteenth century. Addressing a scholarly tradition that has "privileged and mystified Douglass's narrative," McDowell argues that the *Narrative* has been used to serve a "double duty: not only does it make slavery intelligible, but the 'black experience' as well" (38–39). But this is a "black experience" that transforms a singular male experience, a specific narrative, and a corresponding mode of understanding into a set of implicit universal assumptions. "It is this choice of Douglass as 'the first,'" McDowell contends, "as 'representative man,' as the part that stands for the whole, that reproduces the omission of women from view, except as afterthoughts different from 'the same' (black men)" (56).

A comparative reading of these two narratives immediately raises questions about Douglass's "omission of women from view." Jacobs's narrative is famous for the statement in its penultimate paragraph, "Reader, my story ends with freedom; not in the usual way, with marriage" (513). After reading this, one might note that Douglass's *Narrative* quite nearly does end in "the usual way, with marriage," for in the final chapter Douglass writes for the first time of his "intended wife," Anna (321), who follows him north. Douglass briefly tells of the marriage that follows her journey and he reprints the marriage certificate. But this detail in the narrative points to a significant absence of information in the previous chapters. Where and how did Douglass and Anna meet? Did she play a role in his escape? While I offer my students sketchy answers to such questions when they arise (they met in Baltimore, where Anna, who was not enslaved, worked; and she did in fact play a role in his escape), I do not invite them. I emphasize instead the need to recognize the absence of autobiographical information in this autobiographical narrative, and I use that absence to ask questions about Douglass's story of individual struggle.

And Jacobs can help with these questions. As Valerie Smith has noted, "Simply by underscoring her reliance on other people, Jacobs reveals another way in which the story of slavery and escape might be written" (*Self-Discovery* 34). In doing so, Jacobs's story draws our attention to the ways in which Douglass's story is written, returning us to Douglass's mixed portrayal of his relationship with his mother at the beginning of the first chapter and to the suggestive account of the sexual violation and whipping of his Aunt Hester that ends that chapter. Perhaps, too, a reading of *Incidents* can return us with fresh eyes to Douglass's own use of sentimental conventions in his portrayal of his grandmother's fate at the end of chapter 8. My purpose is emphatically not to suggest that Jacobs's *Incidents* is the supplementary text that completes Douglass's portrait of slavery. Rather, my purpose is to suggest that teaching either text alone reduces a challenging *art* to a set of containable *facts* and that teaching them together raises issues of representation (of slavery and of self) that place students in a dynamic relation to the subject—a cultural, historical, and intellectual site in which they must contend with their own relation to the world constructed and sustained by the system of slavery. Students whose initial response to slavery is that we shouldn't dwell in the past come to learn that it is important to recognize the extent to which the past dwells in us.

My title for this essay, "Qualified Knowledge," refers in part to the need to qualify what counts as knowledge of the world of slavery, often a generalized knowledge that focuses on the ownership of human beings, with neat divisions between evil white Southern slaveholders, victimized black slaves, and (at least relatively) good white Northerners. Jacobs draws us into the "all-pervading corruption produced by slavery" and forces us into an understanding of slavery that focuses less on the act of enslavement than on violations of the body, mind, and will—violations that readers are in danger of committing as they read. Accordingly, "qualified knowledge" refers also to Jacobs's argument that without particular experiences of enslavement (*incidents* in an individual life) there can be no understanding of slavery. Not everyone, in other words, is qualified to claim the authority of knowledge. One's task as reader is not to draw information out of the text, but rather to submit to the authority of the text, to learn from it how to learn.

I teach the two narratives in chronological order, looking to Douglass's *Narrative* for an introduction to the subject (and to generalized outrage on the subject) and trusting *Incidents* to return us to the *Narrative* with significant second thoughts. I prepare for this dual reading by contextualizing Douglass's narrative in terms mainly of biography and genre. Usually, I begin the first class on Douglass by placing a paperback version of the *Narrative* on a table, and stacking next to it copies of Douglass's other autobiographies: *My Bondage and My Freedom* (1855); *Life and Times* (1881); and the supplemented *Life and Times* (1892). Noting the difference between the relatively short volume that provides most readers with what they know about Douglass and the great number of pages he devoted over the years to his ongoing life's story and noting also that the difference in length is more than a difference in the number of experiences to be recounted, I ask my students to define *autobiography*. I try to complicate their understanding of autobiography by remarking on its social dimensions—the fact that one tells one's story differently at different stages in one's life (something that all students readily understand and appreciate); that one tells one's story differently to different audiences (something that all teenagers, sons, daughters, and students can appreciate when reflecting on, say, peer, parental, or professorial audiences); and that one reads autobiographies either to learn about known public figures or to learn about relatively unknown figures who have played significant roles in a larger social drama. In other words, one reads autobiographies less for the story of a life than for the cultural story represented by individual life.

With a set of questions about autobiography as a strategic mode of cultural representation, we examine the *Narrative* for significant features in the way Douglass carefully depicts his role in the social drama of the antislavery movement. We look not merely at Douglass's self-representation but also at his portrayal of representative white men and women, constructing a spectrum of cultural roles that extend from our ideal of an enlightened white reader to the representative man of the system of slavery, Mr. Gore. The perfect product of the culture of slavery, as Douglass portrays him, Mr. Gore "was just the man for such a place, and it was just the place for such a man" (267). Others might enter the spectrum of roles elsewhere—for example, Sophia Auld, who enters as "a woman of the kindest heart and finest feelings" (274)—but they will eventually gravitate to Mr. Gore's state of perfection (as Sophia herself soon is transformed into a "demon" [274]). And we follow that spectrum as it extends to the North, where Douglass's motto was "Trust no man!"—and where he "saw in every white man an enemy, and in almost every colored man cause for distrust" (320). Beyond being a description of horrors to inspire moral outrage, Douglass's *Narrative* is a description of the culture of slavery, in which we learn "how a man was made a slave" (294), how slaves are taught to be disgusted by freedom (300), and how to make a "contented slave" (315). As if writing a handbook on enslavement, Douglass tells the story of how cultural roles are scripted, produced, directed, and performed.

When we reach Jacobs's *Incidents*, I hope we are prepared to think carefully about autobiographies and about what Robert Stepto calls "the discourse of distrust" ("Distrust" 304). Specifically, I hope we are prepared to think about the authenticity of artistic representation in the way so ably indicated by Jacqueline Goldsby: "Since, according to Jacobs, 'truth' can be discovered only if it is left 'concealed,'" Goldsby argues, "rules of documentary evidence may not resolve the dilemma that *Incidents*, as a slave narrative, confronts: how to preserve testimony of an experience that is itself beyond representation" (12). I begin by confronting this dilemma directly, presenting what I call Jacobs's paradox, the two driving assertions behind Jacobs's address to her white readers: first, you must understand my experience; second, you cannot understand my experience. Throughout *Incidents*, Jacobs reminds her readers of the second of these assertions, noting in the preface, "Only by experience can any one realize how deep, and dark, and foul is that pit of abominations," "what Slavery really is" (335–36, 335). Believing in "the knowledge that comes from experience" (351), Jacobs emphasizes that her readers necessarily stand apart from that knowledge, as when she is reunited with her son (named Benjamin in the narrative) and exclaims, "O reader, can you imagine my joy? No, you cannot, unless you have been a slave mother" (489). There are many other things readers cannot imagine, though Jacobs asks them to, sometimes calling on them to imagine what they would be like had they similarly been shaped by the experience of slavery: "What would *you* be, if you had been born and brought up a slave, with generations of slaves for ancestors?" (375). But even as she emphasizes that her readers cannot understand her experience, she reminds them that they must, for slavery has, in fact, shaped their experiences socially, economically, politically, morally. I've noted Jacobs's famous proclamation that her story ends "not in the usual way, with marriage"; less often quoted are the important sentences that follow this statement: "I and my children are now free! We are as free from the power of slaveholders as are the white people of the north; and though that, according to my ideas, is not saying a great deal, it is a vast improvement in *my* condition" (513). *Incidents* ends, in other words, where most of its readers live, in a world shaped, and in identities scripted, by the system of slavery.

Douglass's *Narrative*, for all of its instruction about how to create slaves, similarly positions its readers outside the circle of experience that makes knowledge possible. When noting his "painful situation" in the North, having escaped slavery to enter a realm in which human trust was impossible, Douglass says that to understand his situation, "one must needs experience it, or imagine himself in similar circumstances" (320). The long sentence that follows this claim lists the various experiences necessary for understanding. Douglass adds experience upon experience, so that each must be accounted for in its relation to the others, joining the temporal ("at the same time let him feel" [320]) with the cultural ("in the midst of plenty, yet suffering the terrible gnawings of hunger" [320]) and mixing biblical overtones with images of human horrors. And Douglass ends the sentence significantly: "I say, let him be placed in this most trying situation,—the situation in which I was placed,—then, and not till then, will he fully appreciate the hardships of, and know how to sympathize with, the toil-worn and whip-scarred fugitive slave" (321). But can we imagine? No, we cannot, Jacobs might say, for the description itself presses against the limitations of representation, speaking of an unimaginable experience, of unspeakable acts, of the inexpressible that lies beyond Douglass's representation. And not being able to imagine, how can we "know how to sympathize"?

And yet, this is where understanding begins. And such a mode of understanding is not itself unimaginable. Whenever I've started to discuss this mode of understanding, I've found that my students have all had an experience that prepares them for the challenge. I ask them to think of a time when they've experienced something deeply troubling and deeply personal and to think of how they have responded (if only inwardly) to well-meaning friends who have said too quickly, "I understand completely." Speaking for myself, I have not, at those times, found much comfort in such claims. But when someone who knows me well has said, "I cannot even imagine what you've been through," my response might well be, wondrously, "You understand." Sometimes understanding means acknowledging one's inability to understand.

And this mode of understanding can be significant, as was demonstrated to me recently when two of my students—Derek Folan and Shih-Chi Tao— addressed the topic of "Jacobs's paradox." In his essay "Harriet Jacobs's *Incidents in the Life of a Slave Girl*: The Awakening of an Author and a Nation," Derek focuses on Jacobs's shifting narrative "standpoint," and argues that Jacobs tells the story of her own "awakening"—a story "impossible to re-create"—in such a way as to provoke a similar awakening in the reader. Jacobs, Derek maintains, recognized the need to avoid what he terms "the sympathetic reaction"; her task instead is to expose the ignorance of her readers and thereby draw them into a recognition of a need for more knowledge. And this is a point that Shih-Chi developed carefully in class discussions, in her informal writing, and in her essay entitled "Jacobs's Paradox." Recognizing that our distance from Jacobs's experiences keeps us from claims of understanding and sympathy, Shih-Chi argues that our recognition of that distance forces us to examine the commonality of our experience. Noting that "the real state for human beings is to live in contradictions," Shih-Chi examines the ways in which Jacobs shapes readers' understanding of the contradictions—between "moral principles" and "actual practices"—that rule their lives. The result is something more significant and more demanding than the sympathetic outrage we might have brought to the subject of slavery before reading the text. The result, in Shih-Chi's simple but wise formulation, is "intimacy." In intimacy we recognize our dependence on others by which understanding becomes a shared process; in intimacy are the seeds of genuine reciprocity, of dialogue among those of different experiences and perspectives—process rather than conclusion. In this process, among those truly engaged, as Shih-Chi and Derek and other students have shown, learning about themselves in order to meet others in intimacy, understanding can begin.

Doing More than Patrick Henry:
Douglass's *Narrative* and Nineteenth-Century
American Protest Writing

Anita Patterson

I recently taught *Narrative of the Life of Frederick Douglass* in a course called The Uses of Nineteenth-Century American Protest Writing. Such an approach clearly has its limits, since it does not allow for a full exploration of the range of distinctively African American discourses from which the *Narrative* derives. But I have nonetheless found teaching the *Narrative* in an American context to be a richly rewarding classroom experience that does justice to Douglass's achievement as an American protest writer and offers students a vivid, nuanced perspective on his contribution to the formation of a national literature in the United States.

Recent studies such as Eric Sundquist's *To Wake the Nations: Race in the Making of American Literature* have shown that slavery and race were vitally important factors in the creation of a mainstream tradition in American literature. Following this line of thought, for a number of reasons I was attracted to the idea of including Douglass's *Narrative* in a course that traced the emergence of an American tradition in protest writing.

First, I thought that studying Douglass's critical reinterpretation of the American tradition in protest writing would help students rise above the politically correct dismissal of the American canon that has been common in recent years. I wanted students to see for themselves how Douglass drew on the rich conceptual and rhetorical resources of the American mainstream.

Nineteenth-century American intellectuals and activists constantly reminded their audiences that slaves were left without the right to own property and without the protection of law in a brutish, Hobbesian nightmare of life on the Southern plantation. By distilling many of these complex, heated arguments into readable prose, Douglass provided the American public with a fresh and much-needed reassessment of the meaning of democracy at a time when rights rhetoric had already been put to notoriously bad use by Southern planters interested in holding onto their "freedom" to own slaves. Many if not all of the canonical nineteenth-century writers included on my course syllabus were intimately familiar with Douglass's work—we know, for example, that Margaret Fuller reviewed the *Narrative* for the *New York Tribune*—and Douglass's subtle, shaping influence on the philosophy and rhetoric of the American mainstream has yet to be adequately ascertained. By rereading the American canon using Douglass's *Narrative* as a lens, teachers and students in American literature courses can remake their own encounter with canonical works and direct the energies of this process of intellectual discovery into lively and rewarding classroom debates.

Second, I knew that because the student body at my university represented an extremely diverse cross section of "ethnic" Chicago, classes would find Douglass's critical perspective on the meaning of America fascinating and relevant. (Like other courses on ethnic American literature I have taught, this one was designed to give students the opportunity to engage in critical reflections on how "marginal" works of literature are dialectically engaged with the dominant cultural norms.)

Finally, I wanted students to learn about the historical connection between American philosophy and African American activism by exploring how in his *Narrative* Douglass effectively stages his emergence as a public intellectual. The moral and rhetorical burdens of publicity assumed by many intellectuals in contemporary America are matters students can hardly miss, even if they just glance at the lead story in any popular magazine, such as *Harper's Magazine*, the *Atlantic Monthly*, and the *New Yorker*. I hoped that by showing Douglass's commitment to the larger objective of addressing the American public—and, in particular, by creating an understanding of how Douglass's access to publicity and his aspiration to being a "representative" African American are linked to the dream of freedom unfolded in his *Narrative*—students would immediately see the relevance of Douglass's experience to the present-day issues raised in public intellectual life.

Walking into the room on the first day of class, I felt ready to face the challenge of putting my revisionary ideas about the American canon into practice. To back me up I had years of research on Emerson and his influence on the development of twentieth-century African American philosophy from W. E. B. Du Bois to Martin Luther King, Jr. Coming on the heels of the now legendary generation of "sixties people"—the baby boomers, the tenured radicals—I was part of an intellectual cohort who had been trained to read American literature with a critically distanced perspective on the myth of America. I was now ready to show my students that by carefully reading African American and other ethnic American authors, we can understand the paradoxes of protest and the uses of rhetoric: how and when protest has worked to mobilize the American public to acts of reform and how, at times, even the most heartfelt assertions of rights to property and freedom have resulted in rights violations and social injustice.

I handed out my syllabus. The course description printed on the syllabus ran as follows:

> English 460. This course will examine a series of nineteenth-century texts that compose a tradition in American protest writing. Using Locke's *Second Treatise of Government* and Paine's *Rights of Man* as our theoretical backdrop, we will begin by laying out the fundamental philosophical concepts (i.e., rights, rebellion, civil disobedience, obligation, and consent) and distinctive rhetorical strategies associated with exhortations to reform or revolution. We will then read a series of essays, addresses, and treatises by some of the most familiar American authors (Emerson,

Thoreau, Fuller, Whitman, and Lincoln) and discuss the relation between art and public action, paying special attention to the way acts of disobedience have been rendered and critiqued in works of American literature. Finally, we will read works by African-American authors, such as *Narrative of the Life of Frederick Douglass*, and show how African Americans are situated in a strategic relationship of critique with respect to the mainstream American tradition.

The syllabus had been carefully scrutinized, revised, and printed out in an engaging but authoritative font. What, you might ask, could *possibly* go wrong?

Much to my surprise, I found that many of the graduate and advanced undergraduate students who were specializing in the field of nineteenth-century American literature were puzzled by the presence of Douglass (and Martin Delany, Harriet Jacobs, and Booker T. Washington) on my reading list. As students of American literature, they clearly were more comfortable resting within the confines of their chosen field of expertise. Unlike some of the younger, less experienced students, these Americanists were interested to read slave narratives but could not say anything about them when asked except that the narratives effectively document how bad slavery and racism in America really were. This inability to engage with the text of Douglass's *Narrative* seemed to go with a general attitude toward African American literature: that it is about "the race thing" and "the slavery thing," and, viewed as such, it should be read and experienced as something wholly separate from "American" literature.

There has been a tendency in the last decade or so to tack on African American and ethnic American authors at the end of the syllabus in American literature courses as a quick and easy way to give the classroom curriculum a new, revisionary look. I think my students were a little surprised at how central a role Douglass's *Narrative* plays in their exploration of the nineteenth-century tradition in American protest writing.

I told the class that our main intellectual objective in the coming weeks would be to learn how Douglass's emergence as a writer is best understood in the light of his critical engagement with the aesthetic and cultural values of the American mainstream. In our discussions, we would be participating in a much larger, ongoing cultural process, namely, the debate over what "we the people" are supposed, realistically, to look like and the struggle to give a definitive portrait of the representative American by clarifying and revising our national self-image and the terms of Douglass's admissibility into the American literary canon.

In my introductory lecture on Douglass, I emphasized the political and social contexts of his emergence as a published author. That Douglass's *Narrative* was published and introduced to the American public under William Lloyd Garrison's auspices meant that Douglass would play down any philosophical differences he had with Garrison on the "union with slaveholders" issue and, more specifically, with Garrison's rejection of the American Constitution. Six years after the *Narrative* was published Douglass declared his differences with Garrison: the fact that he now believed that dissolution of the Union was not necessary and that the Constitution should be interpreted, in its letter and spirit, as an antislavery document and an instrument for attaining equality and freedom. This declaration is best understood in the light of Douglass's embrace of democratic first principles even at the very outset of his career as a writer.

The portrait of Douglass that emerged over the course of the semester depicted him as bearing all the hallmarks of a quintessential nineteenth-century American protest writer. Although I did refer students to selected works of criticism—for example, in *Frederick Douglass: New Literary and Historical Essays*, edited by Eric Sundquist; *Critical Essays on Frederick Douglass*, edited by William L. Andrews; and Donald Gibson's "Reconciling Public and Private in Frederick Douglass's *Narrative*"—I also reminded them that the approach we were taking to Douglass's *Narrative* was not often given emphasis in recent criticism.

Our most lively and memorable class discussions devolved on four main points about Douglass's creative engagement with the cherished values of the American canon. First, Douglass's *Narrative* gave us fresh insight into the justifications for government and rebellion against tyranny raised in the tradition of American political thought. As Wendell Phillips notes in his introductory letter to the *Narrative*, Douglass was, in a literary sense, assuming risks that were metaphorically comparable to the yoke of slavery borne by America's founding fathers: "They say the fathers, in 1776, signed the Declaration of Independence with the halter about their necks. You, too, publish your declaration of freedom with danger compassing you around" (253). The real and present dangers of publication and public visibility—the risks Douglass ran of being recaptured and returned to slavery—were never far from Douglass's mind. At one point, we discussed Douglass's resolution to rebel against the tyranny of American slavery in the light of the arguments and rhetorical strategies of American revolutionary protest writers:

> In coming to a fixed determination to run away, we did more than Patrick Henry, when he resolved upon liberty or death. With us it was a doubtful liberty at most, and almost certain death if we failed. For my part, I should prefer death to hopeless bondage. (306)

In addition, Douglass's reflections on the nature of power—both "irresponsible power" (274) and the "power to enslave" (275)—contain penetrating insights into the need for legal protection, the nature of and justification for democratic government, and the moral mandate to rebel against tyranny.

I should emphasize, once again, that although the course focused on nineteenth-century authors, I also had the students read John Locke's *Second Treatise of Government* and Thomas Paine's *Rights of Man* and *Common Sense* to give them a theoretical backdrop for thinking about American democracy. I recommended a very good contemporary commentary on liberal democracy and the meaning of social contract—Carole Pateman's *The Problem of Political Obligation: A Critique of Liberal Theory.*

The second major topic for discussion was how Douglass's *Narrative* fits with the traditional poetics and practice of civil disobedience. Here we compared and contrasted Thoreau's critical reassessment of American democratic values in *Walden* and "Civil Disobedience" with Douglass's reaction to reading *The Columbian Orator* and Sheridan's speeches on Catholic emancipation. We spent a great deal of class time discussing Thoreau's meditation on the inadequacies of American government and the role of conscience in public life, in the light of Douglass's comments about the striking similarities between favored slaves on Colonel Lloyd's plantation and "the slaves of political parties" (262) and "the power of truth over the conscience of even a slaveholder" (278), as well as Douglass's account of the unexpectedly "comfortable quarters" he discovered during his night in jail (310). Our discussion culminated in Douglass's famous act of violent resistance, his battle with Mr. Covey, an event that underscores the fact that, as oppressed persons, slaves have no political obligations insofar as those obligations are to the state. To discuss this point, I referred students to an essay by the political philosopher Michael Walzer, "The Obligations of Oppressed Minorities," in the volume *Obligations: Essays on Disobedience, War, and Citizenship.*

Third, we examined Douglass's role as public intellectual, his strategy of casting himself as a "representative" American, in the light of similar attempts undertaken by nineteenth-century authors such as Emerson (in "Self-Reliance," *Representative Men*, and elsewhere) and Whitman (in *Democratic Vistas* and *Song of Myself*). Here we focused on some of the special problems faced by Douglass as a public intellectual: the fact that he could not appear too learned, because some people might doubt he had once been a slave; the dangers of public visibility; the need to deliberately avoid giving details of his escape and his personal life; and the aesthetic compromises necessary to bear the burdens of representativeness and didacticism.

Our fourth main point concerned Douglass's similarities and differences with Abraham Lincoln. Reading excerpts from Lincoln's speeches (such as "A House Divided," the first and second inaugural addresses, the Emancipation Proclamation, the Gettysburg Address, and his last public address in 1865), we compared and contrasted Lincoln's and Douglass's views on the relation between philosophy and public action.

The topic for the final paper in the course was to explore how the meaning of freedom, developed over the course of Douglass's *Narrative*, reflects his critique of the conceptual premises of American democracy. Drawing on what they had learned about nineteenth-century protest writing, many of my students found they had a lot more to say about Douglass's *Narrative* than they did when they first read the book. I directed them to the passages where Douglass discovers his determination and desire to be free. The concept of freedom, which emerged dialectically out of the social condition of slavery, gave Douglass a cherished dream and a reason to live. As Douglass puts it, "I often found myself regretting my own existence, and wishing myself dead; and but for the hope of being free, I have no doubt but that I should have killed myself, or done something for which I should have been killed" (279). On the whole, I think students were fascinated by Douglass's insights into the "care and anxiety" (318), as well as the "duties and responsibilities" (322), of freedom.

Teaching Douglass's *Narrative* in a mainstream American context has convinced me that there is a reasonable solution to the problem of curricular reform. That the debate over the canon is still in progress should be cause for satisfaction rather than despair. By confronting head-on the contentious issue of multiculturalism and by learning to self-consciously design an American literature curriculum that both respects differences and shows the importance of understanding the cherished commonalities and values that unite our national culture, teachers are now in a position to make American literature courses better than ever. The idea of "greatness" has not been done away with; instead, our standards of excellence have simply become more accurate, nuanced, and rooted in the ethnically diverse realities of American history. The path of curricular reform does not necessarily lead into the slough of skeptical relativism or the wilderness of the politically correct. By teaching students to participate in the collective, combative work of asking what it means to be an American, we are encouraging the art of civic participation and helping to ensure that American democracy will be alive for generations to come.

exploratory writings in which they imagine themselves first as nineteenth-century Northern white readers of the text and second, as Douglass himself asks, as fugitive slaves.

Such imaginative leaps across time and space are difficult for any readers but may pose special problems for students from homogeneous communities. The vast majority of our students are white, between eighteen and twenty-two years old, and from small towns and cities in the upper Midwest. Many wish to learn about diverse cultures but simply have not had the experience that would enable them to think about race matters with sophistication. Their writings thus risk oversimplification or misunderstanding, but if I work hard to describe the historical and rhetorical contexts of *Narrative*, I find that their written responses provide a powerful opening to our discussions of how Douglass develops the central theme of his resistance to slavery and his coming to freedom and selfhood.

Moreover, by combining historical awareness with their own personal responses, these student writings enact the kind of sympathetic imagination Douglass calls for and so become the means by which the students not only learn about but exercise their democratic values. For, as Louise Rosenblatt reminds us, "Literature fosters the kind of imagination needed in a democracy—the ability to participate in the needs and aspirations of other personalities and to envision the effect of our actions on their lives" (212).

I begin by describing Douglass's narrative as a specific rhetorical response to American slavery in the mid-nineteenth century. Having already read and discussed excerpts from *The Interesting Narrative of the Life of Olaudah Equiano*, students come to Douglass's text with some understanding of the African roots of African American culture and of the Middle Passage, American slavery, and the slave narrative. I want students to understand especially how slave narratives, beginning in the 1830s, functioned as a tool of abolitionism by offering an alternative to polemical argument and going, as one nineteenth-century editor said, "right to the hearts of men" (qtd. in Andrews, *To Tell* 5); for the differences between eighteenth- and nineteenth-century slave narratives, see Andrews, *To Tell*, ch. 2, or Foster, *Witnessing*, ch. 3). At this point I do not want to burden them with a lot of theory about the rhetorical strategies of either abolitionist sponsors or slave narrators like Douglass. What's important is that students understand (and imagine) who Douglass's readers were and how those readers' prejudices and expectations raised considerable barriers for slave narrators attempting to reach—and influence—an audience that doubted the narrators' very humanity and was skeptical about the authenticity and truthfulness of their accounts. Andrews describes this problem as "the unprecedented and largely unparalleled situation of black self-writers" whose white audience perceived blacks—slave and free—as "an alien population recognizably 'depraved,' 'vicious,' and, for the most part, incorrigible" (*To Tell* 4–5). John Sekora notes that most white northerners were indifferent: "for them slavery was remote, abstract, inconsequential" (495). And

Frances Smith Foster summarizes the challenge for the black writer in this way:

> He had to overcome the incredulity of persons whose surprise that a black could write overshadowed any attempt to understand or to consider what he was writing about. He had to convince his readers to accept the validity of his knowledge and conclusions, which in many instances profoundly contradicted their own. Furthermore, if he was to obtain their sympathy and aid, he had to do this in a manner which did not threaten or embarrass his readers.   (*Witnessing Slavery* [1979] 9)

If students are to enter imaginatively into the consciousness of Douglass's readers, they need to understand in some visceral way the extent to which racial attitudes were different from—and perhaps similar to—those today. To help students do this, I put the following passage on an overhead without revealing the writer and text:

> Are not the fine mixtures of red and white, the expressions of every passion by greater or less suffusions of color in the one, preferable to the eternal monotony, which reigns in the countenances, that immoveable veil of black which covers the emotions of the other race? Add to these, flowing hair, a more elegant symmetry of form, their own judgment in favor of the whites, declared by their preference of them, as uniformly as is the preference of the Oranootan for the black woman over those of his own species. The circumstance of superior beauty, is thought worthy attention in the propagation of our horses, dogs, and other domestic animals; why not in that of man?

Because of the peculiarity of the language, I ask students first to "translate" what it says. I focus especially on the analogy, which students correctly read to the effect that male orangutans prefer the company of black women to that of female orangutans just as blacks prefer the company of whites to that of other blacks. Students are appalled at the crudity of this racism (though it is couched in elegant language) and even audibly gasp when I reveal that the passage is from *Notes on the State of Virginia*, query 14, in which Thomas Jefferson discusses his "observations" of blacks in the context of a bill that would emancipate and colonize slave children on reaching adulthood (264–65). I then discuss how Jefferson commented on what he perceived to be the physical, intellectual, and moral differences of blacks, concluding, "I advance it, therefore, as a suspicion only, that the blacks, whether originally a distinct race, or made distinct by time and circumstances, are inferior to the whites in the endowments both of body and mind" (270).

My point is not to titillate or shock students or even to destroy an icon (though that may be the effect). Jefferson is an important figure to look at for two reasons. First, as Winthrop Jordan points out, Jefferson's views on race and slavery "were of great importance because so many people read and reacted to them. His remarks about Negroes in the only book he ever wrote were more widely read, in all probability, than any others until the mid-nineteenth century" (429). I emphasize that Jefferson's views were descriptive rather than prescriptive of whites' thinking—that he did not create these views but that his writing most clearly represented them. Second, Jefferson's writings reflect the paradox suggested by Douglass's subtitle: *An American Slave*. Students are familiar with the promises of "life, liberty, and the pursuit of happiness" in the Declaration of Independence. When they confront Jefferson's views on race, they understand how deeply embedded that paradox is in the mind-set of one of the nation's founders. (If there is time, having the class read the entire section on race in query 14—about six pages—well prepares them to understand what racial theories Douglass and other black writers, like Benjamin Banneker and David Walker, are claiming their humanity over and against.)

It is also important to point out to students that racism developed historically in conjunction with the increasing economic importance of slavery in the South. As George Fredrickson has shown, the "doctrine of permanent black inferiority began its career" alongside the concept of slavery as a "positive good" that emerged in the 1830s in response to the rise of abolitionism (47). On an overhead I list Fredrickson's conclusions about "the basic white–black supremacist propositions" that virtually all whites—Northern and Southern, abolitionist, slaveholder and in-between—held after the 1830s, namely, that blacks are "physically, intellectually, and temperamentally" different from and inferior to whites; that such differences are "either permanent or subject to change" only very slowly; and that an integrated, egalitarian society is either "completely impossible" or achievable only "in some remote and almost inconceivable future" (321). Lest students distance themselves from such views, I ask them to guess what percent of non–African Americans believe the following, according to a 1990 poll:

> that African-Americans are less intelligent than whites;
> that African-Americans are less patriotic than whites;
> that African-Americans are more violence-prone than whites; and
> that African-Americans are more likely to 'prefer to live off welfare' and less likely to 'prefer to be self-supporting' than whites.

> (qtd. in Terkel v)

The numbers, respectively, are 53, 51, 56, and 62, and when students typically guess close to correctly, we realize together that to enter imaginatively into the racist worldviews of antebellum readers, we need hardly leave today's twentieth-century America.

It is at this point that I ask students to write a one- to two-page exploratory response to the question, "If you were a white Northern reader in 1845, what part or aspect of Frederick Douglass's *Narrative* would most move you to change your mind and perhaps even work for the abolition of slavery?" Students do not know everything about these imagined readers, and I could provide them with more characteristics—for example, that they were Christian and had particular reading habits and values that grew out of popular culture (see Foster, *Witnessing*, ch. 4). Yet I am consistently struck by how thoughtful and deeply felt these initial written responses are, even without that knowledge. Regarding the whipping of Douglass's Aunt Hester, one student, Jen Olson, quoted the passage at length and then wrote:

> As a woman (either now or in 1845), I could not help but feel that no person should be subject to this horrid atrocity. Women have always been more conscious of their bodies, the size of their waists, if they have a full chest, if they are attractive to men, etc.; thus the description of the scene of ripping off a woman's clothes and hanging her naked body for all to see, is almost as painful as the whipping itself. The psychological effect this master inflicted is as damaging as the actual physical act of whipping Aunt Hester. [. . .] The image that forms in one's mind is of one's sister, mother, aunt, friend, or girlfriend. [. . .] I feel this point is what would be the deciding factor for many white Americans, especially for those citizens who had never seen a slave.

A male student wrote of the same passage that while he might be unlikely to be moved by the slaves' poverty—which he would see among Northern whites and blacks as well,

> as a white, Christian Northerner, the most shocking affront to my sense of decency would be the sheer violence of slavery. [. . .] Knowing what it means to be in pain leads to disgust, regardless of racist opinions on ignorance or beauty. [. . . It] is obvious that terrible situations such as this are not only commonplace, but foundational to slavery.

Without my prompting, some students chose to write letters to Douglass or to characters within his narrative or even to Jefferson. And far from needing my guidance, students themselves raise the significant themes or moments of the narrative in their writing.

Student writings from a recent semester focused on the following aspects and passages: Douglass's lack of knowledge of his birth and paternity and his separation from his mother at an early age; the overwhelming and often arbitrary violence in Douglass's experience, especially the whipping of his Aunt Hester and his fight with Covey; Master Auld's attempt to forbid Douglass's education and Douglass's subsequent strategies to learn to read and write, culminating in the writing of the *Narrative*; and Douglass's critique of religion, especially his statement that "[f]or of all slaveholders with whom I have ever met, religious slaveholders are the worst" (302). This last concern may speak to the religious heritage of our college, where more than ninety percent of students identify themselves as Christian.

While some of these student responses may sound naive—as in those who narrate an instant conversion to abolitionism—what is striking is how closely their writings correspond to what critics suggest actual nineteenth-century readers' reactions were. Frances Smith Foster writes:

> While the nineteenth-century reader might not have been greatly concerned by charges that slaves were forced to work and were not fed and clothed in the same manner as himself, he would have been angered by stories of excessive brutality, destroyed families, and violated women. He would think it extreme to deny even the recognition of one's birth into the human race.
> (*Witnessing* 80)

These student writings help the class address through close reading of specific passages how Douglass developed the larger theme of his coming to selfhood, what one student aptly described as Douglass's "redefining of *black worth*, from a person being a piece of property bought with money to a human being with a potential to contribute to any society." But more than that, they open the way for us to examine further how Douglass imprinted his own voice on his story and thus wrested control of his narrative from his abolitionist sponsors. For as Andrews has pointed out, Douglass's writing not only is about liberation but also is in itself an act of liberation (*To Tell* 104).

At this point I describe how abolitionists insisted that the slave narratives follow a particular structure and ordering of facts to establish authenticity and move their intended audience. Such an ordering originated with the first recruitment of ex-slave orators in the mid-1830s (Sekora 496) and was later incorporated into what James Olney calls the "master outline" of the great slave narratives, beginning with a signed portrait, a title page including the claim "Written by Himself," and prefaces by white abolitionists testifying to the veracity of the tale and the character of the teller ("I Was Born" 152–53). When I list the features of this master outline on an overhead, students clearly see how Douglass's *Narrative* fits this plan, beginning with the title page and the prefaces by William Lloyd Garrison and Wendell Phillips. But they can see, too, how Douglass infuses "a sense of an individual authorial personality, the sound of a distinctive authorizing voice" by taking the "brute facts" of slavery and imaginatively manipulating them through a variety of rhetorical strategies to evoke a more intense response in his readers, a response that will influence their perceptions and, especially, their emotions. In short, Douglass creates a "performing self"; he makes himself—his own expressive language and not the program of abolitionists—the focal point and in so doing, "he repossesses autobiography as a self-expressive, not simply a fact-assertive act" (Andrews, *To Tell* 98–99, 134).

As we examine the *Narrative* again, we look to see Douglass's rhetorical inventions and manipulations. On a broad level, they involve the construction of his text as an amalgam of the spiritual autobiography and the American success story (Andrews, *To Tell* 130). The spiritual autobiography begins with Douglass's "entrance to the hell of slavery" when he sees his Aunt Hester whipped and culminates with his "glorious resurrection, from the tomb of slavery, to the heaven of freedom" after his battle with Covey (258, 299). Students recognize Douglass's echoing and subversion of biblical language and imagery, especially his scorching irony on the supposed Christianity of slaveholders, concluding with the poetic parody in the appendix. When I ask how Douglass has shaped his narrative to be a particularly American story that would appeal to his readers, students describe his subjection to an outside power and his struggle to liberate himself from that power, his striving to better himself economically and socially, his respect for hard work, his desire for education and self-knowledge, and his respect for family and the black community.

At a more specific rhetorical level, students can see how Douglass's manipulations both advance the polemic and signify his uniqueness as teller. One such manipulation is Douglass's subversion of Jefferson's analogy of blacks as animals (which students saw in his remarks about the orangutan). Douglass begins by comparing himself to a horse ignorant of his age but extends the rhetoric to describe Covey as a "snake" (291) and slave catchers as "hungry lions," "ferocious beasts of the forest," "hideous crocodiles," and "monsters of the deep" (320). Returning to the whipping of his Aunt Hester, students might be asked to examine how Douglass uses language to provoke a response. Andrews argues that Douglass "repeatedly 'whips' his reader with a word" to put the reader in the place of his aunt. In this way, students may see that "whipping is a fact of slavery of which the white reader must have empathic as well as objective knowledge" (*To Tell* 133).

The students might also come to agree with critics such as Deborah McDowell, who argues that the slave woman in this passage and others is constructed as sexual victim to the point that, "as the Narrative progresses, the beatings proliferate and the women, no longer identified by name, become absolutized as a bloody mass of naked backs" (202). Moreover, McDowell writes, "Douglass's repetition of the sexualized scene of whipping projects him into a voyeuristic relation to the violence against slave women, which he watches, and thus he enters into a symbolic complicity with the sexual crime he witnesses" (203). Thus the earlier concern of a female student about "the scene of ripping off a woman's clothes and hanging her naked body for all to see" can raise larger questions about Douglass's representations of women in his narrative. Critics have noted how Douglass objectifies and silences women in his account (his wife, Anna, barely rates a mention) and equates his selfhood with cultural definitions of manhood and power. As Valerie Smith contends, the very myth of American achievement in which Douglass casts his story— physical power, perseverance, literacy—"lends credence to the patriarchal structure largely responsible for his oppression." By mythologizing "rugged individuality, physical strength, and geographic mobility," Smith argues, "the narratives enshrine cultural definitions of masculinity" (*Self-Discovery* 27, 34). Thus closer critical scrutiny of Douglass's rhetorical choices in constructing his narrative leads not only to appreciation of his "performing self" but also to an understanding of how Douglass himself was historically situated as a male. Students may conclude from this assessment the desirability of supplementing Douglass's *Narrative* with narratives of women writers such as Harriet Jacobs (who, in fact, our course will include this year for the first time).

Finally, Douglass's call for the reader's sympathetic imagination leads to the class's final exploratory writing and opens the way for conversation about our responsibilities as readers and citizens. When toward the end of his narrative Douglass tries to describe his state of mind on arriving in the free states, he says that to understand this "most painful situation" one must experience it "or imagine himself in similar circumstances" (320). Andrews describes this as a signal turning point in slave narratives. "For the first time in Afro-American autobiography," Douglass declared "a new and crucial role for the imagination as a mode of mediation" between the Northern white reader and the fugitive slave writer. Douglass demanded a new discursive relationship of equals, "one based on an active, flexible engagement of the reader with the black text free from preconceived roles, instituted agendas, and programmed responses." In his call for an "imaginative leap into the total situation of the fugitive and the world of the text," Douglass opened up "new rhetorical options for black autobiographers as they had never been explored before" (*To Tell* 137–38).

Together we read this passage that catalogs the terrors of being a fugitive in the North and that concludes, "I say, let him be placed in this most trying situation,—the situation in which I was placed,—then, and not till then, will he fully appreciate the hardships of, and know how to sympathize with, the toil-worn and whip-scarred fugitive slave" (321). I then ask the students (either in class or out) to respond in writing to the questions, "How do you understand what Frederick Douglass wants his readers to do?" "How does this apply to you today—not only as a reader of the *Narrative* but as a citizen in a diverse democracy?"

Students are divided about what Douglass wants from his readers and whether such imaginative sympathy is even possible. One student, Andy Aswegan, wrote:

> I think that Douglass wants to explain something very important to his readers: no matter how much he can give examples about slavery and tell us how he felt, no one could ever understand the suffering unless they were a part of it as a slave. This is very important in his narrative because it sets no limits on the cruelty he talks of. By saying this, it makes slavery even worse than anything we can imagine. And right now I imagine it to be TERRIBLE. I need to keep in mind that I will never fully know how he and other slaves felt in that time. I need to keep my mind open of the atrocities. Instead of taking every last detail and saying "Yep, slavery was pretty bad," I need to know that the unexplainable psychological damage was just that—unexplainable.

Jen Olson agreed, saying:

> White Americans then and now are not able to feel this mental anguish
> that Douglass is experiencing. [. . .] It was not only the slave master that
> was forcing and encouraging slavery, it was and is society. Is this how
> African-Americans feel today, especially on the white Luther [College]
> campus?

But another student felt Douglass's call provoked her in a new way, saying that
it "keeps me removed from the real heart of the problem if I can cite statistics
of people in poverty or homelessness." To begin to see a way to help, she said:

> I must imagine myself in that situation, as a poor person or a homeless
> person. [. . .] This was what Frederick Douglass wanted his readers to
> understand [. . .] to completely involve themselves in the story. Only in
> understanding, in removing the distance from the situation, can a real
> passion for change come about.

These writings led to a lively discussion among students about the possibilities for sympathetic imagination and the implications of saying whether it is
possible. One student said that people say, "I know how you feel," but they
cannot know. Another said that after her mother's death, she felt that only
those who had lost a mother could know how she felt but that the effort of others to understand still meant something to her. A third said that in making the
effort to understand Douglass we fall short, and only in that failure do we
come to understand the terror of the slaves' experience. But another dis-
agreed, saying, "We're selling short the power of the imagination to place us in
other people's shoes. No, we can't be that slave, but Frederick Douglass *is* asking us to imagine."

At the end of this conversation I pointed out that there is a historic prece-
dent for an imaginative leap into the life of a slave. Walt Whitman wrote in
"Song of Myself":

> I am the hounded slave, I wince at the bite of dogs,
> Hell and despair are upon me, crack and again crack the marksmen
> I clutch the rails of the fence, my gore dribs, thinn'd with the ooze of my
>   skin [. . .].   (225)

And such identification continues to be urged by African American writers
throughout the twentieth century. Ralph Ellison writes of the white reader who
"draws his whiteness around himself when he sits down to read":

> He doesn't want to identify himself with Negro characters in terms of our
> immediate racial and social situation, though on the deeper human level,

identification can become compelling when the situation is revealed artistically. The white reader doesn't want to get too close.

(*Shadow and Act* 170)

More recently Derrick Bell has written, "Few whites are able to identify with blacks as a group—the essential prerequisite for feeling empathy with, rather than aversion from blacks' [suffering]. [. . .] Unable or unwilling to perceive that 'there but for the grace of God, go I,' few whites are ready to actively promote civil rights for blacks" (4).

While Douglass, Ellison, and Bell all appeal to white readers' need to project themselves into blacks' experience, their admonitions echo more broadly in our first-year humanities course. We teachers seek throughout the year to help students become better democratic citizens by developing a critical historical consciousness and an empathetic understanding of the lives of others. These goals become particularly compelling for our students during our focus on American diversity, when many students begin to see their family histories implicated in the complex racial drama of the United States and to see themselves as agents of democratic change. More than any other text in the course, perhaps even in the students' college careers, Douglass's *Narrative* confronts accepted notions of what it means to be an American, what it means to be an engaged reader, and—for many—what it means to be white. In this way, Douglass's great work becomes for all of us not just another text but the primary provocation for our continuing democratic response.

Teaching Douglass's *Narrative* in the World Literature Survey

David L. Dudley

Narrative of the Life of Frederick Douglass, an American Slave today enjoys a seemingly unassailable position in two literary canons; almost universally included in both American and African American literature anthologies, it is also widely taught in survey and special topics courses within both fields. Besides its double status as a standard American and African American text, however, Douglass's autobiography has now attained wider popularity—popularity proved by its frequent inclusion in world literature anthologies and its availability in several inexpensive paperback editions. This evidence indicates that instructors who might never have the opportunity to teach an American or African American literature course are nevertheless teaching Douglass in other settings and that thousands of students—most of whom are not literature majors—are reading it. My own experience illustrates the point: although African American literature is my specialty, I get to teach only one or two courses each year in the field, but I teach world literature survey every term, in sections much larger than my upper-division courses. (Such are the teaching realities—the teaching needs, I should say—at my university.) In ten years, I have introduced about 1,250 students to Frederick Douglass's *Narrative* in world literature surveys, but only 200 or so have studied it with me in African American literature courses. Because I strongly believe that all students should be acquainted with Douglass's great work, I am grateful I can teach it in the world literature course; it is an added pleasure that the forceful style, clearly articulated themes, and powerful characterization in the *Narrative* make it a favorite even with unskilled and sometimes uninterested readers.

Texts talk to one another. In the African American literature course, Douglass's autobiography dialogues exclusively with other African American texts. In the world literature course, however, the *Narrative* dialogues with works by authors neither black nor American. This broader context prompts me to teach the text somewhat differently from the way I approach it in an African American literature course. Additionally, the men and women who appear in my world literature sections are as a rule different as students from those who enroll in upper-division, special interest courses like African American literature. These different audiences call for different approaches to the material.

I teach Douglass's *Narrative* in a course prosaically titled World Literature II. This is its catalog description:

A survey of great works of literature from the 1700s to the present. The course studies literary representation and reaction to the rise of science, industrialism, and other forces shaping the modern and postmodern world. Emphasis on critical reading and writing skills.

(Georgia Southern University catalog, 1998–99)

As a rule, Georgia Southern University students express little enthusiasm for the literature requirement in the curriculum. This attitude is understandable because most of them read little in high school and few intend to pursue a degree in the humanities, let alone in literature. The students are primarily from the Southeast, mostly from Georgia, and a significant number come from metropolitan Atlanta. Some choose Georgia Southern because it is smaller and less intimidating than the University of Georgia; others lack the grades or test scores to get into the state university. Many of our students come from small towns, and many represent the first generation in their family to attend a university. When facing forty students in a world literature course on the first day of a term, I accept that many are not readers; I also recognize that, for most, my class will be their last formal exposure to serious literature. Given my knowledge about the typical Georgia Southern undergraduate's background, skills, interests, and career goals, I focus on teaching theme in my world literature classes rather than detailed textual or formal analysis. I tell students my goal is to help them appreciate literature's connections with real life, but my intentions are even deeper than that. Literature has power to influence our thinking and values. Having dedicated my own career to the humanities, I hope to foster—through reading, contemplating, and discussing literature—a humane sensibility within my students that will help them know and accept themselves and become more understanding and accepting of others. *Narrative of the Life of Frederick Douglass* has proved a valuable resource in helping me and my students realize those goals.

For years, I taught World Literature II chronologically, beginning with texts from the age of reason and ending with contemporary works. That approach gives students a clear grasp of various literary periods, but it limits my ability to group texts in ways that allow them to talk to one another. Consequently, I now teach the course thematically, clustering texts from different periods under subject headings such as What Does It Mean to Be Human?, The Individual and God, and The Power of the Past. Currently, the course begins with Human Triumph and Tragedy, a short unit designed to capture the students' interest, help them read intelligently, and let them know my approach to texts. The two texts in the unit, Douglass's *Narrative* and Franz Kafka's *The Metamorphosis*, illustrate two extremes of human possibility: Frederick Douglass offers us an epic of self-creation, and Kafka warns of the consequences that follow when the individual allows humanity to be stripped away.

Let me say immediately that I'm well aware of the dangers and limitations of structuring a literature survey course thematically. I do not push too hard for exact thematic parallels among texts; complex works of art never fit neatly together. Mixing autobiography and fiction raises other questions. Devotees of Frederick Douglass might ask, "Aren't you trivializing his life by comparing it to a short story?" I think not. No one would want students to view Douglass's quest for freedom or his portrayal of the hell of slavery in the same way they look at Gregor Samsa's perversely comical transformation into a gigantic beetle. Douglass's story is true and Kafka's is fiction, yet both convey truths about the human condition. Allowing different kinds of texts to play off one another consistently encourages classroom discussion and provokes thoughtful student essays. The benefits of such teaching outweigh the risks of trivializing any text or reducing its complexity and uniqueness.

On the day we first discuss the *Narrative*, I begin by asking my students to define two words: *slave* and *man* (the second taken as a synonym for human being, not the male of the species). They find *slave* easier to define than *man*, which is precisely what I expect: we will spend an entire term exploring what it means to be human. Then I ask them to imagine how Douglass would have defined the terms, pointing them to the famous sentence that many critics agree lies at the heart of the text: "You have seen how a man was made a slave; you shall see how a slave was made a man" (294). When students remember that Douglass attaches these words not to his actual flight from physical slavery but to his fight with Edward Covey, an event predating his escape by three years, they begin to understand that slavery and freedom are mental states as well as external realities and that the words *slave* and *man* exist—or ought to—in oxymoronic relation.

Next I ask, by what power did Frederick Douglass become a man? Who or what helped him? Students recall that people like Sophia Auld and the street children of Baltimore helped Douglass learn to read and write. His fellow slave Sandy gave him a root to carry, assuring him that no white man could whip him as long as he possessed it. But it's quickly evident that the power to resist slavery's dehumanization came from within Douglass himself. As his autobiography stresses, he did it—he had to do it—on his own. I remind the students of the dangers Douglass faced in resisting Covey. He was a teenager fighting against an adult, a slave battling a white master. Covey could have killed him with impunity. Yet the youth risked everything and thereby found his manhood.

Students side with Douglass in his struggle to free his spirit and his body. How could they not? His eloquence, his attractiveness, his worthiness all bid us take his part. So I ask my students why it is that the vast majority of readers today side with Douglass but that the white slave-owning society in the nineteenth century would not acknowledge the humanity of slaves or agree to their freedom. It's easy to assert smugly that we would never have assented to slavery and its abuses had we lived during its era, yet Douglass—and history itself—reminds us that slavery or any system that gives absolute power to one human being over another ends up dehumanizing not only the victims but their tormentors as well. It happened to Sophia Auld just as it happened to the guards in Nazi concentration camps.

I want readers of Douglass's *Narrative* to realize, as I do more keenly today than ever before, the sheer insanity and the evil of abusing any human being, particularly because that person happens to belong to a certain group. When I read the first volume of David Levering Lewis's monumental biography of W. E. B. Du Bois last year, one detail struck me with surprising force—that while Du Bois was a professor at Atlanta University, he was forbidden by the laws of Georgia to use the Atlanta public library. It didn't matter that he was one of the best educated people in the state (indeed, the entire nation) at that time or that he was a genius. All that mattered to the Jim Crow law was that Du Bois had some African blood in his veins. That alone overrode the reality of Du Bois's intelligence, character, and achievements. But as Du Bois reminds us, race is psychology, not biology, and it was white supremacist society's hatred and fear of an idea of blackness that caused it to embrace and cling to a system of legalized inequality, just as economic self-interest had prompted slave owners to deny the humanity of their victims.

Legalized slavery is not the issue today, but my students come to understand that people are still enslaved and dehumanized when their freedoms and privileges are denied them simply because they are black—or Hispanic or physically handicapped or women or members of any identifiable group that can be singled out for prejudicial treatment. This is why I teach *The Metamorphosis* after *Narrative*. Gregor Samsa faces the same threat to his humanity as Frederick Douglass does, but unlike Douglass, who finds within himself the power to fight back, Samsa is complicit in his dehumanization. He has permitted his family and his employers to treat him like a bug, so his transformation is the appropriate external metaphor of interior reality. Gregor's tragedy ultimately lies not only in his society's efforts to dehumanize him but also in his failure to fight back. Douglass found his manhood while he was still in chains; Du Bois fought with every power at his command to overturn an unjust system of race prejudice. Gregor, a fictional character, warns us of the consequences in real life for people who allow society to dehumanize them.

The second thematic unit of my course I title What Does It Mean to Be Human? Mary Shelley's *Frankenstein* begins the unit, which also includes *Gulliver's Travels*, book 4. *Frankenstein* fits well with Douglass's and Kafka's works, for all center on the theme of transformation. In the *Narrative*, we see how a man becomes a slave and a slave a man. Gregor becomes a monstrous insect; as Kafka's title suggests, the author is presenting us an ironic, modern addition to Ovid's *Metamorphoses*. In Shelley's novel, the creature, endowed with life but not humanity by his creator, is abandoned by Victor Frankenstein on the day of his birth. Yet like Douglass, the creature educates himself; through his reading he discovers, as does Douglass, a sense of the richness of human potential, potential denied him. Discovering within himself the capacity for devotion, he yearns to love and be loved. He wants to be like others. Tragically, his hideous physical form brands him an outcast. Here again, a circumstance of birth, one beyond his control, becomes the predominant reality of a character's life.

Frankenstein's creature, like Gregor Samsa, is a fictional creation; nevertheless, his predicament mirrors the reality that Douglass, Du Bois, and millions of real human beings have faced. True, the creature, spurned and rejected, turns to evil, committing a number of horrible murders. Yet my students sympathize with him more than they do with Victor Frankenstein; they agree that Mary Shelley presents a creature more human than his creator. In contemplating the creature and his fate, the class is invited again to consider our responsibility to accept one another, regardless of our differences, and to examine the consequences that follow when people are rejected and abandoned.

I hope that my approach to teaching Douglass's *Narrative* in the world literature survey and my general strategies in such a course are by now evident. My interest lies in identifying broad humanistic themes in the works and in inviting students to see the applicability of these themes to their own lives and to the world in which they live. Those uncomfortable with this approach might accuse me of turning the college classroom lectern into a pulpit. I recognize and welcome the charge. I teach because I want to influence my students' thoughts and values even more than I want to impart information; if these students want information, they have the library or the Internet. Although I am not a black man, Frederick Douglass, whose portrait hangs in my office, is my hero. I invite students to make him their hero too. I'm outraged that W. E. B. Du Bois was barred from the public library in the capital city of the state in which I live. I want my students to feel that outrage and to vow not to let such things happen today or tomorrow. If this is preaching, then the lectern is my pulpit. In colleges and universities across the country, other teachers are espousing their worldviews, their values and beliefs. I'm going to do the same whenever I have opportunity.

When I teach *Narrative of the Life of Frederick Douglass* in the African American literature survey course, my focus and purpose are somewhat different from those I've outlined above. I'm dealing with students who are majoring in English, minoring in African American studies (the course is cross-listed), or taking the course as an elective. All these students are present because of personal interest; most are practiced readers, and those who are English majors have had some formal training in dealing with texts. Aware that these students are more sophisticated readers than many in the world literature survey and that they have elected to study the material, I feel free to read the *Narrative* in greater detail, discussing Douglass as a writer and his text as a work of literary art. We explore Douglass's purposes for writing his autobiography and how Douglass uses his text to create a distinctly American self, following the tradition established by Benjamin Franklin in his autobiography. I also trace how Douglass's work stands prominently in the African American literary canon, influencing and inspiring later authors as different as Booker T. Washington and Richard Wright. We also analyze in some detail the excellences of Douglass's superb style, illustrating through numerous specific examples from the text how the author wields the structure and substance of the words themselves as weapons against slavery.

Contemplating two contrasting approaches to Douglass's *Narrative*, I realize that both offer satisfactions and rewards. In the world literature survey course, the pleasure is primarily emotional. It feels good when students let me know, either through their comments in class or in the essays they write, that they too have come to admire Frederick Douglass and his astonishing achievement. If even one student hears and answers my plea to help create a more humane world, I consider my teaching in such a class successful. When I focus on a text's structure, its author's rhetorical strategies, its position in the canon as a work influenced by earlier texts and influencing later ones, the pleasures are intellectual. I'm particularly satisfied that when teaching autobiography I can invite students to think about the problems facing the autobiographer—the challenge presented by the limitations of memory, the necessity to dramatize and give shape to one's experience, the inevitable fictionalizing inherent in any act of writing. These elements in autobiography, in Douglass's as much as in any other one, fascinate and challenge me, and it's gratifying to awaken students to questions that arise when they realize that no autobiography is a simple, objective recording of past events. I'm amused when students inadvertently refer to Douglass's *Narrative* as a novel. Such a reference alone is an excellent starting point for a discussion of the relation between factual reporting and the fictionalizing in every act of recollection.

Great works of art invite a multiplicity of interpretive approaches. Douglass's *Narrative* is one such work. I'm grateful for the opportunity to teach it in different ways to different students. The intellectual rewards from presenting the text in the upper-division African American literature course are many, but the emotional rewards of teaching it in the world literature survey course have proved even greater. May this realization inspire and assure all my colleagues who teach a large number of service courses. Such courses, far from being part of the grind, the dues we pay for the privilege of an occasional upper-division class, may actually produce the largest dividends.

Teaching Douglass's *Narrative* in the United States Literature Survey

Bruce Mills

> He who can peruse it without a tearful eye, a heaving
> breast, an afflicted spirit,—without being filled with an
> unutterable abhorrence of slavery and all its abettors, and
> animated with a determination to seek the immediate
> overthrow of that execrable system,—without trembling
> for the fate of this country in the hands of a righteous
> God, who is ever on the side of the oppressed, and whose
> arm is not shortened that it cannot save,—must have a
> flinty heart, and be qualified to act the part of a trafficker
> "in slaves and the souls of men."

William Lloyd Garrison's prefatory comments to *Narrative of the Life of Frederick Douglass* resonate with contemporary student readers. Surprised by abhorrent details of "that execrable system," present-day perusers of the text—except the few of flinty heart or those who seem initially struck silent by their own passionate indignation—often strive to find voice in the righteous current of their anger. Ironically, the successful evocation of such sympathies may lead students to a narrow range of responses. *Analyzing* how the narrative choices contribute to the work's power and thus further illuminate the artful voice scripted from the literal and figurative body of slavery sometimes strikes a discordant note. Are we not in the realm of peroration rather than interpretation? Are we not called on to rise up and strike a blow against the institutional racism still so visible within and beyond the academy rather than to examine particular rhetorical devices with dispassion?

And yet, in a class surveying United States literature through the onset of the Civil War, students also want to understand the text's "literary" place in literary history. Hence, while moved, students might at the same time resist a book used for the seemingly unliterary purpose of abolitionist propaganda. Often prefaced in the reading schedule by the works of Emerson, Fuller, Hawthorne, or Poe (figures whom students nearly unanimously name as key writers of the period), *Narrative of the Life* can seem an interloper, a text that is historically relevant but "straightforward" and thus less intellectually (or imaginatively) engaging. In short, this slave narrative—or, for that matter, those written by Jacobs, Equiano, and others—potentially exists in a kind of nether world of the nation's literature.

Although Douglass's story remains compelling to generation after generation of reader, then, the survey teacher who includes *Narrative of the Life* faces particular challenges. First, a too-insistent refusal to value the emotive power of the text and its relevance to an ongoing struggle to combat racism risks devaluing important individual (and national) concerns and a central intent of the work itself. Second, the powerful rendering of such a historical heritage can divert students from the probing textual analysis that they apply to the poetry and fiction of the antebellum period. It is significant that this lowering of literary expectations in connection with the slave narrative or other autobiographical forms sometimes reaffirms traditional notions of what defines literature, artistic merit, and literary history. To students, the narrative's historical specificity, explicit political and moral agenda, and nonfictional form make it less literary.

In focusing on such conflicting responses to *Narrative of the Life of Frederick Douglass*, my reflections reveal the sometimes intimate concerns that arise in the classroom of small liberal arts colleges and imply a pedagogical philosophy that emphasizes active learning strategies rather than lecture. Yet whether at a small college, research university, or community college, students still predominantly experience the survey (and the text) within the realm of English studies and thus within an academic culture that wrestles not only with what defines the literary but also with how the study of literary expression remains relevant to what are seen as American values and needs. Moreover, the original purpose and power of the text and the shared disciplinary need to survey the literary history of the United States evoke undergraduate reactions that embody common challenges. Without a pedagogical acknowledgment of the moral relevance of the felt text, the teacher devalues a response quite appropriate to the historical intent. And without some attention to the text as an artful rendering of the harsh realities of slavery, teachers risk creating a setting that unconsciously reaffirms notions of literary merit that assign the work secondary status. In the following sections, I reflect briefly on the survey of American literature from the exploration period through the Civil War and describe pedagogical strategies that address the tendency to categorize (even if unconsciously) the *Narrative of the Life of Frederick Douglass* as less artful because of its autobiographical form and overt moral and political agenda.

The Survey of United States Literature

How does the teacher of the early period in American literature create coherence at a time when the nation's literary history is undergoing such profound reformation? With the burgeoning of available readings, what paradigms effectively negotiate apparent curricular chaos and contention? What goals should guide the formation of an American literature survey? To consider how *Narrative of the Life* might fit within such a survey invites some initial reflection on these questions.

Regardless of era or professional ethos, the survey by its nature creates problems of selection and coherence. Even though it devoted sixty percent of its space to eighteen nineteenth-century writers, D. C. Heath's *American Literature: Tradition and Innovation* (1969), a forebearer to the current *Heath Anthology*, offered instructors sixty-two authors; published just over thirty years earlier, the first volume of *The Oxford Anthology of American Literature* (1938) included seventy writers. As revealing of breadth as such a sampling might be, however, it is nonetheless true that the anthologies of the past decades predominantly included male authors and, more generally, that their selections were offered with scant attention to gender, race, and ethnic heritage. After all, it is one thing to choose from a range of Puritan texts and another to integrate Native American oral tradition, exploration narratives, slave narratives, and transcendentalist essays. Clearly, the current problem is not so much one of numbers as one of conceptualization, of finding a paradigm that centers rather than marginalizes new texts. While conventional notions of period (colonial, revolutionary, federalist, and Romantic) can be useful and, as influential models of past years, warrant some representation to students of the discipline, they do not provide paradigms that organically embrace the range of current readings. Practice and theory increasingly confirm that a more coherent accommodation of materials rooted in diverse experiences and traditions arises from organizing content around the literary dialogue rooted in intersecting individual and cultural concerns. Specifically, the multiple dimensions of *Narrative of the Life* emerge more readily in a unit focusing on slavery and the literary imagination or, as in recent editions of *The Heath Anthology of American Literature*, volume 1, on explorations of the "American" self, than in a unit focusing on definitions of the Romantic that hearken back to Wordsworth and Coleridge or to New England transcendentalism. Such thematic designations, after all, gesture toward historical and cultural realities essential to the evolution of the slave narrative. In conceiving of the survey as acknowledging the historical circumstances that inspire literary enterprises rather than as simply representing selected authors and works, teachers will discover coherence in juxtaposition, in comparison, in dialogue.

Ironically, however, reasserting the importance of history and heritage directs students toward questions, concerns, and genres that seem "unimaginative." Again, such a fact is not unique to the decade ushering in the new millennium. From the point in this century when the academy acknowledged American literature as a valid subject of study, the effort to provide some sense of the tradition has led to the inclusion of exploration journals, sermons, captivity narratives, and spiritual autobiographies. Yet, even with a disproportionate emphasis on poetry (including the work of such writers as Bradstreet, Taylor, Wheatley, Bryant, and Whitman) or the weighting of the reading to allow for a fuller integration of nineteenth-century short fiction, historical novels, and romances, students frequently express surprise at the nonliterary nature of the course. Much to the chagrin of many class members, the emerging pedagogical emphasis on cultural context, the predominance of nonfictional genres, and the inevitable need for historical coverage demand a thorough inclusion of forms that strike students as less engaging, or, to quote a favorite term, "dry."

While undergraduates rarely equate *Narrative of the Life of Frederick Douglass* with the likes of Bradford's *Of Plymouth Plantation*, many experience the *Narrative* as a kind of intrusion into their conceptual framework, which is based on limited assumptions about what constitutes literature and literary merit. Unlike the works of Poe or Hawthorne (which students tend to view as classics embodying universal themes and thus as literature positioned in the canon solely on the basis of merit), Douglass's text and the genre it represents conspicuously assert a historical specificity and political intent. In frequently aligning the slave narrative with the nonfictional, historical, and political (of the past century as well as this one) rather than with the literary, students apply a different interpretive lens, raising questions and offering comments that focus on what happened rather than on how such happenings are constructed. After all, has Douglass not simply documented a life rather than artfully arranged a tale? Within the American literature survey, most students consciously and unconsciously place *Narrative of the Life* in the unwelcome company of the Puritans, or, heaven forbid, *The Autobiography of Benjamin Franklin*.

One more dimension of the survey course warrants acknowledgment. Whether in a ten-week quarter or a fifteen-week semester, the need to cover more than two centuries of literary history inevitably leads teachers to select the most representative texts, works that they see as manifesting literary and cultural concerns typical to a period or movement. At a time when the expansion of the canon has sparked curricular and disciplinary restructuring (and challenged the very legitimacy of the survey itself), instructors must often provide students with a working knowledge of traditional configurations of literary history as well as with paradigms that more readily accommodate "additions" with non-Western roots. Such pressures can lead to a kind of tokenism: single texts come to represent an entire movement or tradition.

To address this potential problem in the teaching of Douglass's narrative, it is essential to create a coherent unit, one that establishes the book as part of an ongoing conversation among a series of works responding to specific literary or cultural matters. In a survey I developed for a ten-week quarter, I have a two-to four-week unit entitled Slavery and the Literary Imagination. I begin with *Narrative of the Life*, supplement the discussion with excerpts from Harriet Jacobs's *Incidents in the Life of a Slave Girl*, and conclude with Harriet Beecher Stowe's *Uncle Tom's Cabin*. In another course, I also included sections from Henry David Thoreau's *Walden*. While Thoreau's work might seem an odd inclusion in this cluster of books, its place in such a unit invites fresh readings, a reorientation toward a text traditionally read within other paradigms. Students read *Walden* through a perspective more immediately shaped by Douglass's *Narrative* than by transcendentalist works such as Emerson's "Nature" or "Self-Reliance." One recalls, for instance, Thoreau's early comparison between Northern laborers and Southern slavery in "Economy":

> I sometimes wonder that we can be so frivolous, I may almost say, as to attend to the gross but somewhat foreign form of servitude called Negro Slavery, there are so many keen and subtle masters that enslave both

north and south. It is hard to have a southern overseer; it is worse to have a northern one; but worst of all when you are the slave-driver of yourself.

(4)

Transcendentalist reflections on inner enslavement and self-reliance compare in intriguing ways with narratives rooted in the physical realities of bondage.

While these texts have worked effectively in conjunction with Douglass's *Narrative*, they describe useful groupings rather than prescribe possibilities. Depending on the length of the semester, these works can be supplemented or replaced with poetry and short fiction from American literature anthologies, such as selections from Frances E. W. Harper; Herman Melville's "Benito Cereno"; sections or all of William Wells Brown's *Clotelle; or, The Colored Heroine* or Harriet E. Wilson's *Our Nig*; and the abolitionist writings of David Walker, Lydia Maria Child, and the Grimkés, to name a few possibilities. Creating thematically coherent units throughout the course affirms an important fact of literary history increasingly reflected in the expanding canon: the representative artifacts of United States literature consistently reflect the signs of an ongoing dialogue over intersecting cultural concerns.

Sequencing Lecture and Discussion

Inviting students to articulate their assumptions and attitudes toward overtly political works can lead to some of the most meaningful teaching moments. What may be perceived as a one-dimensional text grows in complexity as students begin to see it outside previous interpretive structures or beliefs. In a discussion of Douglass's narrative, an initial engagement with the historical facts of slavery and of student reactions to them elicits ideas and interpretations that can later be enriched and complicated. To be estranged from "known" beliefs regarding autobiography sets the stage for both a fuller understanding of the literary and political dimensions of Douglass's work and a later reassessment of unquestioned distinctions between fiction and nonfiction—and thus a reevaluation of how one places a text in any literary history.

To invite such an understanding of the links between various layers of *Narrative of the Life*, I have found it useful to conceptualize the presentation of background material, discussions, and writing as forming three cycles. The first two cycles create a dialectic between seeing the narrative as a chronological recording of a life that fosters abolitionist sympathies ("propaganda") and as a thematic ordering of a life that invites an exploration of rhetorical strategies ("literature"). In the third cycle, class activities more consistently encourage reflection on the way the book synthesizes these interwoven elements or purposes of the narrative. By so delineating these cycles, I do not mean to suggest a lockstep sequence or the formation of inflexible boundaries between issues. A rigid unwillingness to deal with questions as they naturally emerge within the specific dynamic of a class can mean disaster. Rather, the model simply builds on the educational assumption that sequencing intersecting concerns invites a smoother movement from analysis to synthesis and thus, for the study of Douglass's *Narrative*, creates more potential for an increasingly sophisticated sense of the text and its place in United States literary history. Finally, given the time limitations of a survey course, these cycles can be divided among three to four class meetings, ideally at least four hours of class, with more time given to synthesis.

Cycle 1   The educational value of Douglass's text emerges in part from its direct acknowledgment of the distinct features of slavery in the United States. In this first cycle, the pedagogical choices seek to supplement students' knowledge of slavery with images that fall within or just outside the borders of Douglass's text. Most library collections have slides or other pictoral documentation of slave ships, slave quarters, advertisements for runaway slaves and slave auctions, and instruments for shackling, branding, or punishing slaves. Moreover, the increasing availability of images on the Internet can keep preparation time manageable. Carefully chosen images establish shared visual texts that illuminate what former slaves had to present in their written depictions of slavery. The recurring image of one man's back scarred from whipping, for instance, provides a painful rendering of how the body serves as a visual manuscript, a text that countless writers from Douglass to Jacobs to Toni Morrison have culled for their own literary purposes.

Through the use of this visual background and the presentation of information on the slave narrative genre, I establish a short list of key points that have arisen from student responses and that will guide discussion of *Narrative of the Life*. In the silence that predictably ensues after the presentation of such graphic images and information, I ask students to consider those episodes in Douglass's text that offer comparable images. Again, as Garrison notes in his preface, if the autobiography inevitably evokes readers' sympathies through its vivid portrayal of the devastating facts of slavery, then productive reflection should center on such responses. When I teach the *Narrative*, I arrange the first day so that students may articulate their reactions orally and in writing. As they struggle for the language to describe and give meaning to the realities of slavery, students begin to sense the problem of finding words for such memories. Having initiated some thought on the difficulty of this literary act, I invite further consideration of why a model or tradition of such narratives is important. Why would a writer in such a situation seek past models? How would these models offer a language and form to express what memory and society might want to veil? What if the model does not entirely fit the content or effectively negotiate readers' resistance to such content?

My initial cycle of discussion, then, includes background on the form, purpose, and popularity of slave narratives; presents visual images documenting the slave trade and slavery; and finally invites students to identify and discuss those images and actions (first from the visual images and then from the text) that most dramatically communicate the horrors of slavery and thus offer the potential to move readers to embrace abolitionist sentiment. To frame reflection, discussion (in large or small groups), or writing, I often supplement the previous queries with the following questions:

> As a slave narrative, *Narrative of the Life of Frederick Douglass* falls within a tradition of texts supporting the immediate and unconditional abolition of slavery. Locate and discuss those images and events that provide a strong argument for immediate abolition. Why do these examples elicit such sympathies for the antislavery cause? Through close attention to the details of the narrative, describe the "argument."

> Construct an abolitionist identity for yourself. Now imagine that, in preparing a speech for an antislavery rally, you wish to reflect on one episode from Douglass's book. Which event would you choose? Why? Consider how your identity or the makeup and assumptions of the audience would affect this choice.

This opening stage of the discussion of *Narrative of the Life* brings forward the sometimes unnamed historical facts of slavery. It does so by emphasizing close description and initial analysis of specific images rather than sustained reflection on the implication of these images to narrative patterns or themes. As I prepare to move students into the next sequence, however, I increasingly encourage them to anchor their responses to specific textual evidence for the purposes of attending to these patterns. Whether solicited through group work, individual journal entries, or brief in-class writings, the list of especially effective images and scenes generated during this cycle of discussion and lecture provides valuable material for considering the narrative's organizing themes.

Cycle 2   To puzzle over the power of compelling scenes within a short time demands an attentiveness to the way in which diction, metaphor, juxtaposition of images, and other narrative choices shape meaning. In effect, students are asked to consider that a narrative arises from organizing the selection of a few events from many. At some point in this transition to an analysis of Douglass's narrative crafting, this truth of the creative act must be emphasized. Whether presented formally in lecture or informally through prefatory comments to discussion, J. Hillis Miller's reflection on narrative offers one way of moving students from an interpretive methodology grounded in simpler conceptions of nonfiction to strategies more consonant with "imaginative" genres such as poetry, fiction, and drama. Miller notes that both fictional and historical narratives are

> closely related forms of "order-giving" or "order-finding," in spite of the fact that fictional narratives are subject to referential restraints in a way very different from the way histories submit themselves to history and claim to represent things that really happened *exactly* as they really happened.   (68)

Students are usually inclined to see the autobiographer as an undiscriminating recorder of fixed events rather than as one who molds the clay of memory. To acknowledge that Douglass is an agent in his own literary making, after all, is to complement a fundamental theme of the text. The meaning and shape of Douglass's experiences result from his refusal to succumb to the chaos of slavery.

Turning to the list generated from students' oral and written comments, I ask a simple but evocative question: If a writer selects and shapes some images and events and not others, what accounts for Douglass's choices? This question consistently begins the students' estrangement from earlier interpretations and initiates their reassessment of the text as being not simply the relating of facts but also the recording of the evolution and naming of the self. Discussion of Douglass's chapter detailing his confrontation with the slave breaker Covey— an episode that clearly engages students and elicits some of the richest analysis (as demonstrated in the critical history of the text)—will demonstrate the meanings that emerge within this cycle of reassessment. Not surprisingly, most lists of significant events underscore the fact that Douglass's experiences with Covey strikingly document particular cruelties associated with slavery. Without initial coaxing, however, students sometimes miss the sophisticated way in which Douglass sets up his "rise" to defeat Covey. For instance, certain images establish the breaking of Douglass from a man to a slave. Posturing himself both literally and figuratively as a man who stands up to slavery, as one who needs to be "broke" or bent to convey inner and outer servitude, Douglass soon shows how his own life is joined with animals, and he increasingly describes his body as lowered to the dirt of field labor. His first whipping occurs after a nearly fatal attempt to lead oxen to and from a grove to collect wood. Just as the oxen are yoked and driven unwillingly to perform strenuous labor, so too is Douglass: "I was broken in body, soul, and spirit. [. . .] [T]he dark night of slavery closed in upon me; and behold a man transformed into a brute!" (293). In emphasizing his literal lowering into the dirt, Douglass means to show readers his need for both physical and spiritual freedom. Moreover, his rise to strike Covey provides the powerful visual icon of his return to humanity. Through careful rhetorical choices, then, Douglass does more than simply relate what happened. The staging of the event and the astute selection of images underscore the connection between inner and outer freedom.

Once the work enters the realm of "story," students feel freed to entertain questions that broaden the scope and intensity of their analysis. Of what narrative importance, I have asked, does Douglass assign the root given him by Sandy Jenkins before Douglass's confrontation with Covey? What does this root come to represent? With whom and with what is it associated? To pause on the meaning of Jenkins's offering is to set up an even more probing reading. Ironically, it is a root drawn from the dirt that Douglass links to his redemption. Student responses to my specific questions suggest that although his struggle does not take the same shape as Harriet Jacobs's rebirth from the womb of her grandmother's garret, Douglass too connects his liberty to the figurative "mid-wivery" of a fellow slave. Because Douglass's *Narrative* is frequently clustered with antebellum texts embodying self-reliant acts and identities, the centrality of community in his work is often overlooked.

The graphic way in which Douglass sketches the scene lends itself to charting (on the board or in handouts) the downward degradation from man to brute and the corresponding rise back to manhood. This charting enhances an understanding of the effect of the narrative choices. While his literary choices may seem self-evident to literature teachers and echo scholarly readings of the chapter, they are still new to most survey students and thus gain clarity through such visual reinforcement of thematic patterns. Finally, the following questions—or variations of them—guide me in generating discussion and writing:

> Given that Douglass has chosen to relate some images and events from among many, discuss a pattern of choices that signals a particular thematic concern. Explore the way diction, metaphor, or other literary devices reinforce this theme.

> Prior to his speaking at an antislavery convention at Nantucket in August 1841, Douglass notes that he "seldom had much to say at the [antislavery] meetings, because what [he] wanted to say was said so much better by others" (325). Reflecting upon the whole of his narrative, identify and discuss those incidents or episodes that reveal Douglass's preoccupation with language, with reading, with thematizing or ordering his life. What models or mentors support his movement toward the construction of voice? What effect does audience or situation have on his ability to speak?

> Using Douglass's narrative as the primary source, compose an antislavery sermon (or Fourth of July oration) to be delivered before a sympathetic audience or, if you wish, an antagonistic audience. Focus the address on a literal incident or aspect of slavery that offers potential for shaping thematic concerns.

Again, students should be urged to address the book as a labor of order finding or order giving and to see that, as another generation of readers, they carry on a similar act of uncovering and discovering meaningful patterns.

Cycle 3 Sequencing these background materials and questions in this way fosters the potential to enter into a more global kind of reflection. The final cycle of discussion continues this building toward such interpretations—the most difficult for students—by asking them to consider how the book manifests a synthesis of reform purposes and literary strategies. Why would Douglass be inclined to order his life as he does, given the historical circumstances within which he was writing? Are there specific narrative choices (image patterns, metaphors, figurative language, etc.) that reflect an artful response to audience assumptions or political needs? Asking students to consider Douglass's use of animal imagery, for instance, might help them discern distinctions between the period's competing designations for bondage, that is, as a patriarchal institution or as chattel slavery. As William Andrews's *To Tell a Free Story*, Joanne Braxton's *Black Women Writing Autobiography*, Henry Louis Gates's introduction to *The Classic Slave Narratives*, and countless other texts have demonstrated, slave narratives consistently relate the way slavery inverts values and relationships expected within a humane social structure. In Douglass's text, to cite one instance, slavery transforms Mrs. Auld, the "pious, warm, and tender-hearted" mistress with a "lamblike disposition," into a cold and suspicious woman of "tiger-like fierceness" (277). As Jacobs relates in *Incidents in the Life of a Slave Girl*, the maternal protection that she should have expected from Mrs. Flint gives way to self-pity and eventual cruelty: "[Mrs. Flint] felt that her marriage vows were desecrated, her dignity insulted; but she had no compassion for the poor victim of her husband's perfidy" (*Incidents*, ed. Yellin, 33). These descriptions conspicuously invert the proper social order, providing an effective rebuttal to slavery apologists who sought to sanctify the institution as protective.

Informing students that Douglass added to and revised his life story in *My Bondage and My Freedom* (1855) and in *Life and Times of Frederick Douglass* (1892)—and briefly characterizing a telling change—further reveals the self-conscious shaping hand of the literary reformer and thus the similarities between creating historical and fictional narratives. Pairing a later draft of an event with its earlier version in *Narrative of the Life* can signal how even lived experiences take on new order and import within different contexts. In the final rendering of his life, for example, Douglass divides the Covey episode into three chapters (chs. 15–17) in a book of three parts (and fifty-three total chapters). The event that forms the center of his initial narrative, while certainly still an important moment in his life, now becomes one defining incident among many. Moreover, considering that the Covey chapter had formed the longest section in the first autobiography, one might now ask whether this section would have been more coherent if it had been more limited in scope. In other words, how does the content and length of the chapter contribute to or limit the effectiveness of the message? In the end, the exploration of well-chosen revisions unveils the way Douglass shapes different stories to capture a maturing sense of self as well as respond to changing cultural circumstances.

Finally, it is also important to compare *Narrative of the Life* with other works in the rich tradition of the slave narrative. Such a strategy, though limited by the need to move quickly to the next reading in the unit, works against the tokenism that slave narratives sometimes suffer in a literary survey. Regardless of its representative features, Douglass's autobiography should not stand as the archetypal rendering of the numerous responses to slavery. One strategy that mitigates against understanding *Narrative of the Life* in this way would be to give students discussion questions or writing assignments that encourage comparisons with other slave narratives. Depending on the episode or two that elicited the most provocative classroom discussions, it is wise to select related scenes or rhetorical devices from Harriet Jacobs's *Incidents in the Life of a Slave Girl* to foster some sense of the gendered places from which Douglass and Jacobs experience and construct their lives. To compare Douglass's description of the Covey episode with Jacobs's articulation of her decision to establish a relationship with the white slaveholder Mr. Sands (ch. 10) or to hide for seven years in her grandmother's garret (ch. 21), for instance, illuminates the way in which conceptions of manhood and womanhood contribute to the thematic structure of the narratives. If Dr. Flint serves the same role as Covey does in threatening a physical and moral degradation, then Jacobs's own rising up against her master provides a revealing juxtaposition to Douglass's fight. Such a comparison might also indicate why Jacobs would be drawn to the genre of the sentimental novel to give shape to incidents in the life of a slave *girl*. Among other reasons, the genre provided the language and form to embody Flint's sexual threats. I have found the following discussion and writing prompts provide ways to elicit a synthesis of central concerns:

> Read Harriet Jacobs's "A Perilous Passage in the Slave Girl's Life," from *Incidents in the Life of a Slave Girl*. Compare her rendering of this central chapter with Douglass's struggles with Covey. What differentiates each person's situation? What difficulties did each face in depicting their experiences? Of what significance is gender to both writers' experiences and to the options each had in relating these private experiences?

> Compare a scene in *Narrative of the Life of Frederick Douglass* with its counterpart in either *My Bondage and My Freedom* (1855) or *Life and Times of Frederick Douglass* (1892). What literary choices differentiate these two scenes? Of what significance are these differences, even the small ones, to the meaning of the event? To what extent do such changes suggest an awareness of new historical circumstances or a growing understanding of how self-definition emerges from and even shapes conceptions of an evolving "America"?

During my first two years of teaching American literature at Kalamazoo College, I noticed that students, while writing insightful and engaging essays focusing on *Narrative of the Life of Frederick Douglass*, often had trouble fitting the text into a critical framework in essays that demanded global reflection on the period. In fact, I was surprised by how many times the text was overlooked. Moreover, when integrating analysis of Douglass's *Narrative* in end-of-the-quarter exam essays and in senior year comprehensive exams, students tended to construct critical frameworks and transitions that set the text apart from rather than within various paradigms, paradigms of their own making or from traditional categories of American literary history.

In central ways, of course, this positioning of the text on the margins marks an accurate assessment, for Douglass's life and narrative embody the experiences of one whom the nation had defined as other. Yet this tendency toward incoherence in student essays and exams alerted me to the need to examine the nature of student responses to the text, to review my own global assumptions about the character of the literary, and, finally, to assess how the structure of the survey supported or undercut the positioning of *Narrative of the Life* as a central work within the early period in United States literature. In my preceding reflections on the survey and my sequencing of lecture and discussion of Frederick Douglass, I offer the outcome of my assessment.

As I continue to teach the *Narrative*, I find myself thinking more and more of a variety of silences regarding the text—silences within the canon of the period as well as in the classroom itself. Caught in such reflections, I am inevitably led back to Douglass's own words. Noting his participation at an antislavery meeting on Nantucket, he concludes the body of his narrative with a moving description of a transition from silence to voice: "I spoke but a few moments, when I felt a degree of freedom, and said what I desired with considerable ease" (326). Although particular teaching contexts, contemporary historical circumstances, and individual passions inevitably shape the design of the United States literature survey and thus the way the *Narrative* engages new generations of readers, teachers must foster a similar freeing in their own students—through course design, discussion, lecture, and writing. Without pedagogical strategies rooted in a conceptual centering of the text, Douglass's and his readers' voices will remained checked and halting.

NOTES ON CONTRIBUTORS

Lindon Barrett is associate professor in the department of English and comparative literature and the program in African American studies at the University of California, Irvine. He is the author of *Blackness and Value*. As associate editor of *Callaloo* he is responsible for literary and cultural criticism.

Russ Castronovo teaches English and American studies at the University of Miami. He is the author of *Fathering the Nation: American Genealogies of Slavery and Freedom* (1995) and is completing a study of embodiment, depoliticization, and United States citizenship.

Gregg D. Crane is assistant professor at the University of Washington and has written on rights discourse, African American literature, and nineteenth-century American legal history. He is completing a book on nineteenth-century figurations of justice, citizenship, and race.

David L. Dudley is associate professor of literature and philosophy at Georgia Southern University. He is the author of *My Father's Shadow: Intergenerational Conflict in African-American Men's Autobiography* (1991).

John Ernest is associate professor of English, director of undergraduate studies for the department of English, and coordinator of the African American studies minor at the University of New Hampshire. He is the author of *Resistance and Reformation in Nineteenth-Century African-American Literature: Brown, Wilson, Jacobs, Delany, Douglass, and Harper*.

Ed Folsom is F. Wendell Miller Distinguished Professor of English at the University of Iowa, where he edits the *Walt Whitman Quarterly Review*. He is the author of *Walt Whitman's Native Representations* (1994) and the editor or coeditor of *Walt Whitman and the World* (1995), *Walt Whitman: The Centennial Essays* (1994), *Walt Whitman: The Measure of His Song* (1981, 1998), and *W. S. Merwin: Essays on the Poetry* (1987).

James C. Hall is assistant professor of African American studies and English at the University of Illinois, Chicago. He is the editor of *Langston Hughes: A Collection of Poems* (1998), coeditor of *Teaching a New Canon: Students, Teachers, and Texts in the College Literature Classroom* (1995), and author of *Mercy, Mercy Me: African American Culture and the American Sixties* (forthcoming).

Laura Hapke is professor of English at Pace University. She is the author of *Daughters of the Great Depression: Women, Work, and Fiction in the American 1930s* (1995). She is writing a history of United States work fiction.

Martin Klammer is associate professor of Africana studies and English at Luther College. His publications include *Whitman, Slavery, and the Emergence of* Leaves of Grass (1995) and other essays and review articles on Whitman.

Ruth Ellen Kocher is assistant professor of English at Missouri Western State College. Her research is primarily about perceptions of identity in twentieth-century American women's literature. She is the author of *Desdemona's Fire* (1999), a collection of poetry that explores racial identity.

Barbara McCaskill is associate professor of African American Literature at the University of Georgia. She is the coeditor of *Multicultural American Literature and Literacies* (1993) and author of the foreword to *Running a Thousand Miles for Freedom; or, The Escape of William and Ellen Craft from Slavery* (1999). She is completing a book, *Designs on the Sign of Race*, on the dialogic interplay of black women and transatlantic abolitionists. She is coeditor of *Womanist Theory and Research*.

Keith D. Miller is associate professor of English at Arizona State University. He is the author of *Voice of Deliverance: The Language of Martin Luther King, Jr., and Its Sources* (1998). His essays have appeared in *PMLA*, *College English*, and *Rhetoric Society Quarterly*. He is working on a book about King's "I Have a Dream" speech.

Bruce Mills is associate professor of English at Kalamazoo College and the author of *Cultural Reformations: Lydia Maria Child and the Literature of Reform*. He is the editor of Child's *Letters from New-York* (1999).

Joycelyn K. Moody is assistant professor at the University of Washington and teaches courses in American literature and women studies. She is writing *True Confessions*, an examination of spiritual narratives by nineteenth-century African American women.

Anita Patterson is assistant professor of English at Boston University. She is the author of *From Emerson to King: Democracy, Race, and the Politics of Protest* (1997). She has published essays on Du Bois, Harriet Jacobs, Thoreau, and Frantz Fanon and is working on a book, *Passage to the Americas: The Poetics of Migration from Whitman to Walcott*.

Elizabeth Schultz is Chancellor's Club Teaching Professor at the University of Kansas. She has published in the fields of African American fiction and autobiography, nineteenth-century American fiction, American women's writing, and Japanese culture. She is the author of *Unpainted to the Last: Moby-Dick and Twentieth-Century American Art* (1995).

Jeffrey Steele is professor of English at the University of Wisconsin, Madison. He is the author of *The Representation of the Self in the American Renaissance* (1987) and *The Essential Margaret Fuller* (1992), as well as numerous articles on American literature.

Arthur Zilversmit is Distinguished Service Professor of History, Emeritus, at Lake Forest College. He is the author of *The First Emancipation: The Abolition of Slavery in the North* (1967); *Changing Schools: Progressive Education Theory and Practice, 1930–1960* (1993). He edited *Lincoln on Black and White* (1971, 1983) and has written on African American history and the history of American education.

SURVEY PARTICIPANTS

Lindon Barrett, *University of California, Irvine*
Geneva H. Baxter, *Spelman College*
B. J. Bolden, *Chicago State University*
Brad Born, *Bethel College*
Harold K. Bush, Jr., *Michigan State University*
David Callahan, *Universidade de Aveiro, Portugal*
Anne Carroll, *University of Maryland, College Park*
Russ Castronovo, *University of Miami*
Gregg D. Crane, *University of Washington*
Jeannine DeLombard, *Philadelphia*
David L. Dudley, *Georgia Southern University*
John Ernest, *University of New Hampshire*
Kevin Eyster, *Madonna University*
Christopher Felker, *Michigan State University*
Audrey Fisch, *Jersey City State College*
Cheryl Fish, *Nassau Community College*
Ed Folsom, *University of Iowa*
Shelley Booth Fowler, *Washington State University*
Granville Ganter, *Graduate Center, City University of New York*
Stephen Hahn, *William Paterson College of New Jersey*
Laura Hapke, *Pace University*
Marilyn H. Harris, *Ledbetter*
Bernice Hausman, *Virginia Polytechnic Institute and State University*
Barbara A. Heavilin, *Taylor University*
Carol E. Henderson, *University of Delaware*
Mark Hennelly, Jr., *California State University, Sacramento*
Evora Jones, *Virginia Union University*
Sandra Kamusikiri, *California State University, San Bernardino*
AnnLouise Keating, *Eastern New Mexico University*
Martin Klammer, *Luther Collge*
Ruth Ellen Kocher, *Arizona State University*
Ellyn Lem, *New York*
Leslie Lewis, *Emporia State University*
Jayne Marek, *Franklin College of Indiana*
Barbara McCaskill, *University of Georgia*
Beth A. McCoy, *Wichita State University*
Christopher Metress, *Samford University*
Keith D. Miller, *Arizona State University*
Stephen Paul Miller, *New York*
Bruce Mills, *Kalamazoo College*
Joycelyn K. Moody, *University of Washington*
Nancy Morrow, *Michigan State University*
William Nelles, *University of Massachussets, Dartmouth*

John Orr, *University of Portland*
Anita Patterson, *Boston University*
Sarah Pelmas, *University of California, Berkeley*
Ted Pelton, *Lakeland College*
Maureen Reddy, *Rhode Island College*
Thomas J. Reynolds, *University of Minnesota*
Alan Rice, *University of Central Lancashire*
Jim Rice, *Central Washington University*
Sarah Robbins, *Kennesaw State College*
Nora Ruth Roberts, *Michigan State University*
Lynne D. Rogers, *Birzeit University, West Bank*
John Daniel Saillant, *Providence*
Richard J. Schneider, *Wartburg College*
Elizabeth Schultz, *University of Kansas*
Saadi Simawe, *Grinnell College*
Virginia Whatley Smith, *University of Alabama, Birmingham*
Jeffrey Steele, *University of Wisconsin, Madison*
Gina Taglieri, *Fashion Institute of Technology*
Linda Tate, *Shepherd College*
C. James Trotman, *West Chester University*
Brenda R. Williams, *University of New Haven*
Eric Wolfe, *University of Mississippi*
Michael Zeitlin, *University of British Columbia*
Arthur Zilversmit, *Lake Forest College*

WORKS CITED

Allen, Julia, and Lester Faigley. "Discursive Strategies for Social Change: An Alternative Rhetoric of Argument." *Rhetoric Review* 14 (1995): 142–72.

Andrews, William L., ed. *African American Autobiography: A Collection of Critical Essays*. Englewood Cliffs: Prentice, 1993.

———, ed. *Critical Essays on Frederick Douglass*. Boston: Hall, 1991.

———. "Narrating Slavery." Graham, *Teaching* 12–30.

———, ed. *Oxford Frederick Douglass Reader*. New York: Oxford UP, 1996.

———. "The Representation of Slavery." McDowell and Rampersad 62–80.

———. "Reunion in the Postbellum Slave Narrative: Frederick Douglass and Elizabeth Keckley." *Black American Literature Forum* 24 (1989): 5–16.

———, ed. *Sisters of the Spirit: Three Black Women's Autobiographies of the Nineteenth Century*. Bloomington: Indiana UP, 1986.

———, ed. *Six Women's Slave Narratives*. New York: Oxford UP, 1988.

———, ed. *Three Classic African-American Novels*. New York: Penguin, 1990.

———. *To Tell a Free Story: The First Century of Afro-American Autobiography, 1760–1865*. Urbana: U of Illinois P, 1986.

Andrews, William, and Nellie McKay, eds. Spec. issue of *Black American Literature Forum* 24.2 (1990).

Aptheker, Herbert. *A Documentary History of the Negro People in the United States*. 7 vols. New York: Carol, 1990.

Attaway, William. *Blood on the Forge*. 1941. New York: Monthly, 1987.

Austin, Allan. *African Muslims in Antebellum America: Transatlantic Stories and Spiritual Struggles*. New York: Routledge, 1997.

Awkward, Michael. "Negotiations of Power: White Critics, Black Texts, and the Self-Referential Impulse." *American Literary History* 2 (1990): 581–606.

Baker, Houston A., Jr. *Blues, Ideology, and Afro-American Literature*. Chicago: U of Chicago P, 1984.

———. *The Journey Back*. Chicago: U of Chicago P, 1983.

———. *Long Black Song*. Charlottesville: U of Virginia P, 1972.

———. *Workings of the Spirit: The Poetics of Afro-American Women's Writing*. Chicago: U of Chicago P, 1991.

Baldwin, James. "Stranger in the Village." *Notes of a Native Son*. 1955. Boston: Beacon, 1984. 159–75.

Barrett, Lindon. "Institutions, Classrooms, Failures: African American Literature and Critical Theory in the Same Small Spaces." Sadoff and Cain 218–32.

Barthelemy, Anthony, ed. *Collected Black Women's Narratives*. New York: Oxford UP, 1988.

Barton, Rebecca Chalmers. *Witnesses for Freedom: Negro Americans in Autobiography*. Oakdale: Dowling Coll. P, 1976.

Bell, Derrick. *Faces at the Bottom of the Well: The Permanence of Racism*. New York: Basic, 1992.

Benjamin, Lois. Introduction. *Black Women in the Academy: Promises and Perils*. Gainesville: UP of Florida, 1997. 1–7.

Bennett, Lerone. *Before the Mayflower*. 5th ed. Chicago: Johnson, 1982.

Berry, Chad, et al. "History from the Bottom Up: On Reproducing Professional Culture in Graduate Education." *Journal of American History* 81.3 (1994): 1137–46.

Berry, Mary, and John Blassingame. *Long Memory: The Black Experience in America*. New York: Oxford UP, 1982.

Blackett, R. J. M. *Beating against the Barriers*. Baton Rouge: Louisiana State UP, 1986.

Blassingame, John. *The Slave Community*. Rev. and enl. New York: Oxford UP, 1979.

———, ed. *Slave Testimony*. Baton Rouge: Louisiana State UP, 1977.

Blight, David W. *Frederick Douglass's Civil War*. Baton Rouge: Louisiana State UP, 1989.

———. Introduction. Douglass, *Narrative*, ed. Blight, 1–23.

Bobo, Jacqueline. *Black Women as Cultural Readers*. New York: Columbia UP, 1995.

Bolton, Ruthie. *Gal*. New York: Harcourt, 1994.

Bontemps, Arna. *Black Thunder*. 1936. Boston: Beacon, 1968.

Botkin, B. A., ed. *Lay My Burden Down: A Folk History of Slavery*. Athens: U of Georgia P, 1989.

Branch, William. *In Splendid Error. Crosswinds: An Anthology of Black Dramatists in the Diaspora*. Ed. Branch. Bloomington: Indiana UP, 1993. 260–308.

Braxton, Joanne M. *Black Women Writing Autobiography: A Tradition within a Tradition*. Philadelphia: Temple UP, 1989.

Brignano, Russell. *Black Americans in Autobiography*. Rev. ed. Durham: Duke UP, 1984.

Brown, Wesley. *The Teachers and Writers Guide to Frederick Douglass*. New York: Teachers and Writers Collaborative, 1996.

Brown, William Wells. *Clotel; or, The President's Daughter: A Narrative of Slave Life in the United States*. London: Partridge, 1853.

———. *Narrative of William Wells Brown, a Fugitive Slave*. Osofsky, *Puttin' On* 173–223.

Buckle, Stephen. *Natural Law and the Theory of Property: Grotius to Hume*. Oxford: Clarendon, 1991.

Burke, Kenneth. *Attitudes toward History*. 1937. Berkeley: U of California P, 1984.

———. *Permanence and Change*. 1954. Berkeley: U of California P, 1984.

Burt, John. "Learning to Write: The Narrative of Frederick Douglass." *Western Humanities Review* 42 (1988): 330–44.

Butler, Joseph. *The Analogy of Religion, Natural and Revealed, to the Constitution and Course of Nature*. 1736. London, 1809.

Butler, Octavia. *Kindred*. Boston: Beacon, 1979.

Butterfield, Stephen. *Black Autobiography in America*. Amherst: U of Massachussetts P, 1974.

Carby, Hazel V. "'Hear My Voice, Ye Careless Daughters': Narratives of Slave and Free Women before Emancipation." Andrews, *African American Autobiography* 59–76.

———. "The Multicultural Wars." Dent 87–199.

———. *Reconstructing Womanhood: The Emergence of the Afro-American Woman Novelist*. New York: Oxford UP, 1987.

Carretta, Vincent, ed. *Unchained Voices: An Anthology of Black Authors in the Eighteenth Century*. Lexington: U of Kentucky P, 1996.

Cassuto, Leonard. "Frederick Douglass and the Work of Freedom: Hegel's Master-Slave Dialectic in the Fugitive Slave Narrative." *Prospects* 21 (1996): 229–59.

Castronovo, Russ. *Fathering the Nation: American Genealogies of Slavery and Freedom*. Berkeley: U of California P, 1995.

Catterall, Helen, ed. *Judicial Cases concerning American Slavery and the Negro*. Washington: Carnegie Inst., 1926.

Chay, Deborah C. "Rereading Barbara Smith: Black Feminist Criticism and the Category of Experience." *New Literary History* 24 (1993): 635–52.

Child, Lydia Maria. *An Appeal in Favor of That Class of Americans Called Africans*. Ed. Carolyn Karcher. Amherst: U of Massachusetts P, 1996.

———. *The Freedmen's Book*. Boston: Ticknor, 1865.

Christian, Barbara. "Diminishing Returns: Can Black Feminism(s) Survive the Academy?" Goldberg 168–79.

———. "The Race for Theory." *Feminist Studies* 14.1 (1988): 67–79.

Cohen, Morris. *Legal Research in a Nutshell*. N.p.: West, 1996.

Conroy, Jack. *The Disinherited*. 1933. Columbia: U of Missouri P, 1991.

Cornelius, Janet. *When I Can Read My Title Clear: Literacy, Slavery, and Religion in the Antebellum South*. Columbia: U of South Carolina P, 1992.

Costanzo, Angelo. *Surprizing Narrative: Olaudah Equiano and the Beginnings of Black Autobiography*. Westport: Greenwood, 1987.

Cover, Robert M. *Justice Accused: Antislavery and the Judicial Process*. New Haven: Yale UP, 1975.

Craft, Ellen. Letter. *Anti-slavery Advocate* Dec. 1852: 22.

Craft, William, and Ellen Craft. *Running a Thousand Miles for Freedom*. London, 1860.

Dana, Richard Henry, Jr. 1840. *Two Years before the Mast*. New York: Penguin, 1986.

Davidson, Cathy N. "Critical Fictions." *PMLA* 111 (1996): 1069–72.

Davis, Angela. *Women, Race, and Class*. New York: Vintage, 1983.

Davis, Charles H., and Henry Louis Gates, Jr., eds. *The Slave's Narrative*. New York: Oxford UP, 1985.

Delany, Martin. *Blake*. 1859. Boston: Beacon, 1970.

Dent, Gina, ed. *Black Popular Culture: A Project by Michelle Wallace*. Seattle: Bay, 1992.

Dix, Dorothea. "The Strong Claims of Suffering Humanity." *The Reform Impulse, 1825–1850*. Ed. Walter Hugins. New York: Harper, 1972. 68–73.

Dorsey, Peter A. "Becoming the Other: The Mimesis of Metaphor in Douglass's *My Bondage and My Freedom*." *PMLA* 111 (1996): 435–50.

Douglass, Frederick. "American Prejudice and Southern Religion." *Frederick Douglass Papers* 1: 9–13.

———. *Autobiographies*. Ed. Henry Louis Gates, Jr. New York: Lib. of Amer., 1994.

———. "The Church Is the Bulwark of Slavery." *Frederick Douglass Papers* 1: 17–20.

———. "The Dred Scott Decision." *Frederick Douglass Papers* 3: 163–83.

———. *Frederick Douglass Papers*. 5 vols. Ed. John Blassingame et al. New Haven: Yale UP, 1979–92.

———. "The Free Church Connection with the Slave Church." *Frederick Douglass Papers* 1: 156–64.

———. "The Free States, Slavery, and the Sin of the Free Church." *Frederick Douglass Papers* 1: 186–89.

———. "I Am Here to Spread Light on American Slavery." *Frederick Douglass Papers* 1: 39–45.

———. "Learn Trades or Starve!" 1853. Foner and Lewis 118–20.

———. *Life and Times of Frederick Douglass*. Ed. Rayford Logan. New York: Collier, 1962.

———. *My Bondage and My Freedom*. New York, 1855.

———. *My Bondage and My Freedom*. New York: Arno, 1968.

———. *My Bondage and My Freedom*. New York: Dover, 1969.

———. *My Bondage and My Freedom*. Ed. William L. Andrews. Urbana: U of Illinois P, 1987.

———. "My Slave Experience in Maryland." *Frederick Douglass Papers* 1: 27–34.

———. *Narrative of the Life of Frederick Douglass, an American Slave, Written by Himself*. Norton Critical Edition. Ed. William L. Andrews and William S. McFeely. New York: Norton, 1997.

———. *Narrative of the Life of Frederick Douglass* [. . .]. Ed. Houston A. Baker, Jr. New York: Penguin, 1982.

———. *Narrative of the Life of Frederick Douglass* [. . .]. Ed. David W. Blight. New York: Bedford–St. Martin's, 1993.

———. *Narrative of the Life of Frederick Douglass* [. . .]. Gates, *Classic Slave Narratives* 243–331.

———. "The Proclamation and a Negro Army." *Frederick Douglass Papers* 3: 549–69.

———. "Southern Slavery and Northern Religion." *Frederick Douglass Papers* 1: 23–27.

———. "The Southern Style of Preaching to Slaves." *Frederick Douglass Papers* 1: 15–17.

Duberman, Martin. *The Antislavery Vanguard*. Princeton: Princeton UP, 1965.

Du Bois, W. E. B. *Black Reconstruction*. Millwood: Kraus, 1976.

duCille, Ann. *Skin Trade*. Cambridge: Harvard UP, 1996.

Dudley, David. *In My Father's Shadow: Intergenerational Conflict in African-American Men's Autobiography*. Philadelphia: U of Pennsylvania P, 1991.

Eaton, Clement. *The Growth of Southern Civilizaton*. New York: Harper, 1963.

Elizabeth. *Memoir of Old Elizabeth, a Coloured Woman*. Andrews, *Six Women's Slave Narratives* 1–19.

Elkins, Stanley. *Slavery: A Problem in American Institutional and Intellectual Life.* Chicago: U of Chicago P, 1959.

Ellison, Curtis, and E. W. Metcalf, Jr., eds. *William Wells Brown and Martin Delany: A Reference Guide.* Boston: Hall, 1978.

Ellison, Ralph. 1952. *Invisible Man.* New York: Vintage, 1972.

———. *Shadow and Act.* New York: Vintage, 1990.

Emerson, Ralph Waldo. *Essays: First Series.* Ed. Joseph Slater and Alfred R. Ferguson. Cambridge: Harvard UP, 1979. Vol. 2 of *The Collected Works of Ralph Waldo Emerson.*

———. *Nature, Addresses, and Lectures.* Ed. Alfred R. Ferguson, Robert E. Spiller, and Waldron P. Belknap. Cambridge: Harvard UP, 1979. Vol. 1 of *The Collected Works of Ralph Waldo Emerson.*

Epstein, Dena. *Sinful Tunes and Spirituals: Black Folk Music to the Civil War.* Urbana: U of Illinois P, 1977.

Ernest, John. *Resistance and Reformation in Nineteenth-Century African American Literature.* Jackson: UP of Mississippi, 1995.

Fanon, Frantz. *Wretched of the Earth.* New York: Grove, 1963.

Farrison, William Edward. *William Wells Brown: Author and Reformer.* Chicago: U of Chicago P, 1969.

The Federalist Papers. New York: Penguin, 1987.

Fehrenbacher, Don. *The Dred Scott Case: Its Significance in American Law and Politics.* New York: Oxford UP, 1978.

Ferguson, SallyAnn H. "Christian Violence and the Slave Narrative." *American Literature* 68 (1996): 297–320.

Fetterley, Judith. *The Resisting Reader: A Feminist Approach to American Fiction.* Bloomington: Indiana UP, 1978.

Fields, Barbara Jeanne, *Slavery and Freedom on the Middle Ground.* New Haven: Yale UP, 1985.

Filler, Louis. *The Crusade against Slavery, 1830–1860.* New York: Harper, 1963.

Finke, Laurie A. "The Pedagogy of the Depressed: Feminism, Poststructuralism, and Pedagogical Practice." Sadoff and Cain 154–68.

Fisher, Walter. "Narration as a Human Communication Paradigm." *Communication Monographs* 51 (1984): 1–22.

Fishkin, Shelley Fisher. "Interrogating 'Whiteness,' Complicating 'Blackness': Remapping American Culture." *American Quarterly* 47 (1995): 428–66.

Fitzhugh, George. *Sociology for the South; or, The Failure of Free Society.* Richmond, 1854.

Fleischner, Jennifer. *Mastering Slavery: Memory, Family, and Identity in Women's Slave Narratives.* New York: New York UP, 1996.

Floan, Howard. *The South in Northern Eyes, 1831–1861.* New York: McGraw, 1958.

Floyd, Samuel. *The Power of Black Music: Interpreting Its History from Africa to the United States.* New York: Oxford UP, 1995.

Fogel, Robert. *The Rise and Fall of American Slavery.* New York: Norton, 1989.

Foley, Barbara. *Radical Representations: Politics and Form in U.S. Proletarian Fiction.* Durham: Duke UP, 1993.

Folsom, Ed. "Appearing in Print: Illustrations of the Self in *Leaves of Grass.*" *The Cambridge Companion to Walt Whitman.* Ed. Ezra Greenspan. Cambridge: Cambridge UP, 1995. 135–65.

Foner, Philip S. *Frederick Douglass.* New York: Citadel, 1969.

———. *Frederick Douglass on Women's Rights.* Westport: Greenwood, 1976.

———, ed. *Frederick Douglass: Selections from His Writings.* New York: International, 1964.

———. *The Life and Writings of Frederick Douglass.* 5 vols. New York: International, 1950.

Foner, Philip S., and Ronald Lewis, eds. *Black Workers: A Documentary History from Colonial Times to the Present.* Philadelphia: Temple UP, 1988.

Foster, Frances Smith. "Adding Color and Contour to Early American Self-Portraitures: Autobiographical Writings of Afro-American Women." *Conjuring.* Ed. Marjorie Pryse and Hortense Spillers. Bloomington: Indiana UP, 1985. 25–38.

———. *Witnessing Slavery: The Development of Ante-bellum Slave Narratives.* Westport: Greenwood, 1979. Exp. ed. Madison: U of Wisconsin P, 1994.

———. *Written by Herself: Literary Production by African American Women, 1746–1892.* Bloomington: Indiana UP, 1993.

Franchot, Jenny. "The Punishment of Esther: Frederick Douglass and the Construction of the Feminine." Sundquist, *Douglass* 141–65.

Franklin, John Hope, and Alfred A. Moss, Jr. *From Slavery to Freedom.* 7th ed. New York: Knopf, 1994.

Franklin, V. P. *Living Our Stories, Telling Our Truths.* New York: Scribners, 1995.

Fredrickson, George M. *The Black Image in the White Mind: The Debate on Afro-American Character and Destiny, 1817–1914.* Hanover: Wesleyan UP, 1971.

Fuller, Edmund. *A Star Pointed North.* New York: Harpers, 1946.

Fuller, Margaret. *The Essential Margaret Fuller.* Ed. Jeffrey Steele. New Brunswick: Rutgers UP, 1992.

Gaines, Ernest J. *The Autobiography of Miss Jane Pittman.* New York: Bantam, 1971.

Garfield, Deborah, and Rafia Zafar, eds. *Harriet Jacobs and* Incidents in the Life of a Slave Girl: *New Critical Essays.* New York: Cambridge UP, 1996.

Garnet, Henry Highland. *Address to the Slaves of the United States. The New Cavalcade: African-American Writing from 1760 to the Present.* Ed. Arthur Davis, J. Saunders Redding, and Joyce Ann Joyce. Vol. 1. Washington: Howard UP, 1991. 115–22.

Gates, Henry Louis, Jr., ed. *The Classic Slave Narratives.* New York: Mentor, 1987.

———. "A Dangerous Literacy: The Legacy of Frederick Douglass." *New York Times Book Review* 25 May 1995.

———. *Figures in Black.* New York: Oxford UP, 1987.

———. "From Wheatley to Douglass: The Politics of Displacement." Sundquist, *Douglass* 47–65.

———. "James Gronniosaw and the Trope of the Talking Book." *Southern Review* 22.2 (1986): 252–70.

———. *The Signifying Monkey: A Theory of Afro-American Literary Criticism*. New York: Oxford UP, 1987.

Gates, Henry Louis, Jr., et al., eds. *The Norton Anthology of African American Literature*. New York: Norton, 1996.

Genovese, Elizabeth Fox. *Within the Plantation Household*. Chapel Hill: U of North Carolina P, 1988.

Genovese, Eugene. *Roll Jordan Roll: The World the Slaves Made*. New York: Vintage, 1976.

Gibson, Donald. "Christianity and Individualism: (Re-)Creation and Reality in Frederick Douglass's Representation of Self." *African American Review* 26 (1992): 591–603.

———. "Faith, Doubt, and Apostasy: Evidence of Things Unseen in Frederick Douglass's *Narrative*." Sundquist, *Douglass* 84–98.

———. "Reconciling Public and Private in Frederick Douglass's *Narrative*." *American Literature* 57 (1985): 549–69.

Goddu, Teresa A., and Craig V. Smith. "Scenes of Writing in Frederick Douglass's *Narrative*: Autobiography and the Creation of Self." *Southern Review* 25 (1989): 822–41.

Goldberg, David A., ed. *Multiculturalism: A Critical Reader*. Cambridge: Blackwell, 1994.

Goldsby, Jacqueline. "'I Disguised My Hand': Writing Versions of the Truth in Harriet Jacobs's *Incidents in the Life of a Slave Girl* and John Jacobs's 'A True Tale of Slavery.'" Garfield and Zafar 11–43.

Goodell, William. *American Constitutional Law*. Freeport: Books for Libraries, 1971.

Graham, Maryemma, et al., eds. *Teaching African American Literature: Theory and Practice*. New York: Routledge, 1998.

Gray, Thomas. *"The Confessions of Nat Turner" and Related Documents*. Ed. Kenneth S. Greenberg. Boston: Bedford, 1996.

Griffin, Farah. *Who Set You Flowin': The African-American Migration Narrative*. New York: Oxford UP, 1995.

Hall, Kim. *Things of Darkness: Economies of Race and Gender in Early Modern England*. Ithaca: Cornell UP, 1995.

Harding, Vincent. *There Is a River*. New York: Harcourt, 1981.

Hayden, Robert. "Frederick Douglass." *Collected Poems*. New York: Liveright, 1985. 62.

Hedin, Raymond. "The American Slave Narrative: The Justification of the Pícaro." *American Literature* 53 (1982): 630–45.

Heermance, J. Noel. *William Wells Brown and* Clotelle. Hamden: Archon, 1969.

Henderson, Mae G. "Speaking in Tongues: Dialogics, Dialectics, and the Black Woman Writer's Literary Tradition." *Changing Our Own Words: Essays on Criticism, Theory, and Writing by Black Women*. Ed. Cheryl A. Wall. New Brunswick: Rutgers UP, 1989. 16–37, 215–21.

Hicks, John D., *The Federal Union: A History of the United States to 1865.* Boston: Houghton, 1948.

hooks, bell. *Black Looks: Race and Representation.* Boston: South End, 1992.

Houchins, Sue, ed. *Spiritual Narratives.* New York: Oxford UP, 1988.

Huggins, Nathan. *Slave and Citizen: The Life of Frederick Douglass.* Boston: Little, 1980.

Hughes, Langston. *Not without Laughter.* 1930. New York: Scribner, 1995.

Humez, Jean, ed. *Gifts of Power: The Writings of Rebecca Cox Jackson, Black Visionary, Shaker Eldress.* Amherst: U of Massachusetts P, 1981.

Hurston, Zora Neale. *Their Eyes Were Watching God.* 1937. New York: Harper, 1990.

Jackson, Blyden. *The Long Beginning, 1746–1895.* Baton Rouge: Louisiana State UP, 1989. Vol. 1 of *A History of Afro-American Literature.*

Jackson, Joyce. "The Changing Nature of Gospel Music." *African-American Review* 29 (1995): 185–200.

Jackson, Rebecca Cox. *Gifts of Power: The Writings of Rebecca Cox Jackson.* Ed. Jean Humez. Amherst: U of Massachussets P, 1987.

Jacobs, Harriet. *Incidents in the Life of a Slave Girl. Written by Herself.* 1861. Gates, *Classic Slave Narratives* 333–515.

———. *Incidents in the Life of a Slave Girl.* Ed. Valerie Smith. New York: Oxford UP, 1988.

———. *Incidents in the Life of a Slave Girl.* Ed. Jean Fagan Yellin. Cambridge: Harvard UP, 1987.

Jameson, Fredric. *The Prison-House of Language.* Princeton: Princeton UP, 1972.

Jefferson, Thomas. *Notes on the State of Virginia.* Ed. William Peden. Chapel Hill: U of North Carolina P, 1995.

———. *Writings.* New York: Viking, 1984.

Johnson, Clifton H. *God Struck Me Dead: Voices of Ex-Slaves.* Cleveland: Pilgrim, 1993.

Johnson, Paul E., ed. *African American Christianity.* Berkeley: U of California P, 1994.

Jones, Gayl. *Corregidora.* Boston: Beacon, 1986.

Jones, Jacqueline. *Labor of Love, Labor of Sorrow: The Black Family in Slavery and Freedom.* New York: Vintage, 1986.

Jordan, Winthrop D., *White over Black: American Attitudes toward the Negro, 1550–1812.* Chapel Hill: U of North Carolina P, 1968.

Judy, Ronald. *Disforming the American Canon: Afro-Arabic Slave Narratives and the Vernacular.* Minneapolis: U of Minnesota P, 1993.

Katz, William Loren, ed. *Flight from the Devil: Six Slave Narratives.* Trenton: Africa World, 1996.

Keckley, Elizabeth. *Behind the Scenes; or, Thirty Years a Slave and Four Years in the White House.* Ed. James Olney. New York: Oxford UP, 1988.

Kennedy, William Sloane. *The Fight of a Book for the World.* West Yarmouth: Stonecroft, 1926.

King, Wilma. *Stolen Childhood: Slave Youth in Nineteenth-Century America*. Bloomington: Indiana UP, 1995.

Kolchin, Peter. *American Slavery, 1619–1877*. New York: Hill, 1994.

Lampe, Gregory P. *Frederick Douglass: Freedom's Voice, 1818–1845*. East Lansing: Michigan State UP, 1997.

Lane, Lunsford. *The Narrative of Lunsford Lane. Five Slave Narratives*. Ed. William Loren Katz. New York: Arno, 1969.

Larison, C. W. *Silvia DuBois*. Ed. Jared Lobdell. New York: Oxford UP, 1988.

Laurie, Bruce. *Artisans into Workers: Labor in Nineteenth-Century America*. New York: Farrar, 1989.

Leaves of Grass *Imprints*. Boston, 1860.

Lehuu, Isabelle. "Sentimental Figures: Reading *Godey's Lady's Book* in Antebellum America." Samuels 73–91.

Leverenz, David. *Manhood and the American Renaissance*. Ithaca: Cornell UP, 1989.

Levine, Bruce, et al. *Who Built America?: Working People and the Nation's Economy, Politics, Culture and Society*. Vol. 1. New York: Pantheon, 1989.

Levine, Lawrence. *Black Culture and Black Consciousness*. New York: Oxford UP, 1977.

Levine, Robert. *Martin Delany, Frederick Douglass, and the Politics of Representative Identity*. Chapel Hill: U of North Carolina P, 1997.

Lévi-Strauss, Claude. "The Structural Study of Myth." *Contemporary Literary Criticism*. Ed. Robert Con Davis. New York: Longman, 1986. 307–22.

Lincoln, Abraham. *The Essential Abraham Lincoln*. Ed. John Gabriel Hunt. Avenel: Portland, 1990.

Litwack, Leon F., *Been in the Storm So Long: The Aftermath of Slavery*. New York: Knopf, 1979.

Litwack, Leon, and August Meier, eds. *Black Leaders of the Nineteenth Century*. Urbana: U of Illinois P, 1988.

Locke, John. *Two Treatises of Government*. New York: Cambridge UP, 1988.

"Los Angeles Sweatshops Are Thriving, Experts Say." *New York Times* 5 Aug. 1995: A6.

Lott, Eric. *Love and Theft: Blackface Minstrelsy and the American Working Class*. New York: Oxford UP, 1993.

Mabee, Carlton. *Black Freedom*. New York: Macmillan, 1970.

MacKethan, Lucinda. "From Fugitive Slave to Man of Letters: The Conversion of Frederick Douglass." *Journal of Narrative Technique* 16 (1986): 65+.

Martin, Waldo E. *The Mind of Frederick Douglass*. Chapel Hill: U of North Carolina P, 1984.

Mattison, Hiram. *Louisa Picquet, the Octoroon: A Tale of Southern Slave Life*. 1861. Barthelemy [2nd narrative].

Mayberry, Katherine J., ed. *Teaching What You're Not: Identity Politics in Higher Education*. New York: New York UP, 1996.

McCall, Nathan. *Makes Me Wanna Holler*. New York: Vintage, 1994.

McCaskill, Barbara. "Designs on the Sign of Race: Nineteenth-Century African-American Women in the National Imagination." Unpublished book manuscript.

——. "A Stamp on the Envelope Upside-Down Means Love; or, Literacy and Literature in the Multicultural Classroom." *Multicultural Literature and Literacies: Making Space for Difference*. Ed. Suzanne M. Miller and McCaskill. Albany: SU of New York P, 1993. 77–102.

——. "'Yours Very Truly': Ellen Craft—the Fugitive as Text and Artifact." *African American Review* 29.4 (1994): 509–29.

McDowell, Deborah. "In the First Place: Making Frederick Douglass and the Afro-American Narrative Tradition." Andrews, *African American Autobiography* 36–58; Andrews, *Critical Essays* 192–214.

McDowell, Deborah, and Arnold Rampersad, eds. *Slavery and the Literary Imagination: Selected Papers from the English Institute, 1987*. Baltimore: Johns Hopkins UP, 1989.

McFeely, William S. *Frederick Douglass*. New York: Norton, 1991.

McKay, Nellie Y. "A Troubled Peace: Black Women in the Halls of the White Academy." Benjamin, *Black Women* 11–22.

Melville, Herman. *Redburn*. New York: Penguin, 1986.

Miller, Douglass, ed. *Frederick Douglass and the Fight for Freedom*. New York: Facts on File, 1993.

Miller, J. Hillis. "Narrative." *Critical Terms for Literary Study*. Ed. Frank Lentricchia and Thomas McLaughlin. 2nd ed. Chicago: U of Chicago P, 1995. 66–79.

Mintz, Sidney W., and Richard Price. *The Birth of African-American Culture: An Anthropological Perspective*. Boston: Beacon, 1992.

Mohanty, Chandra Talpade. "On Race and Voice: Challenges for Liberal Education in the 1990s." *Between Borders: Pedagogy and the Politics of Cultural Studies*. Ed. Henry A. Giroux and Peter McLaren. New York: Routledge, 1994. 145–66.

Moody, Joycelyn. "Ripping Away the Veil of Slavery: Literacy, Communal Love, and Self-Esteem in Three Slave Women's Narratives." *Black American Literature Forum* 24 (1990): 633–48.

Moon, Michael, and Cathy N. Davidson, eds. *Subjects and Citizens: Nation, Race, and Gender from Oroonoka to Anita Hill*. Durham: Duke UP, 1996.

Morison, Samuel Eliot, and Henry Steele Commager. *The Growth of the American Republic*. Rev. and enl. ed. 2 vols. New York: Oxford UP, 1937.

Morrison, Toni. *Beloved*. New York: NAL, 1987.

Moses, Wilson J. *The Golden Age of Black Nationalism*. New York: Oxford UP, 1988.

——. "Writing Freely? Douglass and the Constraints of Racialized Writing." Sundquist, *Douglass* 66–83.

Mullen, Harryette. "Runaway Tongue: Resistant Orality in *Uncle Tom's Cabin, Our Nig, Incidents in the Life of a Slave Girl,* and *Beloved*." Samuels, *Culture* 244–64.

Murray, Albert. *The Omni-Americans: Black Experience and American Culture*. New York: Outerbridge, 1970.

Nelson, Dana. *The Word in Black and White: Reading "Race" in American Literature, 1638–1867*. New York: Oxford UP, 1992.

Newbury, Michael. "Eaten Alive: Slavery and Celebrity in Antebellum America." *ELH* 61 (1994): 159–87.

Newton, James E., and Ronald L. Lewis, eds. *The Other Slaves: Slave Mechanics, Artisans, and Craftsmen*. Boston: Hall, 1978.

Northup, Solomon. *Twelve Years a Slave: Narrative of Solomon Northup*. Osofsky, *Puttin' On* 225–406.

Oakes, James. *The Ruling Race: A History of American Slaveholders*. New York: Knopf, 1982.

Olney, James, ed. *Autobiography: Essays Theoretical and Critical*. Princeton: Princeton UP, 1980.

———. "'I Was Born': Slave Narratives, Their Status as Autobiography and as Literature." Davis and Gates 148–74.

Osofksy, Gilbert. *Harlem: The Making of a Black Ghetto: Negro New York, 1890–1930*. 1966. Chicago: Dee, 1996.

———, ed. *Puttin' On Ole Massa: The Slave Narratives of Henry Bibb, William Wells Brown, and Solomon Northup*. New York: Harper, 1969.

The Paideia I Reader. Ed. Jyoti Grewal. Decorah: Luther Coll., 1997.

Painter, Nell Irvin. "Representing Truth: Sojourner Truth's Knowing and Becoming Known." *Journal of American History* 81.2 (1994): 461–92.

———. *Sojourner Truth: A Life, a Symbol*. New York: Norton, 1997.

Palumbo-Liu, David. "Historical Permutations of the Place of Race." *PMLA* 111 (1996): 1075–78.

Pateman, Carole. *The Problem of Political Obligation: A Critique of Liberal Theory*. Berkeley: U of California P, 1979.

Pennington, James W. C. *The Fugitive Blacksmith. Great Slave Narratives*. Ed. Arna Bontemps. Boston: Beacon, 1969.

———. *The Fugitive Blacksmith. Five Slave Narratives*. Ed. William Loren Katz. New York: Arno, 1969.

Peterson, Carla. *"Doers of the Word": African-American Women Speakers and Writers in the North (1830–1880)*. New York: Oxford UP, 1995.

Petrie, William, ed. *Bibliography of the Frederick Douglass Library at Cedar Hill*. Fort Washington: Silesia, 1995.

Phillips, Caryl. *Crossing the River*. New York: Vintage, 1995.

Phillips, Ulrich B. *American Negro Slavery*. 1918. Gloucester: Smith, 1959.

Pike, Martha, and Janice Gray Armstrong. Prologue. *A Time to Mourn: Expressions of Grief in Nineteenth-Century America*. Ed. Pike and Armstrong. Stony Brook: Museums, 1980. 11–14.

Potkay, Adam, and Sandra Burr, eds. *Black Atlantic Writers of the Eighteenth Century*. New York: St. Martin's, 1995.

Preston, Dickson J. *Young Frederick Douglass*. Baltimore: Johns Hopkins UP, 1980.

Price, Richard. *Clockers*. New York: Avon, 1983.

Prince, Nancy. *A Narrative of the Life and Travels of Mrs. Nancy Prince, Written by Herself*. Barthelemy 1–89.

Quarles, Benjamin. *Frederick Douglass*. New York: Atheneum, 1968.

Raboteau, Albert. *Slave Religion*. New York: Oxford UP, 1980.

Rawick, George, ed. *The American Slave: A Composite Autobiography*. Westport: Greenwood, 1972.

Reed, Ishmael. *Flight to Canada*. New York: Atheneum, 1989.

"Refugees from Recession Fill Hotel's Payroll." *New York Times* 1 March 1992: A1.

Reichlin, Elinor. "Faces of Slavery." *American Heritage* 28 (1977): 4–5.

Reising, Russell J. *The Usable Past: Theory and the Study of American Literature*. New York: Methuen, 1986.

Richards, David A. J. *Conscience and the Constitution: History, Theory, and the Law of the Reconstruction Amendments*. Princeton: Princeton UP, 1993.

———. *Foundations of American Constitutionalism*. New York: Oxford UP, 1989.

Ritchie, Barbara, ed. *Mind and Heart of Frederick Douglass*. New York: Crowell, 1968.

Rogers, William. *"We Are All Together Now": Frederick Douglass, William Lloyd Garrison, and the Prophetic Tradition*. New York: Garland, 1995.

Rose, Willie Lee, ed. *A Documentary History of Slavery in North America*. New York: Oxford UP, 1976.

Rosenblatt, Louise M. *Literature as Exploration*. New York: MLA, 1995.

Rowan, Richard. *The Negro in the Steel Industry*. Philadelphia: U of Pennsylvania P, 1968.

Sadoff, Dianne F., and William E. Cain, eds. *Teaching Contemporary Theory to Undergraduates*. New York: MLA, 1994.

Saks, Eva. "Representing Miscegenation Law." *Raritan* 8.2 (1988): 39–69.

Samuels, Shirley, ed. *The Culture of Sentiment: Race, Gender, and Sentimentality in Nineteenth-Century America*. New York: Oxford UP, 1992.

Sánchez-Eppler, Karen. "Bodily Bonds: The Intersecting Rhetorics of Feminism and Abolition." Samuels 92–114.

———. *Touching Liberty: Abolition, Feminism, and the Politics of the Body*. Berkeley: U of California P, 1993.

"Scattered Violence Erupts on Drivers' Picket Lines." *New York Times* 8 April 1994: A19.

Scott, Joan W. "The Evidence of Experience." *The Lesbian and Gay Studies Reader*. Ed. Henry Abelove, Michèle Aina Barale, and David M. Halperin. New York: Routledge, 1993.

Sekora, John. "Black Message / White Envelope: Genre, Authenticity, and Authority in the Antebellum Slave Narrative." *Callaloo* 10.3 (1987): 482–515.

Sekora, John, and Houston Baker, Jr. "Written Off: Narratives, Master Texts, and Afro-American Writing from 1760–1945." *Studies in Black American Literature I: Black American Prose Theory*. Ed. Joe Weixlman et al. Greenville: Penkevill, 1984. 43–62.

Sekora, John, and Darwin T. Turner, eds. *The Art of Slave Narrative*. Macomb: Western Illinois UP, 1982.

Sennett, Richard, and Jonathan Cobb. *The Hidden Injuries of Class*. New York: Random, 1983.

Shange, Ntozake. "Wow Yr Just like a Man." *Nappy Edges*. New York: St. Martin's, 1978. 13–16.

Smith, Adam. *The Theory of Moral Sentiments*. Indianapolis: Liberty Fund, 1984.

Smith, Sidonie. *Where I'm Bound: Patterns of Slavery and Freedom in Black American Autobiography*. Westport: Greenwood, 1974.

Smith, Valerie. "Loopholes of Retreat: Architecture and Ideology in Harriet Jacobs's *Incidents in the Life of a Slave Girl*." *Reading Black, Reading Feminist*. Ed. Henry Louis Gates, Jr. New York: Meridian, 1990. 212–26.

———. *Self-Discovery and Authority in Afro-American Narrative*. Cambridge: Harvard UP, 1987.

Southern, Eileen. *The Music of Black Americans: A History*. 3rd ed. New York: Norton, 1997.

Spooner, Lysander. *The Unconstitutionality of Slavery*. Boston, 1853.

Stampp, Kenneth M. *The Peculiar Institution: Slavery in the Ante-Bellum South*. New York: Knopf, 1956.

Starling, Marion. *The Slave Narrative*. Boston: Hall, 1981.

Steinbeck, John. *Grapes of Wrath*. 1939. New York: Penguin, 1997.

Stepto, Robert B. "Distrust of the Reader in Afro-American Narratives." *Reconstructing American Literary History*. Ed. Sacvan Bercovitch. Cambridge: Harvard UP, 1986. 300–22.

———. *From behind the Veil: A Study of Afro-American Narrative*. Urbana: U of Illinois P, 1991.

Stepto, Robert B., and Dexter Fisher, eds. *Afro-American Literature: The Reconstruction of Instruction*. New York: MLA, 1979.

Sterling, Dorothy. *We Are Your Sisters: Black Women in the Nineteenth Century*. New York: Norton, 1984.

Stewart, Alvan. *Writings and Speeches of Alvan Stewart on Slavery*. Ed. Luther Marsh. New York: Negro UP, 1969.

Still, William L. *Underground Rail Road*. Philadelphia, 1877.

Stone, Albert, ed. *American Autobiography*. New York: Prentice, 1981.

———. *Autobiographical Occasions and Original Acts*. Philadelphia: U of Pennsylvania P, 1982.

———. "Identity and Art in Frederick Douglass's *Narrative*." *CLA Journal* 17 (1973): 192–213.

Stowe, Harriet Beecher. *The Key to* Uncle Tom's Cabin. New York: Arno, 1969.

———. *Uncle Tom's Cabin*. New York: Vintage–Lib. of Amer., 1991.

Stroyer, Jacob. *My Life in the South*. Katz, *Flight* 155–218.

Stuckey, Sterling. *Slave Culture: Nationalist Theory and the Fundamentals of Black America*. New York: Oxford UP, 1988.

Sundquist, Eric. "Frederick Douglass: Literacy and Paternalism." *Raritan* 6 (1986): 108–24.

————, ed. *Frederick Douglass: New Literary and Historical Essays*. New York: Cambridge UP, 1990.

————. *To Wake the Nations: Race in the Making of American Literature*. Cambridge: Harvard UP, 1983.

Tatum, Beverly Daniel. "Teaching White Students about Racism: The Search for White Allies and the Restoration of Hope." *Teachers College Record* 95.4 (1994): 462–76.

Terkel, Studs. *Race: How Blacks and Whites Think about an American Obsession*. New York: New, 1992.

Thomas, Brook. *Cross-Examinations of Law and Literature: Cooper, Hawthorne, Stowe, and Melville*. New York: Cambridge UP, 1987.

Thomas, Herman. *James W. C. Pennington: African-American Churchman and Abolitionist*. New York: Garland, 1995.

Thompson, John. *An Authentic History of the Douglass Monument*. Freeport: Bks. for Libs., 1971.

Thoreau, Henry David. Walden *and* Civil Disobedience. New York: Norton, 1966.

Tillich, Paul. *Dynamics of Faith*. New York: Harper, 1957.

Tompkins, Jane. "Sentimental Power: *Uncle Tom's Cabin* and the Politics of Literary History." *Sensational Designs: The Cultural Work of American Fiction 1790–1860*. New York: Oxford UP, 1985. 122–46.

Trachtenberg, Alan. *Reading American Photographs: Images as History, Mathew Brady to Walker Evans*. New York: Hill, 1989.

Traubel, Horace. *With Walt Whitman in Camden*. Vols. 1–3. 1906–14. New York: Rowman, 1961.

Truth, Sojourner. *Narrative of Sojourner Truth*. Ed. Jeffrey C. Stewart. New York: Oxford UP, 1991.

Tuck, Richard. *Natural Rights Theories*. New York: Cambridge UP, 1987.

Tushnet, Mark. *The American Law of Slavery, 1810–1860: Considerations of Humanity and Interest*. Princeton: Princeton UP, 1981.

Tyler, Samuel. *Memoir of Roger Brooke Taney*. Baltimore, 1876.

Van Leer, David. "Reading Slavery: The Anxiety of Ethnicity in Douglass's *Narrative*." Sundquist, *Douglass* 118–40.

Voss, Frederick S. *Majestic in His Wrath: A Pictorial Life of Frederick Douglass*. Washington: Smithsonian, 1995.

Walker, Peter F. *Moral Choices: Memory, Desire, and Imagination in Nineteenth-Century American Abolition*. Baton Rouge: Louisiana State UP, 1978.

Wallace, Maurice. "Constructing the Black Masculine: Frederick Douglass, Booker T. Washington, and the Sublimits of African American Autobiography." Moon and Davidson 245–70.

Wallis, Brian. "Black Bodies, White Science: Louis Agassiz's Slave Daguerreotypes." *American Art* 9 (1995): 38–61.

Walters, Ronald G. *American Reformers, 1815–1860*. New York: Hill, 1978.

Walzer, Michael. *Obligations: Essays on Disobedience, War, and Citizenship*. Cambridge: Harvard UP, 1970.

Washington, Booker T. *Frederick Douglass*. New York: Haskell, 1968.

Wells, Ida B. *The Memphis Diary of Ida B. Wells*. Ed. Miriam DeCosta-Willis. Boston: Beacon, 1995.

Wheat, Ellen Harkins, ed. *Jacob Lawrence: The "Frederick Douglass" and "Harriet Tubman" Series of 1938–1940*. Seattle: U of Washington P, 1991.

Whelchel, L. H. *My Chains Fell Off*. Lanham: UP of Amer., 1985.

White, Deborah Gray. *Ar'n't I a Woman: Female Slaves in the Plantation South*. New York: Norton, 1987.

Whitman, Walt. *Complete Poetry and Collected Prose*. New York: Lib. of Amer., 1982.

Wiecek, William. *The Sources of Antislavery Constitutionalism in America*. Ithaca: Cornell UP, 1977.

Wilson, Harriet. *Our Nig*. 1859. New York: Vintage, 1983.

Wilson, William Julius. *When Work Disappears: The World of the New Urban Poor*. New York: Vintage, 1997.

Wright, Richard. 1940. *Native Son*. New York: Harper, 1993.

Yacovone, Donald. "Abolitionists and the 'Language of Fraternal Love.'" *Meanings for Manhood: Constructions of Masculinity in Victorian America*. Ed. Mark C. Carnes and Clyde Griffen. Chicago: U of Chicago P, 1990. 85–95.

Yee, Shirley. *Black Women Abolitionists*. Knoxville: U of Tennessee P, 1992.

Yellin, Jean Fagan, and Cynthia Bond, eds. *The Pen Is Ours: A Listing of Writings by and about African-American Women before 1910*. New York: Oxford UP, 1991.

Zafar, Rafia. "Franklinian Douglass: The Afro-American as Representative Man." Sundquist, *Douglass* 99–117.

Zilversmit, Arthur. *First Emancipation: The Abolition of Slavery in the North*. Chicago: U of ßChicago P, 1967.

INDEX

Modern Language Association of America
Approaches to Teaching World Literature
Joseph Gibaldi, series editor

Lafayette's The Princess of Clèves. Ed. Faith E. Beasley and Katharine Ann Jensen. 1998.

Lessing's The Golden Notebook. Ed. Carey Kaplan and Ellen Cronan Rose. 1989.

Mann's Death in Venice *and Other Short Fiction*. Ed. Jeffrey B. Berlin. 1992.

Medieval English Drama. Ed. Richard K. Emmerson. 1990.

Melville's Moby-Dick. Ed. Martin Bickman. 1985.

Metaphysical Poets. Ed. Sidney Gottlieb. 1990.

Miller's Death of a Salesman. Ed. Matthew C. Roudané. 1995.

Milton's Paradise Lost. Ed. Galbraith M. Crump. 1986.

Molière's Tartuffe *and Other Plays*. Ed. James F. Gaines and Michael S. Koppisch. 1995.

Momaday's The Way to Rainy Mountain. Ed. Kenneth M. Roemer. 1988.

Montaigne's Essays. Ed. Patrick Henry. 1994.

Novels of Toni Morrison. Ed. Nellie Y. McKay and Kathryn Earle. 1997.

Murasaki Shikibu's The Tale of Genji. Ed. Edward Kamens. 1993.

Pope's Poetry. Ed. Wallace Jackson and R. Paul Yoder. 1993.

Shakespeare's King Lear. Ed. Robert H. Ray. 1986.

Shakespeare's The Tempest *and Other Late Romances*. Ed. Maurice Hunt. 1992.

Shelley's Frankenstein. Ed. Stephen C. Behrendt. 1990.

Shelley's Poetry. Ed. Spencer Hall. 1990.

Sir Gawain and the Green Knight. Ed. Miriam Youngerman Miller and Jane Chance. 1986.

Spenser's Faerie Queene. Ed. David Lee Miller and Alexander Dunlop. 1994.

Stendhal's The Red and the Black. Ed. Dean de la Motte and Stirling Haig. 1999.

Sterne's Tristram Shandy. Ed. Melvyn New. 1989.

Swift's Gulliver's Travels. Ed. Edward J. Rielly. 1988.

Thoreau's Walden *and Other Works*. Ed. Richard J. Schneider. 1996.

Voltaire's Candide. Ed. Renée Waldinger. 1987.

Whitman's Leaves of Grass. Ed. Donald D. Kummings. 1990.

Wordsworth's Poetry. Ed. Spencer Hall, with Jonathan Ramsey. 1986.

Wright's Native Son. Ed. James A. Miller. 1997.